4275

Weeks, Bob.
    The Brier : the history of Canada's most celebrated
curling championship / Bob Weeks. -- Toronto :
Macmillan Canada, c1995.
    xiv, 240 p. : ill.

Includes index.
07636865   ISBN:0771573057

1. Canadian Curling Championship - History. 2. Curling -
Tournaments - Canada - History. I. Title

4231   95JAN02   06/ex   1-01038568

THE BRIER

THE BRIER

The History of Canada's Most Celebrated Curling Championship

BOB WEEKS

Macmillan Canada
Toronto

Canadian Cataloguing in Publication Data

Weeks, Bob
The brier

Includes index
ISBN 0-7715-7305-7

1. Canadian Curling Championship — History.   2. Curling — Tournaments — Canada — History.   I. Title.

GV845.W44   1995   796.964'0971   C94-932678-X

Macmillan Canada wishes to thank the Canada Council, the Ontario Ministry of Culture and Communications and the Ontario Arts Council for supporting its publishing program.

Macmillan Canada
A Division of Canada Publishing Corporation
Toronto, Canada

1   2   3   4   5   99   98   97   96   95

Printed in Canada

To my father,
who taught me how to curl,
and to my son, whom I one day
hope to teach as well.

The Canadian Curling Association

From the earliest days of the Dominion Curling Association to the present Canadian Curling Association (CCA), which is responsible for the growth and development of curling in Canada for both genders, all ages and every level of ability, the management of curling has matured just as its premiere championship property—the Labatt Brier—has.

With in excess of 1.2 million Canadians who participate in curling annually, approximately 1250 curling facilities across the country, a viewing audience which can reach in excess of 2 million for the finals of The Scott Tournament of Hearts and Labatt Brier, a curling television broadcast schedule that is in excess of 150 hours over a four-month season effective 1995 and the attainment of Olympic status effective 1998, curling has emerged as an amateur sport of significant stature in Canada.

The demands, challenges and opportunities of this growth make the future for curling in Canada, and indeed throughout the world, look very, very bright. The optimism for our sport's future, however, is built to a large degree on the strong traditional roots of our past.

Contents

Acknowledgements

Putting together a book on the Brier was one of those projects that seemed like a great idea until I actually started doing it and discovered how big its history actually is. While media guides have condensed a list of winners into a couple of pages, the stories behind each of those championships seem endless, and trying to track down each of these tales is a task that could take a lifetime. As I delved more and more into the research, it became obvious that, if a complete history was to be recorded, I would need to write several billion words. So, right from the start, I apologize to the many people, winners included, whose stories are not told in this book. I hope that what is here is representative of the great traditions of the Brier, and that you can understand no omissions were consciously intended.

While I'm busy apologizing to some, I must also thank the many others who gave up spare hours to talk with me and point me in the right direction. If there was one consistent theme that ran through the hundreds of interviews I conducted for this book, it's that every one of the curlers shares a deep emotional attachment to the Brier. Not one of them ever had a bad word to say about the event —only, perhaps, about the ice!

Special appreciation goes to Peter Birchard, Alf Phillips, Jr., Ken Thompson and Donna Dilschneider, the four publishers of the *Ontario Curling Report*, who gave me my first chance to write about this great game and then allowed me to join them (replacing

Donna) as a publisher, and to take over as editor. Your encouragement and friendship will always be special. David Langford, the sports editor of the *Globe and Mail*, also took a great chance on me a few years back, giving an untried young writer a weekly column in Canada's national newspaper. That opportunity gave me a huge audience, a lot of freedom and plenty of responsibility, all of which I take seriously and for which I will be forever grateful. Thanks, Dave.

To my employers at Canadian Controlled Media Communications, especially Randy McDonald and Kim Locke, thanks for looking the other way as I battled through this project and other curling ventures. I owe you one (or two or three . . .).

There were some other especially helpful people I can never thank enough. Tom and Anne Fisher at the Curling Hall of Fame and Museum of Canada were always there with a name, a date, a story and, when I visited them at their home, a sandwich, a smile and a beer. I hope you will very soon get the permanent Hall of Fame—along with some respect from the curlers—that you so richly deserve.

Doug Maxwell, who at the time of writing had just finished attending his 35th consecutive Brier, was also there whenever I had a question to be answered, as was Breathless Bill Good, who set the record among Brier attendees with 45.

To my buddies on the bench—Ray Turchansky, Robin Brown, Teresa Kirkpatrick and Murray McCormick—thanks for putting up with my historical babbling over the past few years. A special note of appreciation goes to Tom Slater, who has not only sat beside me at the last umpteen Briers but actually curled with me for a few years and is now crazy enough to golf with me throughout the summer.

Jeff Timson has always made life easy for me with his work at the Brier and he, too, went out of his way to help me during the writing of this book. Denise Schon at Macmillan, the person who had enough faith to give this project the go-ahead, was understanding with extensions for a naive rookie author. And Kirsten Hanson, editor extraordinaire, taught me the book business while I gave her a full dose of curling. Lorne Rubenstein doesn't know an in-turn from an out-turn, but he was always willing to listen to my latest problem. Ruth Howey was a great courier and always managed to get me to smile. And my own team, Brian Trepanier, John Henderson, Mark Pierog and Bob Wallace, tolerated my schedule and always seemed to find a spare.

My father, the man who introduced pebble to Germany, spent a lot of time reading over the drafts and, along with my mother, encouraged me every step of the way. I love you both.

Finally, to my wife, Joanne, and my son, Christopher, thanks for putting up with me while I was holed up in my office working on this book. Joanne changed too many diapers, cooked too many meals, missed too many nights out and didn't say anything when our phone bills hit four figures.

Christopher, who attended his first Brier in Ottawa at the age of five months, learned to do a lot of things while his dad was busy typing. It's impossible to make up lost time, but for you two, I'll try.

Bob Weeks, October 1994

Foreword

Anyone who visits Benito, Manitoba, my hometown near the Saskatchewan border, would probably not mistake it for Vancouver or Toronto or any other big or medium-sized city in this country. It's a quaint and peaceful place where everyone knows everyone else. There's a lot of heart in Benito and a lot of pride, especially in winter when the ice goes in at the curling club. Just as the harvest celebrates the end of the farming season, the throwing of the first rock kicks off winter.

It was in this environment that I first came to realize there was a Canadian curling championship, an event that would later play a big part in my life. As I became more aware of it, I followed the big names such as Matt Baldwin and the Richardsons as they competed each March. I listened intently on the radio and followed the play in the newspapers, tracking each round with great enthusiasm.

Like every young curler, I thought there would be nothing better in the world than to play in the Brier. And unlike the Stanley Cup or the Grey Cup, there was something very appealing about it because I knew I had a chance to make it there. Even though I was from a small Prairie town, I could follow a long road and eventually get to the greatest curling event in the world.

That, I think, is what makes the Brier special. Everyone starts out at the same level in curling clubs across the country and has to work to get to the finish line. When the season begins, no one is further ahead than anyone else. Even last year's Brier winner has to make it out of his club.

The other appeal is that, more often than not, those who do get to the Brier aren't from the big centers, but from small towns and communities like Benito. And the event itself has been played in locales that would never host a football or hockey championship of the same calibre. It's not necessarily a small-town affair, but it is an open one, which allows people from places of all sizes to come together and share their enjoyment of the roaring game.

I have been lucky enough to make it to the Brier eight times and, on each occasion, there is a real sense of excitement. Certainly, the curling is a big part of that, but anyone who thinks the Brier is just about rocks going up and down the ice is sadly mistaken. Even for the players, the Brier is a time of fun and, sometimes, craziness. Yes, we work hard, but it is rare that a curler playing in the national championship won't take time to enjoy the festivities that go along with every Brier. Ask anyone with a Purple Heart what his fondest memory of a Brier is, and you probably won't hear a story that has to do with some miraculous shot. It will likely be about some humorous incident that took place off the ice.

That's really what the Brier is all about: a week-long festival that brings together people who love curling from all parts of the country. It doesn't matter what you do, where you come from or whether you're watching or playing; once you are there, you are a curler and part of a special fellowship.

With so many wonderful stories about this great championship —both on and off the ice—I was always saddened that there wasn't a record of it. This book will fill that void, preserving, and in some cases revealing, many of the great moments from Briers past. I can think of no better person to write this account than Bob Weeks. I have curled with Bob over the years, and even won a cashspiel or two with him, but I think even he'll admit he's a better writer than a curler. (He dumps his out-turns!)

Because he has some talent on the ice, however, he is able to sense what the curlers are feeling and bring those emotions to the reader. He is able to understand the game from the perspective of the best players and describe their experiences to a once-a-week curler in a downtown industrial league. Most importantly, there's a passion in Bob's words; it's easy to see that he writes from the heart.

So whether it's his heart, a Purple Heart, or the heart of curling fans across the country, that heart has played a part in making this book very special for those who gather every March, either in person or in front of their television sets, for the Brier, Canada's greatest sporting event.

Ed Werenich, July 1994

Prologue

The Dream Never Dies

It's a bitterly cold January evening in Huntsville, Ontario. Steam is filtering up from the street sewers and the ice squeaks under the boots of the people who dare to venture outside and risk frostbite. The wind whips one of the few traffic signals in this town of 12,000 tucked into Ontario's cottage country, about two hours north of Toronto, but there are few cars on the road to heed its flashing colors.

On most nights such as this, residents are bundled up in their homes, perhaps in front of a roaring fire, resting up for another onslaught of skiers and snowmobilers who will arrive the next morning for a day of winter fun. But tonight is different. Just off the main drag, a parking lot is overflowing. Cars are parked on every inch of the street and a steady stream of parkas and toques is entering the doors of an odd-shaped building.

The scene suggests one of those clown cars from the circus, only backwards: more and more people are going into this building, even though it must be bursting at the seams.

What could attract so many people on such a cruel night?

Inside the packed house, the answer is obvious—curling. But not just any curling: tonight is the second step on the arduous road to the Brier, the Canadian men's curling championship. These games are part of the storied playdowns. Players on 16 teams have come from clubs in the surrounding area to do battle in the zone competition. Two teams will emerge from this weekend of play to

1

travel on to the next level. Each team has come out of its own club, the first step, with hopes of reaching the finals of the ultimate Canadian sporting event.

And this scene is being played out in 1,300 curling clubs from coast to coast. In Cranbrook, British Columbia, and Gander, Newfoundland, all the way up in Whitehorse, Northwest Territories, and down in Windsor, Ontario. In Estevan, Saskatchewan, and Crapaud, Prince Edward Island, men are slipping on their sliders, stretching out their limbs, cleaning off their brooms and preparing to knock heads in a sport brought to Canada hundreds of years ago by transplanted Scots.

Close to 50,000 men will begin play, but only four will stand atop the podium early in March, a golden tankard held high above their heads. Along the way, dreams will die and hearts will break. A wick here and a rub there will send one team to the next game and another to the sidelines, there to wait for next year, when the dream can start all over again.

The Brier is the most nationalistic sporting event in Canada. It has become an important piece of a sporting culture that Americans and Europeans have continually invaded. It transcends politics and regional barriers, bringing together representatives from every province and the territories.

Its structure defies logic. It lasts for nine days and is held, not in large urban centers, but in places such as Red Deer, Alberta, Brandon, Manitoba, and Kamloops, British Columbia. If this decentralization is not testament enough to what an unusual event the Brier is, consider that, aside from the players, the most important person at this competition is the icemaker, the person who lays down and keeps the playing surface—only in Canada could someone earn prestige by freezing water.

Thousands of loyal fans will make the trek to the host city to take part in the festival that has grown around the Brier. They become as much a part of the event as the players, participating in decades-old rituals such as Ontario's North-South party, "morning classes" and provincial cheers. For nine days, they will pull for their team and wonder if the skip took too much ice or should have played the hit instead of the draw. Between draws, they will sing songs in the Brier Patch, the huge bar that has become a fixture at the tournament, and mix with curling lovers from every corner of the country. Francophones will dance with Anglos, Albertans will join arms with Ontarians, Newfoundlanders will buy folks from Saskatchewan a beer and no one will pay the slightest attention to the GST, sovereignty association or cod fishing.

Together, they will watch the best curling in the world performed by players from their club or their town or their province.

And make no mistake: there are no professionals participating in the Brier. In fact, there is no prize money, just a crest, a trophy and a medallion at the end of this winter rainbow. There are no multi-year agreements, no threats of strikes by players and, until recently, no agents or players' unions.

There are no American entries or expansions. Every competitor in the Brier is Canadian. There is no import rule, but none is needed, for the best curlers in the world are Canadian and the Brier is the top event of its kind in the sport. Only at the Canadian championship will you see such an assembly of superlative rock throwers.

And these players are not pampered athletes. When the Brier is over, they will return to work as firefighters, lawyers, accountants, farmers and waiters. But if they have made it, if they have worked themselves into the fraternity of Brier competitors, they will forever be held in high regard in any curling club in the country by virtue of a simple, heart-shaped purple crest that will adorn their sweater or jacket. It signifies participation in this pinnacle of curling, and represents a sort of sainthood among those who worship at the House of Granite.

Visions of that Purple Heart, the crest given to provincial champions, are dancing in the heads of curlers on the ice at the Huntsville Curling Club. For some, it is just that—a vision. They know they will never make it to the Brier without a ticket. But they still enter, year after year.

For one player here, however, the Brier is a realistic goal. It is also the reason why the cozy confines of the club are jammed to overflowing.

Tonight, the fans have come to see the Wrench.

In the last 20 years, no curler has been more at the forefront of the game than Ed "the Wrench" Werenich. A roly-poly man in his mid-forties with a thick mustache and graying hair, he is the unlikely star of curling. He looks no more like an athlete—let alone a Canadian and world champion—than someone's 100-year-old grandfather, but his deft touch and keen strategic mind have taken him to eight Briers and won him two.

Tonight, along with his teammates John Kawaja, Pat Perroud and Neil Harrison—fellow world champions—he is quite easily the class of the field. The appearance of the team seems to exude its talent. Nattily attired in athletic jackets emblazoned with the name of the team's sponsor, Adidas, the four stand out fashionably on an ice surface full of down vests, baseball caps and sweaters bearing crests of long-ago club bonspiel wins.

The smooth deliveries and keen communication are also indicators that this team is here with a purpose. While others on the ice have a choppy pattern to their play, Werenich's squad works together seamlessly, shooting, sweeping, calling, discussing and shooting again. There is no rushing, no guessing. The confidence is clear and every motion is deliberate.

For these four players, the Brier is not an apparition but a target. Making it there will determine if they have had a good year. Despite the $50,000 they have won in the 10 previous weeks of playing cash competitions in every part of the country, competing at the national final is the ultimate purpose of their winter.

And for Werenich, this year is vitally important. At 46, he knows he is running out of time if he hopes to capture another Brier. A third win would put him in exclusive company, alongside the likes of Howard Wood, Ken Watson, Matt Baldwin, Ron Northcott and the famous Richardson clan. Although he still shows signs of youthful exuberance, the grind of competitive curling has begun to grow old for Werenich. The fire that once drove him has burned down to flickering embers of desire.

Werenich has lived to curl and, to a certain extent, curled to live. The game has controlled the structure of his entire life. In his house, all the toys—the VCRs, the televisions, the computers—are a result of the game. Every piece of furniture has been purchased with curling money. In fact, the house is virtually paid for with prize money from curling. All Werenich's friends are curlers, and he chose his career as a firefighter at the suggestion of a curling cohort.

The sport has consumed him for more than three decades, and although he has sacrificed a great deal to play, he is aware that the choices he has made may not have been the wisest. He worries that the options he has chosen may also devour the lives of his two sons, Ryan and Darren.

"At one time, it was all I ever cared for," Werenich says of the game that is still his passion. "It was in my blood. Unfortunately, I think that's what's happening to my kids. It's becoming the only thing they really give a damn about. It hasn't done any harm to me, but I wonder if they aren't putting a little too much emphasis on it."

The Wrench's worries come from experience. He knows that very few have managed to make a living at curling. Only four people can win the Brier each year although so many make it their goal. For those who are successful, there can be rewards. For those who fail, the despair can be immense. Werenich has seen the broken hearts littered in clubs from coast to coast. These are the victims of desire who have put so much effort into reaching the Brier, only to find that it will never be possible. The lives of many have been changed because of an insatiable hunger to get to this Holy Grail of curling. Jobs have been abandoned, marriages have ended and fortunes have been spent all in the cause of getting to the Brier. Merv Mann is known throughout the curling world, not because he won the Brier, but because he is probably the greatest curler never to get there. For more than a quarter of a century, he battled it out in Saskatchewan for the small purple crest. While he won countless other events, his record is indelibly marked by his failure to reach the national final.

This is the intensity that worries Werenich. Although curling and the Brier have been good to him, he knows his sons must realize that there is more to life than this game of rocks and ice. But once bitten, very few escape the craving of just one more battle on the Brier trail. That is exactly what happened to Werenich.

He was born in Benito, Manitoba, a farming community of 500 people just a stone's throw from the Saskatchewan border. His Ukrainian parents had come to Canada in 1939 from eastern Europe, where the storm clouds of war were gathering. They were grain farmers, and Werenich and his two older brothers spent most of their time working the land. The basic values of agrarian life are still important to him.

It was not a privileged childhood, and Werenich always despised the class structure that saw wealthier neighboring communities look down on Benito. He took great delight in being able to show up some of those he called snobs.

At age 10, he accompanied his Grade 5 class to a curling rink, where he was introduced to the roaring game by his teacher, Miss Koroluk. From that moment, there was no turning back. Werenich was hooked and began playing at every chance.

"My mother couldn't understand why we were always throwing these tea kettles up and down the ice," Werenich recalled. "She didn't understand the game, but she always asked us what we won for prizes."

Along with his brother Tony, Werenich zipped around the Prairies in the family car, curling in any small town that had a bonspiel. When he wasn't competing, he was practicing, throwing hundreds of rocks daily, constantly refining his touch and looking for some sort of edge to the game.

After finishing high school, the Wrench packed up for the big city and moved to Toronto to find a little action. He took stabs at work and tried continuing his education at Ryerson, but everything took second place to curling. His infatuation with the game persisted, and he thought nothing of quitting jobs that restricted his bonspiel schedule.

By his own admission, Werenich was a rough farm boy in the city, without much more than a great curling touch and a pool cue from which he managed to eke out a living. But he knew he was home. He understood that Toronto was where he had to be. And so he managed to sweet-talk his girlfriend from Benito into coming to Toronto, and the former Linda Goulsbra eventually became Mrs. Wrench.

But the turning point in Werenich's life came in 1972 when he joined up with Paul Savage, a bon vivant and rising star on the Toronto curling scene. Savage had been the Ontario Schoolboy champion in 1965, and in 1970, at 22, had skipped his province in the Brier. Gradually, he had succeeded Alfie Phillips, Jr., the 1967 Canadian champ, as Ontario's dominant player.

While perhaps opposites in their upbringing—Paul was raised in suburban Toronto in an upper-middle-class neighborhood—Werenich and Savage were kindred spirits. Both existed for curling, parties and little else. Although it was a rare occasion when the two didn't argue on the ice, they were quite clearly made to curl together and became close friends.

With Savage at skip, Werenich playing second and a host of others filling in the gaps, they barnstormed across Ontario, playing in big events, carrying on until the wee hours and learning to win early morning games with raging hangovers.

By 1973, the team, which also included Bob Thompson and Ron Green at third and lead respectively, was good enough to be considered the favorites at the Ontario final. They won that event handily, and Werenich was off to his first Brier.

"I remember when we won," he says. "I was so excited, I couldn't do anything. There was a big party going on, but I just had a couple of beers, went to bed and lay there with my eyes wide open and a big smile on my face."

Unfortunately, three weeks later, his inaugural visit to the Brier became a huge disappointment. The Brier in Edmonton was a disaster of pitiful ice. It became known, in fact, as the Bad Ice Brier. There were puddles on the sheets and the surface became almost unplayable except for a small patch down the center. Where it wasn't melting, the frost buildup resembled a car's windshield after an ice storm. The temperature a foot above the ice level soared to an unbelievable 72 degrees Fahrenheit, and it was all the icemaking team could do not to lose the ice. On the sides, players could throw a rock as hard as physically possible and still not move an opposition stone from the rings.

"You had to let the rock go at your heels," recalls Morley Harry, the vice of the Northern Ontario team that year. "If you held onto it at all, you had no chance of getting it to the other end."

The Ontario team, used to the quick ice in eastern Canada, relied a great deal on delicate touch shots, but those became almost impossible under the conditions. For Werenich, it was too much to take. He became disinterested and spent some of the time during the games leaning against the side boards, eating hot dogs. Halfway through the week, after recording the third loss against two wins, he ditched his teammates, went back to the hotel and began packing his bag. "At that point, I didn't care if I ever curled again," Werenich remembers.

Livid with Werenich because he had missed a luncheon hosted by the Ontario Curling Association, Savage finally located his second, now somewhat cooler thanks to a few beers, and tore a strip off him. Werenich, who was not one to back down from anyone, fought back. The two stood toe-to-toe, screaming at each other for almost an hour before finally settling things over a few more beers.

The Savage-Werenich combination went back the next year to the Brier in London, Ontario, where conditions weren't much improved. Only a steady diet of partying kept them interested in the competition that year. They did manage to beat the eventual champions, the Hec Gervais rink of Alberta. If nothing else, that win was significant because the second on the championship team was Warren Hansen, who would become director of competitions for the Canadian Curling Association and Werenich's combatant in many future battles.

In 1977, the Ontario team returned to the Velodrome in Montreal and managed to tie for second in what Werenich described as another lackluster Brier. But the close finish made it very clear they could win the title.

However, the bickering between Werenich and Savage proved too much for the team to survive. Although close to winning the coveted Tankard, the two were on divergent paths when it came to strategy and curling philosophy.

And so, in 1981, Werenich left Savage to skip his own team, won Ontario and made it to the Brier semifinals, where he lost to Saskatchewan's Bob Ellert. Two years later, he enticed Savage to reunite, this time with Werenich skipping. That team, which also included Kawaja and Harrison, became known as the Dream Team. Pundits predicted the combination of egos and personalities on the rink would lead them to win everything or kill each other. Fortunately, the former prevailed and Werenich had his first Brier title.

From that high point, Werenich slowly fell into a curling funk. After another good season in 1984, when he and his Dream Teamers lost the Brier final to Manitoba's Mike Riley, the team began to unravel. By the end of 1985, the four players had split, Werenich, Savage and Kawaja all moving out to skip their own rinks.

Werenich made it back to two Briers during the next four years, but the magic was not there. Finally, in 1990, reunited with Kawaja and a front end of Ian Tetley and Pat Perroud (who had won the Brier in 1985 with Al Hackner of Northern Ontario), the Wrench captured a second championship in Sault Ste. Marie. Since that appearance, however, he has been stymied in his attempts at another Purple Heart.

But, like an addict, he wants one more hit, and that is what has brought him onto Sheet Two tonight in Huntsville. Although he is a class above the other teams, he is fully aware that, unlike in any other sport, a two-time world champion like himself can be side-lined by a hot team. A weekend golfer is unlikely to go out and beat Jack Nicklaus, a once-a-week tennis player could never handle Andre Agassi, but one of the pick-up teams in Huntsville might have a chance against Werenich.

Some funny ice, bad rocks or maybe a lucky angle-raise-double-wick-through-the-port could quickly spell the end for anyone.

Savage has already suffered just such a fate in his playdowns at Toronto's Avonlea Curling Club, losing at the hands of two club-level teams.

"You let down, the intensity isn't there," Werenich explains. "Being through it as many times as I have, I've lost to teams that I never should have. I know the chance of losing is there more so than in most sports, but you can't just say, 'Okay, come on guys, let's be intense.' It doesn't work that way. But I've seen some club teams that have come up and whacked guys they shouldn't have."

A good example is Werenich's competition on this Friday evening, Gary Smockum from Barrie, Ontario. Twelve months earlier, Smockum, who can be described as a semi-competitive player, needed only to hit an open stone and keep his shooter in the rings to knock off Russ Howard, a former Brier winner and the country's most successful team over the previous three years. Smockum made the hit, but rolled out of play and then lost in an extra end. He drove back to Barrie, heartbroken. Howard went on to win the world championship.

That's how quickly things can turn, how unpredictable curling can be. And so Werenich must keep his mind sharp and his game at its peak.

Although unlikely, one of those teams that could hand him a defeat this weekend sits on the next sheet to the Werenich-

Smockum game. David Lankin has been to the Brier, as a spectator. His winters are not spent crisscrossing the nation in search of curling competitions, but rather in Orillia, Ontario, where he works as a schoolteacher. His biggest victory came more than 30 years ago, when he won the 1962 Ontario university championship.

These days, Lankin is a once-a-week curler who plays for the camaraderie of the sport. While Werenich still practices almost daily, Lankin's regimen of preparation is a couple of slides from the hack moments before his game. His team has been curling together just a few months and merely signed up for the Brier playdowns because he and his friends thought it would be fun.

Lankin began throwing rocks on natural ice at the age of 12 and, like all young curlers, dreamed of playing in the Brier. Now, however, at 51, he knows he is unlikely to make it past this level of play. Still, he enters annually to see how far he can get on the playdown route and to enjoy the friendship of curlers from around the area.

And for this brief moment, Lankin is at the same level as Ed Werenich. One is a fellow who might have a hard time winning a Christmas mixed half-day bonspiel; the other has been champion of the world twice. But the two are traveling the same road leading to the Brier, and despite their varying skills and backgrounds, neither one is any further ahead. There are no shortcuts to the Brier. Every game must be played, every end contested.

That is part of the beauty of the event. There is a feeling that anyone could win the Brier. At the very least, each team has a chance. Whatever his record or past history, anyone who signs up could get to the Brier. These same people would never enter a nation-wide competition of 100-meter dashers, or pole vaulters or speed-skaters, because, in those events, they know they would never stand a chance. While the same is probably true in the Brier, there is at least a glimmer of opportunity that in a simple game, somehow, sometime, they might just have a chance.

Realistically, of the 50,000 competitors entered in the playdowns, 49,000 are probably like Lankin. They enter knowing they don't have a hope of seeing a Purple Heart, but understanding that everyone, including Werenich or Howard, still has to get out of his club, past his zone, through his district and win the provincial.

"I can relate to Rick Folk and Russ Howard when I see them in the Brier final on television," Lankin states, "because I know I was playing in that same competition. I know they started out just like I did."

Well, maybe not quite like Lankin. In his first game of the zone playdown, he is trailing 7–1 after five ends, although few people in the Huntsville Curling Club have noticed. Most eyes are focused on Werenich's ice. As they look on, the Wrench calmly draws his final stone of the fifth end around some guards and up to the corner of the four-foot circle to take three points. As the rock settles on its target, the crowd buzzes with amazement. For them, a cold draw to the center of the sheet is an extremely difficult task. For Werenich, it is expected.

Meanwhile, Lankin calls himself for a takeout but throws the rock so light it fails to remove the opposition stone. No one in the crowd hoots at this obvious gaffe. They have seen this mistake too often in their own games.

Prophetically, perhaps, on a strip of wall separating the two viewing windows of Sheet Two and Sheet Three hangs a small sign with the title "Curler's Prayer." It reads: "Give me the wisdom, and half the class, as those bastards, behind the glass."

As the evening wears on, the spectators continue to marvel at the play of the Werenich team. With each delicate shot, pockets of appreciative comments filter up from all over the club. For these folks, watching the playdowns is like going to the movies. It's a night of entertainment, an evening of fun and laughter. And like seeing an Oscar-nominated movie, the attraction of the Brier playdowns and the presence of Ed Werenich assure them of a good evening.

By the eighth end of his scheduled 10-end contest, Werenich has enough of a lead that Smockum has conceded. The eight players shake hands and retire to the lounge to go over the game.

With the feature contest over, many fans head out. Others make a beeline for the bar, where they order up one more. Only a few continue to watch Lankin begin an incredible comeback.

After 10 ends, he has managed to tie the score at 10. As he plays an extra end, even Werenich, a rye and coke in hand, is taking notice behind the glass as the decisive rocks are thrown. Although he is light-years ahead in skill and strategy, the Wrench can still find pleasure in watching the outcome of Lankin's match. Like the people who were sitting in the same seats an hour earlier watching him, he comments on the shot selection and the outcome of each stone.

Unfortunately, the comeback falls short. With his last stone, Lankin fans an open hit to win the game.

The next morning, Lankin will again lose in the double-knockout competition, and his Brier playdowns will have ended for another year. Like so many other teams, however, he will return again in 12 months to do it all over, almost certain that he has no chance of getting to the national final.

Werenich will waltz through this stage and the next. But, like Lankin, his season will end prematurely. At the Ontario final, he will find himself one win shy of a play-off spot and will watch from the sidelines as Russ Howard claims his fourth consecutive Brier berth. Howard, too, will fall a game short, losing in the national final to British Columbia's Rick Folk.

For the 64th time, the Brier has one winner and many, many losers. And although no one will remember David Lankin or others like him, they are an important part of the competition. Along with the crowds who watch at the club and in arenas, and members of the press who cover the events, the tens of thousands of curlers who have dreamed of hoisting the trophy high above their heads have helped to make the Brier into an unparalleled and unique Canadian sporting tradition.

1

Setting the Foundation

Tracing the roots of curling in Canada and exploring the history of the national championship that grew from them is a speculative process at best. Some romantics claim that soldiers serving under General Wolfe curled on the St. Lawrence River as far back as 1759, using melted-down cannonballs for stones. While that story may or may not be true, it is certain that Scottish immigrants brought the game to Canada as early, perhaps, as the 1750s, where it flourished as a pastime during the long winter months.

Soon the curlers began to formalize their favorite pursuit. The oldest organized sporting club in North America, the Royal Montreal Curling Club, was founded in 1807 by 20 prominent businessmen in Montreal, and more clubs quickly followed in Lower Canada. As new immigrants moved westward, more and more clubs were created, although it was some time before there were formal associations to link them in any way.

By the turn of the century, curling was growing in popularity, and major tournaments such as the Manitoba Bonspiel (begun in 1888 and the world's largest annual curling event today), the Quebec Bonspiel and the Toronto Bonspiel were firmly entrenched in the winter calendars of most sporting enthusiasts. Teams traveled in either large groups or individual rinks to many of these championships, and ties began to strengthen between curlers in different Canadian centers.

In 1902, the first tour of Scottish curlers came to Canada to play a series of matches against Maritime, Quebec and Ontario teams, as well as several teams in the northeastern United States. In 1909, a group of Canadians went to Scotland for a reciprocal expedition.

Although teams from various parts of the country were on this tour and regularly played against each other at the big bonspiels, it was not until the end of the First World War that any thought was given to a national championship. As the 1920s arrived, Canada was basking in the pride of a maturing nation. The horrors of the war, if good for nothing else, had instilled a nationalistic spirit from coast to coast, and Canadian soldiers had returned home to find a country determined to stand on its own. The economy was booming and there was a general feeling of optimism everywhere. The time was ripe to set up a Canadian championship.

But there were still major obstacles to bypass. While curling was played across the country, it was a different game in different regions. In the West, the sport was supported by the rural communities, with farmers passing the long, cold Prairie winters by tossing granite stones. Small two-sheet, natural-ice clubs dotted the landscape in most communities with more than 100 residents. The curling club was the hub of the winter social scene until it was time for farmers to return to the fields in the spring.

In Quebec and Ontario, curling was more of an elitist sport. Many clubs were found in urban centers and had exclusive memberships, catering to the upper classes. And in Quebec, especially, irons were the instruments of choice (were they the descendants of Wolfe's cannonballs?). Curling irons, as their name suggests, were made of iron and weighed about 20 pounds more than the granite stones used in western Canada. They were also almost impossible to move with a takeout. Even when the shooter was thrown with enough weight to travel through the back wall of most clubs, an iron would hardly budge. So, not only was the equipment different, the style of the game was distinct. Those who played with the irons relied almost exclusively on a draw game, while hitting became an accepted part of the strategy out west.

Although they were used sporadically in Montreal, granites were looked down on in Quebec. Tradition reigned, despite the fact that many players believed the granite game provided more entertaining sport. In the haughty clubs of Lower Canada, most thought granites to be inferior and almost brash. There was certainly no thought given to switching, even if it would mean parity with the rest of the country.

Because most of them continued to use irons, Quebec curlers did not often compete outside their own province. In its own backward manner, this tradition may have had a hand in starting the Brier.

By 1924, the Manitoba Bonspiel was the most significant curling championship in the country, and teams would travel from various parts of Canada to play in it. While the event annually drew hundreds of entries, the organizing committee was determined to keep increasing the field, and looked to Montreal as a natural place from which to draw a few more rinks. One of the bonspiel's council members, George J. Cameron, offered to help.

Cameron was the president of W.L Mackenzie and Company, the representatives for Macdonald Tobacco in western Canada. He regularly traveled to Montreal to meet with officials at the head office of the tobacco company and said that on his next trip, he would ask some of the granite players in Montreal if they would be interested in making the trip west for the big spiel.

Cameron had been born near London, Ontario, in 1881 and moved to Winnipeg in 1900. Four years later, he took up curling and became, if not the most proficient of players, certainly one of the most enthusiastic. What Cameron lacked in ability on the ice, he made up for in administrative talent, dedicating himself to the betterment of the sport he loved. He sat on numerous committees, and in 1928, became president of the Manitoba Curling Association.

A dedicated volunteer, during his lifetime Cameron was also president of the Winnipeg Board of Trade, the Aquatic Club of Lake Winnipeg and the Winnipeg Rotary Club, a national councillor of the Canadian Chamber of Commerce and a life member of the Manitoba Rifle Association. A strong nationalist who used his ties in various parts of the country to help strengthen his business, he held strong convictions about Canada and was quick to offer them to anyone who would listen.

While in Montreal on his recruiting mission, Cameron sent back a good news–bad news wire to the Manitoba committee.

Unfortunately, due to their previous commitments, he was unable to attract any teams to the bonspiel. But he had succeeded in convincing Macdonald Tobacco to put up a trophy for the Manitoba Bonspiel that included a unique prize: the winner of the new trophy would receive an all-expenses-paid trip to eastern Canadian cities for a series of goodwill curling matches, and the tobacco giant would pick up the tab.

The Manitobans quickly accepted the Macdonald company's kind gesture and decided that a special playdown among teams in the big bonspiel would determine the winner of the new prize. It was agreed that rinks reaching the quarter-finals of the four primary events would be eligible for the new prize, and 14 teams entered for the inaugural playdown.

When the extra competition had concluded, the team of Howard "Pappy" Wood, John Erzinger, Jr., Victor Wood and Lionel Wood, accompanied by a small contingent of officials and media, headed east.

Organizers could not have hoped for a better ambassador than Wood, a boisterous, vivacious man who had ruled the ice in Winnipeg for many years. Wood began his curling career in 1903 on a backyard rink built by his father, who had been president of the Manitoba Curling Association in 1900-01. In 1908, Wood entered the Manitoba Bonspiel for the first time and, incredibly, competed in the tournament for 70 consecutive years, a feat that has found a place in the *Guinness Book of Records*. He won numerous championships, including the Manitoba Bonspiel Grand Aggregate eight times. In 1947, he had the distinction of capturing the first-ever car bonspiel—he and his team drove home from Nipawin, Saskatchewan, in four new Hudsons.

Wood was an outgoing man who was always shaking hands and slapping backs. He spread the gospel on his eastern trip and became a popular guest. The fact that he could curl with such expertise only helped to build his reputation.

The tour began in Montreal and visited Quebec, Ottawa, Toronto, Hamilton and Detroit, and became a marathon not only of curling but of banquets and hospitality, as each host club attempted to outdo the previous one.

The weather for the March jaunt was unseasonably mild, and one game in Toronto was actually contested on the lawn bowling pitch of the Granite Club—using lawn bowls, not stones—when the ice proved unplayable. The Winnipeg rink also experienced its first earthquake when a minor rumble passed through Quebec City, although the only thing that continued to shake was the nerve of its opponents as Wood's team won most of its games.

In all, the trip lasted two weeks and two days and fostered strong ties between eastern and western curlers. Many of the leaders of the Quebec curling community used the tour to pull for a national association of clubs. They wished to see western organizations set up branches of the Royal Caledonian Curling Club of Scotland (the mother club of curling, which had established the rules of the sport) as they had done in Quebec. The idea was to have a national body organized under the RCCC to deal with national and international competitions. For the Westerners, however, that idea was still premature.

One of the other accomplishments of the journey was showing the appeal of the granite game to the iron players in Quebec. If there was to be a national body, there had to be only one type of stone in use, and the play of the Wood rink may have begun to upset the balance in favor of granites.

Significantly, just a few weeks after the Winnipeggers left Montreal, a large open bonspiel using granite stones was held at the Forum, where the artificial ice—a rarity for curling at that time —was used for a grand finale to the curling season. The bonspiel was deemed a huge success and won many converts from the irons.

In 1926, the winning team of the Macdonald-sponsored event was another Winnipeg rink, this time skipped by George Sherwood. If the Wood team felt overwhelmed by its itinerary a year earlier, then the Sherwood team, which included C.A.V. Edge, L.S. Tinling and R.L. Vincent, must have wondered if the opposition was trying to gain an edge by celebrating it into the ground. The records reveal that the team was away for 17 days, traveled 3,700 miles, played 19 games (winning 18 of them)—and attended no fewer than 19 banquets.

At the quiet request of Cameron, the second tour featured more competitive games, including play by the Winnipeggers in the Quebec City Bonspiel, where they won the Holt Renfrew event. Cameron felt that, if the tour was to grow, more than goodwill had to spur it on. The first tour saw the Wood team compete against curlers who were well known but perhaps not well skilled. Cameron pushed to instill a good-natured but keen sense of rivalry that would increase the profile of future visits. However, it was hard to think about competitive games when the Winnipeg team walloped most of its opponents, sometimes by more than 20 points, losing only to Ross Hartstone of Hamilton.

If the 1925 tour had planted a seed for a national championship, then the second tour allowed that seed to germinate. Knowing what to expect in 1926, the Manitobans sent an additional dozen travelers, all of them leading curling officials of one sort or another. Most had joined the caravan with the aim of building on the tour. They were met by an equal number of curling enthusiasts in Ontario and Quebec, who wished to reach the same conclusion.

At one significant meeting held at Toronto's King Edward Hotel, the idea of a national championship was put forth for discussion. It became quite clear that all parties wanted the same thing: a championship that would bring together the best curlers in the country for national honors.

That meeting was chaired by Thomas Rennie, then the president of the Ontario Curling Association and an influential man in Toronto business circles. Rennie worked for his father's seed company, the William Rennie Company, and eventually became the firm's president. He worked the business into the most successful of its kind in the country.

An experienced curler, Rennie had started playing the game at the age of five in 1873, using wooden blocks on a backyard rink. He graduated to win Ontario's most prestigious event, the Silver Tankard, eight times, and finished second on three other occasions. He reached the final of the Toronto single-rink championship 16 times, winning 10 of those matches. He was also a lawn bowler of some distinction, leading a Canadian team to an international victory against squads from England, Wales, Scotland and Ireland in 1913.

Playing out of the Granite Club, Rennie was a regular visitor to the Manitoba Bonspiel and knew many of the officials on the 1926 tour. At the Toronto meeting, he and Cameron worked the room to get all attendees on side for the common goal: a national championship. The plan was for Cameron to go to the Macdonald Tobacco Company and, after showing it how successful inter-provincial games between competitive rinks had become in two short years, ask the company to upgrade its support to a national bonspiel.

The reaction at the Montreal office to the Cameron-Rennie plan was positive, primarily because of the people running the company. Curlers may not have realized it then, but they were about to begin a long association with Macdonald Tobacco and its president, Walter M. Stewart.

Stewart had started with the company as a clerk, working for founder Sir William Macdonald. The latter gentleman was one of the great philanthropists of 19th-century Canada, donating funds to assist education and medicine. Macdonald College, part of McGill University, was built with his support, and help was also given to what is now the University of Guelph. He created grants that led to the establishment of the Royal Victoria Hospital in Montreal and other medical and educational facilities throughout the country.

When he died, Macdonald left the company to Stewart, who ruled the business with a domineering presence. Somewhat of a paranoid eccentric, he had the only key to the company door and all mail crossed his desk. If he decided a letter or a piece of correspondence should be dealt with, he passed it on. If not, it was never seen by the addressee. In later years, Stewart would not even allow his son, David, to have a phone in his office. David Stewart became an important part of Macdonald Tobacco, but when he wanted to make a phone call, he had to use a pay phone on the street.

Walter Stewart did, however, continue his mentor's generous ways. Of prime interest to the new president was supporting events, organizations or structures that promoted Canada. Caught up in the euphoria of the 1920s, Stewart made it the corporate philosophy to build the nation through example and support, always acting as a good citizen.

In addition to continuing the medical and educational grants, Stewart believed that sports fit neatly into the company's philosophy. One of his first actions was to put up a trophy for the best in Canadian rifle shooting at the Connaught ranges in Ottawa.

Shortly after, Cameron approached Stewart with the curlers' new idea. Although he had never curled, Stewart was a keen sportsman and became taken with the idea of assisting the rock throwers in their efforts to form a national championship. He was also likely influenced by his brother, Howard, an active player in the Montreal area (who would go on to play in six Briers), and one of the biggest supporters of the transition to granites.

So staunch a believer in granites was Howard Stewart that he actually offered to buy new Ailsa Craig stones for any Montreal curler who wished to replace his or her irons. He ended up purchasing more than 200 pairs and is given credit for convincing many players to make the switch.

"Uncle Howard went from iron to granite rocks," recalled David Stewart in a Brier program decades later. "He became very enthusiastic and began promoting granites in the East. George Cameron, Macdonald's western representative, was interested in an inter-provincial competition. Cameron had no difficulty selling my father on the idea because it was precisely the type of thing he had been moving towards all his life."

Walter Stewart did have some stipulations about the event that would bear the company's name. He said the competition had to strive to be national in scope, attracting entries from every region, and also that it maintain its simplicity. Most emphatically, he wanted the atmosphere to be one of fun and sportsmanship, and hoped that, as the event grew in stature, the publicity surrounding it would be used to promote the game across the country.

Despite his overbearing control of the business, Walter Stewart was a reclusive and guarded man. Incredibly, he never attended a Brier. As well, he never considered his support for the Brier a form of sponsorship for Macdonald Tobacco. He said the company was assisting the curlers with their game and helping to build the nation. In the 50 years in which the company funded the Brier, the money was never budgeted as advertising. Moreover, when the championship was moved to various locales in later years, Stewart never even considered removing existing advertising from competitors from the facilities.

Nevertheless, the name of the tournament came from a brand of Macdonald tobacco known as Brier. Ads in newspapers of the day read: "Everywhere! Brier smoked by more men than any other brand in Canada. It's the tobacco with heart." Each cut plug came with a small tin heart stuck in the middle. That symbol was the progenitor of the Purple Heart, first presented to provincial winners in the early 1930s. The competition was originally known as the Dominion Curling Championship for the Macdonald's Brier Tankard, but as years went on, the name "Brier" came to be synonymous with the event.

How or why the name Brier was chosen for the curling trophy is unknown (the Macdonald Brier trophy was first handed out to the winners of the Manitoba Bonspiel in 1925), but as a shrewd businessman, Walter Stewart certainly did not seem to have any aversion to using it, despite his prohibition against referring to the company's help as sponsorship. But other sports sponsorships in later years also made use of Macdonald's brand names, including an East Coast hockey team known as the British Consols, and company correspondence suggested concern when certain outlets refused to use these brand names when reporting on an event.

While the company's funding may have seemed like a generous, well-intentioned donation, it was probably, in fact, the start of brand marketing in sports. Stewart's strong public stand on making the money a donation and not advertising could very well have been tactical—a ploy to get media to proclaim Macdonald Tobacco's benevolence. Indeed, reports of the day did refer to the company's "quiet generosity."

Aside from his few stipulations, Stewart removed himself completely from the operation of the new event. Instead, he placed his trust in those who knew the game, naming three trustees to oversee the competition in its entirety. Years later, David Stewart outlined his father's philosophy to writer Doug Maxwell in the book *The First Fifty*: "He was an intensely shy man and believed that you should get good people to run the event, give them a philosophical framework in which to operate and let them do the job."

The three appointees were all well-known curlers. Rennie was the first chairman of the Brier trustees, as the group became known, and was joined by Lt. Col. Peter Lyall of Montreal, who made four appearances in the Brier as a player, and Senator Jack Haig of Winnipeg.

These trustees and their successors ran the Brier, plain and simple, until Macdonald Tobacco bowed out in 1979. Only at that time did the Canadian Curling Association effectively assume full control of the competition.

In the early years, this troika became the most powerful group in

Canadian curling, shaping the way in which the national championship grew and making decisions that would eventually have a great impact on the sport.

Yet absolute power did not corrupt absolutely. The three trustees were appreciated and respected by most, perhaps no more so than in the inaugural year of the championship. Without script or precedent, they had to shoulder the great responsibility of ensuring the event was worthy of a national title.

Some decisions about the Dominion Curling Championship came easily for the trustees. First, they decided to make the competition a round-robin, thus guaranteeing a true national champion. The second issue was location. Because Macdonald was picking up the tab for bringing in all the teams, Toronto, as the most central location, seemed the obvious choice. And the opulent new Granite Club, billed as "the largest single covered expanse of artificial ice on the American continent," was perfect for a host site. Just a year old, the club, near the intersection of Yonge Street and St. Clair Avenue, was also large enough to accommodate the expected crowds and had facilities to host the various functions that were planned. There were even a few rooms where some of the lucky teams could stay during the competition.

The third decision was stickier: selecting the teams. The trustees opted to make the 1927 championship an invitational event. They sent requests to eight curling associations, some provincial, some city (Montreal and Toronto), to send teams to the initial competition. Because many of the provinces did not have official single-rink provincial championships (at that time, many provincial titles were double-rink competitions in which two teams played against two teams in a total-points format), many representatives were the winners of big bonspiels. Toronto, for example, sent the winners of the Canada Life trophy. Ontario sent the champions of the Ontario Silver Tankard, an event held regularly since 1875.

That Ontario team, from Sarnia, almost didn't accept the invitation. Skip Col. John Mackenzie, along with the team's vice, Bill Watson, had left for Florida to wait out the winter shortly after claiming the Silver Tankard title. The team's second, Mel Hunt (father of noted Toronto sportswriter Jim Hunt), and lead Harry Watson (grandfather of *Hockey Night In Canada* broadcaster Harry Neale) managed to locate the snowbirds and sent a wire telling them the team had been selected to participate in the new Canadian championship. The two sent back their positive intentions and arrived in Toronto just four days before the start of the event—they had gone more than a month without throwing a stone and were now vying for a Canadian title!

Other squads were handpicked by the regional associations. One of those was the Nova Scotia team skipped by Professor Murray Macneill. Those in charge of making the selection felt it would be fair to choose the four best players and send them to carry Nova Scotia's colors. The Montreal team was also an amalgamation rink made up of Lyall at skip and Howard Stewart at second. They were chosen just two days before the Brier's start, and rushed to Toronto to prepare.

The idea of inviting teams from Montreal and Toronto may seem unusual when looking at today's Brier fields, but all the entries were, in effect, more regional than provincial. Teams even played under their city names, such as Sarnia, Saint John and Montreal (representing the Granite Curling Association). In fact, to this day Northern Ontario has a separate entry. It was seen as a distinct region and had its own curling council, so it was granted an entry in the Brier. (Because of the large travel costs involved in holding an all-Ontario final, the arrangement was never changed.) That team—Emmet Smith and his rink from Haileybury—was invited and, in newspaper reports, referred to as the New Ontario team.

There was only one entry from western Canada the first year, and that came from Yellow Grass, Saskatchewan. Skipped by the outgoing Ossie Barkwell, the team had defeated Jimmy Congalton to win the Manitoba Bonspiel. Complete with their own rocks, the Barkwell team left the next week for Toronto and the Brier to compete under the weighty banner of western Canada. What they saw when they arrived at the Granite Club must have amazed them.

In 1927, there was no curling rink like the Granite. For one thing, there were no dividers between the sheets, a standard feature in the West. Many curlers today may think the boards dividing the sheets were used to prevent rocks from spilling onto adjacent sheets, but that was not the case. In the West, most rinks were not built near running water, so there were no places to hook up hoses.

To flood these rinks, a frame of the curling sheet's dimensions was first constructed and large water barrels were placed around the outside. Manned by two "tippers," the barrels were all tipped into the frame at the same time.

Things were a little different at the Granite Club. It was a curling palace, and it attracted the game's elite. The club had started in the 1880s when a group of players split from the Toronto Curling Club because not enough emphasis was being placed on curling. Those breakaway members certainly couldn't complain now. The first national bonspiel was being held on their ice.

And so, with everything in place, the Dominion Championship began. The affair started with an opening banquet (a tradition still observed) with the Lieutenant-Governor of Ontario, W.D. Ross, and Premier Howard Ferguson welcoming the players. Noted Canadian golfer and cricketer George S. Lyon (who was not as well known for, but was equally adept at, curling) also said a few words.

The first day of play, March 1, 1927, drew large and curious crowds. The *Toronto Star* heralded the start with the headline, "Brilliant Play Marks Opening of Dominion-Wide Event," although it relegated the story to the back of the sports section, behind reports of women's college hockey, badminton and Babe Ruth signing a new contract for $210,000. But there was a definite excitement in the air among the curling fans, who were anxious to see the players from other parts of the country.

The diverse styles of curling immediately attracted attention, but no rink stood out more than Ossie Barkwell's. Curlers in the East had never seen a deliberate hitting game such as that of the Westerners. It drew responses of shock, bewilderment, amazement and even laughter. But it did seem to work.

The *Globe* commented on Barkwell's unusual strategy: "Of the many features that marked the curling yesterday, the playing of Ossie Barkwell's rink from the prairies of sunny southern Saskatchewan was in marked contrast to the method employed by the Maritime and Ontario and Quebec rinks . . . The Barkwell team has no patience with the calm, deliberate method of building up ends with fine draws such as the eastern rinks depend on. They can draw shots when the occasion demands but they favor the running shot, the beef and the brawn of the curling game."

While Barkwell smashed his way to a 3-4 record, it was two eastern teams that fought it out for the championship. Macneill gained a big advantage on the field with his play on the second day when he skipped his Halifax team to three wins in the 14-end games, moving his record to 4-1. He was followed closely by New Brunswick's Johnny Malcolm, who was also skipping a composite rink made up of players from four different clubs.

In the sixth round, Macneill, who had been picked because of winning the Johnson Cup, a significant event in Nova Scotia, came back from an eight-point deficit to knock off the Montreal entry. That sealed the title, and the handpicked Nova Scotia team became the first winner of the Dominion Curling Championship for the Macdonald's Brier Tankard.

In the main room of the Granite Club, Macneill and his mates, Al MacInnes, Cliff Torey and Jim Donahue, were presented with silver tea sets and gold medallions.

Back in Halifax, news of the victory spread quickly. The *Halifax Herald* ran a large page-one headline proclaiming, "Local curlers win Canada Championship," and added head shots of the newly crowned winners.

For Macneill, it was the culmination of a long curling career. He had started playing the game in his backyard while a boy in Saint John, New Brunswick. He cut the end off large poles to make rocks and inserted wire into the middle of the wooden disks for handles. He even pebbled the ice and held big bonspiels, gathering the boys from his neighborhood to play.

Always competitive and usually a winner, Macneill continued his game for many years, graduating to the adult ranks where he became one of the top players on the East Coast. His win at the first Dominion Curling Championship assured him of fame, perhaps even immortality, among the curling fraternity.

The process of bringing together the top rinks in the country had proven a huge achievement. Large crowds marveled at the curling, billed in the *Globe* as "the best Toronto has ever seen." With this kind of momentum behind it, it was almost certain the competition would become an annual affair, and when Walter Stewart gave the event his company's blessing, the Brier was officially born as the Canadian Curling Championship.

2

The Early Years

By the time the teams arrived for the second Dominion Curling Championship for the Macdonald's Brier Tankard, several significant changes had occurred.

First was the addition of two teams from the West. Manitoba and Alberta joined Saskatchewan, increasing the field to 10 and the round-robin to nine games.

Second, with the exception of Montreal, Toronto and Northern Ontario, entries were provincial representatives, not regional. Third, at the suggestion of Ossie Barkwell following the first Brier, the games went from 14 ends to 12. Twelve was becoming the standard in many competitions, and the wear and tear on the Brier players after the first year was often criticized. With two more games to play in 1928, this change was almost a necessity.

Finally, by the end of the second national championship, curling would have its first star, Gordon Hudson of the Strathcona Curling Club in Winnipeg.

Nicknamed Poker Face, Hudson was a popular player among the curling brethren. A large man with ruddy features, he had been successful in the Manitoba Bonspiel for many years, winning various events and many big games. He made his debut in that bonspiel at the age of 15 in 1909 and went on to capture a total of 27 trophies in various events, including five Grand Aggregates or overall championships.

Hudson was a quiet man who kept his words to a minimum,

preferring to let his curling speak for him. He showed little emotion on the ice or off, but was respected throughout his club and beyond. Like the rest of the players of his day, Hudson performed in a shirt and tie, covered by a large, shawl-neck sweater. A peaked cap always sat atop his head, in contrast to the fedora worn by most competitors.

What made him so talented at curling was his delicate touch and keen eye. "He had all the shots," said clubmate and rival Leo Johnson. "He was a really finished product as a curler and it never hurt to lose to a curler like him."

Hudson arrived on the scene as the Roaring Twenties were turning into the Great Depression. Mackenzie King had just been elected for a second term in office and the country was hunkering down into a deep funk. More and more, people turned to sport to take their mind off the sad state of the economy; in addition to Foster Hewitt's nation-wide broadcasts of hockey, which had begun in 1922, the scoring exploits of Montreal Canadiens' Howie Morenz and the Olympic skating of Norway's Sonja Henie, winter sports enthusiasts looked to curling—and to Hudson.

Despite his stoney expression, Hudson was a perfect attraction to take curling out of the clubs and into the Canadian sporting scene. One of the reasons he became so popular was his delivery. The big Winnipegger was one of the first Brier players to leave the hack when he threw his stone. He would slide out all the way to the back of the eight-foot on the side of his shoe in what became known as the Strathcona delivery. He also started the style, whether by accident or intent, of keeping his trailing foot turned down so the ankle rested on the ice.

His smooth, flowing, graceful delivery proved very accurate, and Hudson was described by reporters at the second Brier as "Lindbergh on ice," after the famed aviator of the day.

Hudson's rink of Sam Penwarden, Ron Singbush and Bill Grant was also one of the first to work as a team instead of as four good curlers. Each player knew his duties and concentrated solely on that task. However, that did not mean they didn't enjoy the friendly spirit of the roaring game.

C.O. Knowles of the *Toronto Telegram* wrote of the dominant team, "Not only are they good players, but good sports. The score is never written on their faces. If they get a bad break, they keep on plying the same steady, consistent game just the same as if everything was coming their way. They are perfectly disciplined, the skip knows his business and the other players know that he knows and don't waste time arguing or suggesting that perhaps he is wrong."

The Manitoba entry powered its way through the first seven games of the 1928 championship without a loss. On the second day of the competition, it outscored the opposition 47-9 in easily winning three of those contests. By the time Hudson knocked off Toronto's Charlie Snow in the seventh round, the talk was of a perfect record. The team seemed unbeatable; certainly, no one could find a weak spot.

But Hudson did finally stumble, losing 9-8 to Alberta in the eighth round and then dropping his final game by the same score to Ontario. That set up a three-way play-off for first between Manitoba, Alberta and Toronto.

Snow's Toronto rink from the Lakeview Curling Club had won the Canada Life Trophy a few weeks earlier and was the crowd favorite at the Granite Club. Huge throngs filled the facility in hopes of seeing a hometown victory.

The Alberta rink was a bit of an anomaly. Although playing under the Alberta banner, the team, skipped by the colorful Hellfire Joe Heartwell, was actually from Rosetown, Saskatchewan. Heartwell had entered the Saskatchewan playdowns but lost out. Undaunted and noticing a loophole in the rules, he took his team to Alberta and won that province's championship. Following that slipup, the trustees amended the rulebook to prevent such a thing from happening again.

The Manitoba team was also popular with the fans, although more because of the team's prowess. The spectators knew this was the best team and marveled at its ability, especially the powerful and effective sweeping.

"Compare the sweeping style of the Hudson rink with the others," enthused the *Toronto Telegram*. "The brooms are plied with a precision and vigor that makes a vacuum cleaner look, by comparison, like an antiquated carpet sweeper."

These three teams finishing in a tie not only ensured a dramatic finish but also left the organizers in a bind. While a two-team play-off had been thought out, the Brier trustees were unprepared for a three-way tie and scrambled to devise a suitable format to determine the Canadian champion. They elected to play a mini round-robin, with each team playing two games. Only after play had begun did someone point out that this arrangement could produce another three-way tie if all three teams went 1-1.

Thankfully, Hudson rescued the trustees from any further embarrassment when he rallied to beat Alberta 12-7 and Toronto 10-6.

The two games were notable for more than just their score. Hudson stunned the Toronto crowd in the game against Alberta by throwing his final stone in the 11th end through the rings to give up a point, but retain last rock in the final frame. Although not uncommon out west, this strategy was unheard of in eastern Canada and caused a buzz among the officials.

"The Eastern folk saw something most of them never saw before," wrote the *Winnipeg Tribune*. "It was the giving away of a point to retain the last rock. Down here, they don't place half as much importance on the last rock as they do out West."

In the final match versus Toronto, Hudson notched his place in Brier history by drawing cold to the four-foot 10 times in a performance that was called "magical" by one paper. The new champions were feted at the Granite Club that night and received silver tea services and gold medals from Lieutenant-Governor W.D. Ross.

While the victory was certainly a highlight, when he returned home to Winnipeg the following week, Hudson was still in awe of something else—Niagara Falls. The new champion had convinced prominent Ontario curler Ross Hartstone to drive the team to the falls the day after the win. Hudson was apparently as inspired by the natural wonder as by the Brier win, because he couldn't stop talking about it when he arrived home.

One sidelight to the 1928 championship was the first talk of a national curling body to look after the sport's affairs. Representatives of the 10 entries all received notices that stated, "A meeting has been called for Friday afternoon to discuss the advisability of forming a dominion curling association. This would ensure uniform rules throughout Canada and a maximum weight of rocks."

While it was encouraging, the meeting did not produce any concrete national body, primarily because none of the attendees had been empowered to vote on such a matter. One of the Brier trustees, Jack Haig, did resolve a motion that the various associations return to the 1929 championship with the power to cast such a vote. From this small, informal meeting, the roots of the Canadian Curling Association were born.

Even as the representatives returned to Toronto the following year, so did the defending champion of the Brier. Hudson was quite obviously the favorite in 1929 and even became a bit of a celebrity among the media and fans, who once again flocked to the championship.

But the team, this time with Don Rollo at vice replacing Sam Penwarden, who had passed away, still concentrated on the task at hand.

Hudson won his first five games and then came up against Nova Scotia. Although the Winnipeger won the game handily 13-4, it should be noted that Nova Scotia skip, H. St. Clair Silver, was a spry 71 when he took to the ice. And if his age was not a disadvantage, then his tools of the trade were. The Nova Scotia rink arrived at the Granite Club with 38-pound rocks, nine pounds lighter than those of every other team. Needless to say, takeouts were a difficult task for the Bluenosers.

Early on, it was clear that the four Manitoba curlers would not be distracted by older players or fan hoopla, and they rolled to a perfect 9-0 mark, winning a close match against Saskatchewan in the final round to clinch the title.

Always with a flair for the dramatic, Hudson came to throw his last rock in the 12th end and found himself up four but facing four Saskatchewan counters. The Strathcona skip made a double takeout and saved his shooter to squeak out a 14-9 victory.

One other significant event took place in the final round of play at the 1929 championship. The Montreal entry, skipped by George Kent, defeated Toronto 14-10 for that city's first Brier win in three years of play. Following the victory, a mock celebration took place at the Granite Club with the Montreal players hoisting Kent up onto their shoulders to the good-natured applause of spectators.

By 1930, the Brier was firmly established as the highlight of the Canadian curling scene. Traditions were being set and rules smoothed out to ensure competitive play. While it wasn't exactly a well-oiled machine at this time, it was gathering steam. Many curling fans returned each year to witness the fine play.

Another familiar sight was that of Howard "Pappy" Wood, who had skipped the western team in the 1925 pre-Brier tour of the East. Wood went on to win the 1930 championship with a stunning 12-9 play-off win over Alberta's Bobby Munro, giving Manitoba its third national championship in four years of Brier competition.

At the official awards presentation, another Brier custom was established when the winners were each given a pair of stones as a prize. A small metal plate with the winner's name and the year of the championship was attached to the handle, and carrying cases were provided for the return journey.

In the next few years, more often than not, those rocks traveled home to Manitoba. In 1931, Bob Gourlay and another Strathcona Club team won the Brier, setting a scoring record in the eighth round when they trounced the Montreal team 22-6. A year later, it was Jimmy Congalton leading his squad from the Winnipeg Granite Curling Club to the title. Congalton had played third for Howard Wood on the championship team in 1930, and Wood politely returned the favor by throwing third stones for Congalton this time around. Once again, Manitoba had to defeat the Alberta team of Art Hallonquist in a play-off to clinch the Brier.

The 1932 championship was marked by a change in the lineup. Owing partly to their poor performance (especially the Montreal entry) and the need to establish a more national perspective, the city entries (the Montreal and Toronto teams) were dropped. That left the field at eight and meant a return to a seven-game round-robin.

Even at that time, however, the trustees were eyeing expansion. Prince Edward Island had formally requested an entry in 1933, but the powers-that-be decided against an odd-numbered field at that time. They had hoped to include a team from British Columbia to bring the number back to 10, but curling had been slow to catch on in the westernmost province and a provincial association was not yet in place.

Manitoba's string of five consecutive Brier wins ended in 1933 with Alberta's triumph. Cliff Manahan of Edmonton's Royal

Curling Club beat Manitoba's John Douglas in the final round for his province's first Brier win. The championship that year was highlighted by a visit from the Governor General, His Excellency Lord Bessborough, who graciously had his photo taken with the competing teams and stayed around to watch the opening afternoon of competition.

The growing stature of the Brier was clear by 1934. The annual opening banquet, still a tradition to this day, had become a significant event not only in Toronto but across the country. Media reported on it from coast to coast, and the annual speech, given by a prominent Canadian, was often front-page news. The 1934 dinner included on its guest list Prime Minister R.B. Bennett and Mackenzie King, then leader of the opposition. Both gave speeches that emphasized the importance of Canada and paid tribute to the Brier for strengthening the nation.

On the ice, the strongest team was again Manitoba as Leo Johnson eked out an extra-end win over Ontario's Gordon Campbell in the final round to claim the Tankard. The Ontario team had dropped a massive six in the third end of the final game, but rallied to tie the score at eight after 11 ends. A dramatic last-rock draw in front of 2,000 fans gave the win to Johnson.

In 1935, the increasing competitiveness forced officials to firm up more rules. The weight of the stones was reduced to conform with Ontario's standard 45 pounds. That allowed many teams to pick up rocks from Toronto clubs rather than bring in their own. Sweeping was further defined to begin no earlier than the first hog line and when the rock hit the far tee line. And the practice of flipping a coin to decide last rock in extra ends was also abandoned in favor of giving first rock to the team that scored the last point.

The winner of the 1935 championship was the Ontario team and one of the first of many family rinks to take the title. Gordon Campbell, along with brothers Duncan at lead and Don at third, were joined by Gord Coates in one of the most powerful rinks of their era. They had finished runners-up the previous two years and finally took top honors in 1935 with a sparkling 7-1 record.

The profile of this team showed how the sport was changing, thanks in large part to the Brier. Up until this point, curling had been the preserve of older gentlemen, but it was beginning to attract the younger set. While the average age of Brier competitors was probably more than 50 in 1935, the Campbells were all still in their twenties. They were among the first of an influx of younger, more dynamic players.

Gordon Campbell had been a stellar athlete in his hometown of Hamilton. Like many young Canadian boys, he had been a football, baseball and hockey player, and had not given curling much thought. But convinced by family friend Dr. Tom Bertram, Campbell went out to the Hamilton Thistle Club to give the game a try in 1929. He found it boring and uneventful, calling it "just another bowling alley game" because in many places, such as the Thistle, the rocks were merely flung down with little regard for ice, weight or position of other stones. Compared to hockey, curling was downright snoozy, and Campbell soon gave up on it.

A year later, the young athlete agreed to drive Dr. Bertram to the Brier in Toronto so Bertram could watch some of the action. Somewhat sheepishly, Campbell accompanied his friend inside the Granite Club in a move that would change his life. He watched the competition with the enthusiasm of a child on Christmas morning. What he saw on the ice that day opened his eyes. It was as if he had suddenly found the key to a new language. The sport was entirely new to him, nothing like what he had played back in Hamilton.

"I saw Gordon Hudson's team play and I got the idea that this could be a game, a real game, when it's played the way it should be," Campbell remembered. "I realized what we had done before was not curling, not like these guys were playing it."

With renewed vigor, he went back to Hamilton and convinced brother Don and Coates to join him on a team skipped by Bertram. Taking what he had learned at the Brier that day, Campbell instructed his two mates and concentrated on what he believed to be the fundamentals of the game. Despite the good intentions of many members at the Thistle Club, Campbell told his rink not to listen to advice from anyone but him. If they were to succeed, they would have to curl the way the Brier players had, not in the fashion that had turned him off the game a year earlier.

Campbell had realized his team needed to be good sweepers and accurate throwers. From that fateful day at the Brier, Campbell had stored in his memory Hudson's Strathcona slide, and the team copied it with such proficiency that the great Manitoba curler later told them, "You deliver a stone the way I think I do." And while their skip didn't teach them many throwing or sweeping techniques, Bertram did instill a sense of what the game was about in his young charges. Most importantly, the players learned the concept of team play, an idea that had not been prevalent in eastern Canada up to that point.

After Gordon, Don and Gord Coates had played a year with Dr. Bertram, Gordon Campbell elected to try things on his own, passing up an opportunity to spend another year under an experienced skip. He obviously knew he had some talent and so did his clubmates. In those days, skips and vices in the club chose teams for provincial competitions by voting at the start of the season. Although he had yet to skip a game, Campbell, who now had younger brother Duncan on board at lead, was chosen to represent the Thistle Club in the prestigious Governor General's competition.

While it was highly unusual to send a green team into such a strong event, the Campbells didn't disappoint, winning it handily. At one point in the competition, however, the team learned a valuable lesson. In the semifinal, the Hamilton boys had been playing one of their best games, placing rocks virtually wherever they wanted. When another stone stopped perfectly behind a guard, Coates turned to Campbell and said, "Why don't you just save time and place your next rock where you want to throw it now?" That comment drew a few chuckles from the Campbells, but up behind the glass, Dr. Bertram, who had become the team's mentor, went purple with rage. When the game was over, he called the four aside and sternly warned them against gloating.

"Never, ever compliment yourselves," he told the four, "because when you do that, you deprive your opposition of the privilege of doing so."

That was a lesson the Campbells never forgot. For the rest of their careers, they played with dignity and respect for their opposition—even when they were trouncing them.

They continued their success for the next few years, winning almost every bonspiel or event in which they played. In 1933, they managed to win provincial honors and went to their first Brier— just three years after taking up the game.

The Campbells quickly developed a reputation as a team that

could score at will. They posted huge victories, usually winning by 10 or 15 points. In the six games they won in the 1933 Brier, they never scored fewer than 12 points. They defeated Nova Scotia by an incredible 22-8 margin.

However, when the round-robin had finished, the Ontario team was a game back of the champion Alberta. They did defeat Manitoba in a play-off for second place, in a practice that was common in the early days of the Brier.

In 1934, the Campbells lost the final game to Manitoba in a match that decided the winners. Gordon Campbell says the famous six that Leo Johnson hung on them in the third end was a result of Campbell stubbornly sticking to a strategy that was clearly failing.

But a year later, after winning the right to represent Ontario for the third consecutive year (the team attended the Brier from 1933 to 1936 before losing a game in the Ontario playdowns), the Campbells finally broke through and took home their province's first championship. The boys from the Thistle Club won their first six games and, when they went out on the ice against Saskatchewan in the last round, they already had the Brier title in hand.

There was a huge crowd at the Granite Club to witness the first championship by an Ontario team, and spectators spilled out onto the ice, standing beside the sheet on wooden planks and over the end boards. They almost encircled the playing surface and, as Campbell remembered, there was no room for him to sit down at the back of the sheet.

"I think every person I knew was there," he recalled. "You'd go up on the sheet and see all your friends standing there—it was tough to concentrate. They'd be cheering you on and giving you pats on the back."

In addition to their impressive curling, the Campbells have a place in Brier history for establishing what is arguably the most famous emblem in Canadian sport—the Purple Heart. The now-famous crest, given to every provincial champion, did not exist for the first six years of the championship. But during the seventh Brier, the Ontario team arrived wearing lavish crests that identified them as the Ontario champions. Senator Haig noticed the impressive patches and asked Gordon Campbell about them. "I think we should do something like that," was Haig's reply, after learning their significance. The next year, after consultations with Walter Stewart and others at Macdonald Tobacco, the Purple Heart crest was created and given to every competitor. Curlers from earlier Briers also received crests to go along with the small pins that they had originally been given.

Ironically, the first crests were not purple, but red. They did have their famous shape, however, which was also the logo used for the Brier brand of tobacco, "the tobacco with heart." To continue with the theme of using the Brier name on the trophy, the pins and crests all took the heart shape. Macdonald Tobacco was ahead of its time with what might now be called vertical marketing integration.

Considering the conditions in the early days of the Brier, the Campbells' winning streaks were quite an achievement. The curling was anything but predictable. By today's standards, ice conditions were horrendous and the equipment was almost useless. Every curling club had different hacks because there were no standards, and players depended on the icemaker to build them. Thus the players competing in big events had to be able to adjust to unusual footholds at each club.

Brooms resembled those now used for sweeping the kitchen floor. At the Brier, brooms were given to each player, provided by the sponsor free of charge. The Buffalo brand was the standard; it was more than a foot wide and tightly bound from top to bottom. While it took great effort to make these oversized cornstalks effective, some teams learned ways to improve the results. They would remove the bottom stitch and cut out part of the straw in the middle with a razor blade. Then the corn could be whipped back and forth with some rhythm.

One factor that could not be corrected was the ice. It was generally filled with runs. "You knew there were going to be falls in the ice," recalled Gordon Campbell in early 1994, who, at 88, is the oldest living Brier champion. "You just hoped that you figured them out before the other guy."

The inconsistent ice meant the skip's job was exceptionally difficult as he tried to read the ice and determine how the rocks would react. In more recent times a warm-up is permitted and a player can get a feel for a particular sheet, but the teams at the early Briers never threw any stones before the start of the game. They went in cold, hoping to make sense out of the imperfect frozen water before them as the first stone went down the sheet.

Off the ice, 1935 was a busy year and a memorable one. After many false starts, dating back more than 50 years, the Dominion Curling Association was born, largely as a result of initiatives put forward by the Ontario Curling Association. At its 1931 annual meeting, the OCA had put forth a motion that it would "appoint a committee to meet with the representatives of other provinces, in March 1933, in Toronto, with the purpose in view of forming a Dominion Curling Association as a governing body of all associations in the Dominion of Canada."

The OCA's movement was met with agreement at the 1933 Brier, and a year later, the 12 curling associations in Canada, which represented about 600 clubs, returned to the table to prepare the final documents. They also chipped in a total of $320 to provide a working bank account. A constitution was written, and on March 6, 1935, the Dominion Curling Association was created.

The national association's main purpose at the start was to standardize rules. It had very little to do with the operation of the Brier and this detachment would not change until Macdonald Tobacco ended its sponsorship in 1979. While the DCA (which would change its name to the Canadian Curling Association in 1967) took an ever-increasing role in the sport, the tobacco company held a tight grip on its championship. In later years, Macdonald allowed two association representatives on the Brier board, but with three trustees and three directors appointed directly by the sponsor, it was clear who was in charge. However, the creation of the national body likely would have taken much longer had it not been for the Brier, and the development of rules and international competitions would also have lagged far behind.

In 1936 there were three new and important additions to the Brier. Prince Edward Island and British Columbia joined the fray, giving the country its first true, coast-to-coast national championship. "This is the first time all curling Canada has been brought together, and may it be an object lesson as to what can be accomplished within the fellowship of the game of curling," stated the Honorable Jack Haig, announcing the teams at the competition's beginning. The two new teams brought the field back to 10 and the round-robin to nine games. They also meant an extra day's play and a need for more sponsorship dollars to bring in and accommodate the eight extra players and their entourages.

The third addition was the appearance of the second big star of the roaring game, a man who has to be considered one of the most important ever to lace on a curling boot. Ken Watson walked out onto Brier ice for the first time at the Toronto Granite Club that year and changed curling forever. In the coming decades, his influence on Canadian and international events would be unsurpassed as he almost single-handedly took the sport from innocence to maturity. His touch and prestige carried curling further in a short period of time than it had gone before.

He was 32 when he made his first appearance at the national championship, an age that was still under the average at the time. His team of brother Grant at third, second Marvin McIntyre and lead Charlie Kerr were considered youngsters back then. Curlers and fans thought them too inexperienced to play in the Brier, especially to represent the powerful province of Manitoba. But, like Gordon Campbell's rink, they personified the new wave of dynamic, youthful players with aggressive strategy and strong team play.

All were solid athletes, another characteristic of the new breed of curler. Grant Watson, for instance, had been a western Canada tennis champion, while Kerr was a terrific baseball player who had managed to hit a double off the legendary Lefty Grove in an exhibition game in Winnipeg. More and more, athletically inclined youth, especially in Winnipeg, were leaving the hockey rinks for the curling ice. And with them came increased competition, better play and a new look to the sport.

Ken Watson had already built a name for himself in Winnipeg. In 1935, his rink was playing a match against Ab Gowanlock, another powerful Manitoba player of the day, along the provincial playdown route. Curlers were so excited about the game between these two titans that they literally crawled into the Winnipeg Granite Club through the windows when the management shut the doors after filling the club to what it considered to be capacity. So packed was the club that the body heat generated by the crowd began to melt the ice before the end of the game.

A year later, these same two teams hooked up in the final of the Manitoba playdowns. The curling association wisely moved the match to the Winnipeg Arena, offering seats on a first-come, first-served basis. Ninety minutes before the scheduled start of the contest, the 5,000 seats were full and 2,000 more people, waiting outside, were turned away.

The Watson players had a huge impact on their peers. They showed them, first and foremost, that curling was not a sport for old geezers. They also altered the game in great measure with their fervor, talent and—more than anything else—their slides.

Prior to 1936, curlers who used a slide in their deliveries imitated Gordon Hudson, rarely going past the back of the eight-foot. More than anything else, their slides were a small push from the hack. Most people continued to play with toe rubbers on their shoes to provide traction and always kept one foot in the hack when throwing the stone.

But Watson and his team were different. By removing their rubbers and sliding on the leather sole of their shoes, they had perfected a slide that would take them out to the top of the rings. In later years, they were even given credit for devising the slide, but the origins of this technique go back long before Watson made it to the Brier. At the turn of the century, the top curler in Manitoba was R.H. Dunbar. He easily beat all the rest, including a frustrated chap by the name of Frank Cassidy, who longed for nothing else but to defeat Dunbar. One of Cassidy's limitations was in delivering the stone. He had great trouble getting the swing of the rock so that it traveled down the ice on target. He found that, if he pushed off from the hack with his leg and slid along the side of his shoe, he had better direction. So he practiced this strange way of delivering the stone and, in the 1910 Manitoba Bonspiel, finally beat Dunbar using it. The younger curlers looking on quickly realized the potential of the new method (especially since it had taken Cassidy to the Bonspiel championship), and soon after, they were all practicing the slide. Among the converts was Hudson, whose slide would later become the inspiration for Watson's.

At the start, Watson attempted to recreate the Hudson slide, but his ankles weren't strong enough to hold him up on just the side of his foot. By chance, one of the curlers at his club threw off his toe rubber and tried to slide on a flat foot. He landed promptly on his posterior, but the young curlers were on to something, and before long, they had perfected their own version of the slide.

In effect, therefore, while they were the first to travel any distance from the hack, the Manitoba players of 1936 were actually third-generation sliders. In Toronto, however, no one had seen anything like it and when Kerr threw his first team's stone in that memorable competition, laughter broke out behind the glass. The spectators thought the slide was some kind of joke and most certainly a contravention of the rules.

But the laughter quickly changed to outrage when the Manitobans racked up an opening-draw win over the host Ontario team by a margin of 21-3. Although none of the other competitors lodged any complaints, protests did surface from provincial representatives. Some said the slide was breaking the spirit—if not the rules—of the game. But others were in favor of it. In general, the feeling split across generations: the younger players found it entertaining and acceptable, while the older, more traditional curlers were appalled. They felt players should deliver the stone while still in the hack. A letter to the editor of the *Globe* explained these conflicting sentiments:

"It looks like the Winnipeg rink will win the competition and I'd like to see you censure the old-timers who are criticizing their style," the letter stated. "I don't mind admitting, as an old-timer myself, that the only reason we older men don't copy them is that we are too old to do so. Why, if they made a rule that there had to be a minimum slide, we'd all be lost."

The real problem with the slide was that no one was sure what was legitimate because there was no national rulebook. In Watson's Manitoba, sliding was considered legal, while in Ontario, no one had used the lengthy delivery before.

At a luncheon following the opening round, Senator Haig, who in addition to being a Brier trustee was also president of the fledgling Dominion Curling Association, decreed that the stone must leave the hand at the tee, and added that a rule would be in place after the DCA's annual meeting, scheduled for later that same week.

But the Watson rink, which was being hailed in headlines as the "Sliding Schoolteachers" (the two Watsons and Kerr were teachers), kept using its new method in the second game against Alberta. Early in the competition, many people figured the Brier would come down to these two teams, and the slide proved to be the difference. Early in the game, Alberta skip Scotty Wanless had a stone at the top of the four-foot and another at the back. Watson slid way out to the side of the sheet and, having the angle, threw his rock perfectly in between the two to sit shot. Wanless was never able to remove that rock, and Watson went on for a 14-6 thrashing of the Albertans.

After that game, the DCA formally warned the team, telling their provincial rep, Hugh McKenzie, that if the Manitobans kept on with such long sliding, they might incur a penalty. After a minor setback, in which the players tried to shorten their slides, they returned to what they knew best.

And with nothing in the rulebook to stop him, Watson kept sliding—all the way out into the far 12-foot—and kept winning. The crowd swelled with each draw, intent on seeing the now-famous slide, which the DCA finally admitted it was powerless to stop.

Watson won five of his first six games, including a 23-4 lambasting of the Quebec entry, before coming up against the fledgling Prince Edward Island team. The squad from Charlottetown Curling Club was winless to this point and things weren't about to improve. The Manitoba entry, sensing an easy game, may have let up a bit. Just before the match, *Winnipeg Tribune* sportswriter Johnny Buss handed Charlie Kerr a cigar, which the powerful lead smoked during the match.

In the first end, with Ken Watson sitting five, Grant Watson threw a draw that appeared to be perfect, if perhaps a little light. Kerr and McIntyre put the brooms to it, and just as it approached the rings, an ash from the cigar dropped in front of the stone and it ground to an immediate halt inches away from the target. When the next two Manitoba stones found the house, the team had a seven-ender that might have been eight—something never achieved in Brier play—if not for the cigar ash.

After smoking Prince Edward Island 25-5, Manitoba humbled Saskatchewan 15-7 and moved into the last round tied with New Brunswick's Reg Shives. Both teams were at 7-1, and by the luck of the draw, they faced each other in the last game.

The largest Brier crowd in history jammed into the Granite Club to watch the big match and witness the crowning of Watson, but the play wasn't cut and dried by any means. Shives and his team put up a gallant fight, and with Watson's final stone of the game left to be thrown, they had a chance to win. But the Manitoba skip calmly drew his rock cold to the full four-foot to cut the New Brunswick team out of three and take an 11-9 decision. Although a thrilling ending, the game was described by most papers as being rather lackluster. However, Watson had arrived.

It took Watson another six years to make it back to the Brier, but in the interval, he molded his game and tried to advance the sport through innovations such as a slider made of solder that allowed him to glide even farther down the sheet. His team also continued to win big games throughout Manitoba and in neighboring provinces. Finally, in 1942, along with a new front end of Charlie Scrymgeour and Jim Grant, Watson made it back.

As the war in Europe was preoccupying everyone, there was a decidedly different atmosphere to this Brier. The fun and frivolity of past competitions were gone. In their place was a concentration on the task at hand, made more difficult by the tricky, almost unplayable ice conditions of the Citadel Arena in Quebec.

But Watson again proved his skill by racking up an 8-1 record. It was not all domination, however, as on three occasions Watson had to come from behind in the final end to win. In one memorable contest, the Sliding Schoolteachers counted four in the 12th to win 11-10 over Alberta. They sealed the championship with a 14-3 win over Prince Edward Island in the last round.

There was an interesting development with the runner-up teams that year. Because the arena had to be used for a hockey game the next evening, second place could not be decided by the traditional tiebreaker game. That circumstance may have prevented a family feud as Ontario's Gordon Campbell ended up with an identical record to that of his brother, Don, who had been on the 1935 championship team but was now skipping British Columbia.

The Watson brothers found a place in the record books with their third victory in 1949, something that had not been achieved by any other curler. Again, the team had a different front end, with Lyle Dyker and Charles Read filling in at second and lead respectively. They won with a perfect 9-0 record, although they needed a last-round win against Reg Stone's B.C. entry to win the title. Both teams came into the final game undefeated with eight wins.

Stone was a different sort of character, rarely uttering a word and literally racing through his games. He would never stop to discuss a shot, but would put his broom down where he wanted it and run to the other end. Once in the hack, he'd wipe off his stone with a quick brush and was almost instantaneously in his backswing. During one contest, his front end was still getting in place when they realized their skip's rock was on its way. The audience roared with laughter as the two scampered to catch up.

When these two teams came to the last game in search of the Brier title, Watson was looking for a place in the record book while Stone was hoping to defeat the already famous Manitoba curler. Early on, it appeared the British Columbia team would get its way as it scored three points in the first end. Watson looked shaky but stormed back, scoring singles in each of the next three ends and two deuces over the next five ends to take command. In the final frame, Watson elected to keep everything clean and took out any rock—even his own—that came into play. The final score was 14-9, and the Watson brothers had their record.

That would be Watson's last appearance in the Brier, but nothing diminished his love for the roaring game. A year after his third win, Watson wrote what is still considered the bible of the game: *Ken Watson on Curling*. At that time, many people considered it sacrilege for an amateur player like Watson to expect to profit from such an instructional book. A number of outspoken curlers, including members of the Dominion Curling Association, reviled Watson for his brash attempt to make money from the game.

In truth, though, Watson was merely trying to pass on some helpful instruction to other players. Curling was booming at this time, and he hoped that his book would help increase its popularity.

In 1959, Watson again drew the wrath of the DCA when he helped set up the first world curling championship, the Scotch Cup, without consulting the governing body. He arranged with Scottish curling authorities to ship the Brier winners over for a challenge against Scotland's best. The Scotch Cup led to the creation of today's world championship, an event that Canadian players consider second in importance only to the Brier.

Watson was also a dedicated developer of junior curling, serving as chairman of the DCA's junior committee from 1942-50. Perhaps after watching the excitement created among youngsters by his slide in that 1936 Brier, he realized how important it was to attract and develop young players. When he was a teacher, he also worked to expand curling in high schools. He had started the first high school curling bonspiel in 1920 while still a student—and won it, as well.

Watson was a successful promoter for many reasons, but chiefly because of his stature among the curling and even non-curling communities. In 1945, he had become such a celebrity that an insurance company persuaded him to join its staff. He gave up 20 years' tenure as a teacher to do so. Watson went on to become the top insurance salesman in western Canada—after all, in a curling-mad place such as Manitoba, who wouldn't want to buy insurance from Ken Watson?

Years later, when asked what it took to be a successful curler, Watson revealed a five-point plan. First, he said that a curler was at his best between the ages of 30 and 35; second, that it's stability—not brilliance—that counts in curling; third, that it takes 10 years to learn stability; fourth, that after the age of 35 a player learns how to make his shots do the most work; and, finally, that teamwork is all-important.

These points were certainly true of Watson and his teams. Over the three Briers in which he competed, his teams compiled an amazing 27-2 record. From 1941 to 1949, in the Manitoba Bonspiel, Watson had an outstanding 139 wins against just 13 losses. Considering his work off the ice, which included writing the first syndicated curling newspaper column, it is unlikely that anyone has ever been more worthy of the nickname "Mr. Curler."

Watson also had a strong, although somewhat bitter view of the Brier remaining in Toronto. In the pre-war era of the late 1930s, there had been increasing calls to take the championship out of the Granite Club and hold it in other locations around the country. As time went on, the voices became louder—even downright nasty.

"Originating back in the days when the 'cut plug' was still found on the tobacconists' shelves," wrote Watson in the 1960s, "this single-rink competition, emblematic of Canadian curling supremacy, was held for 13 long years in the palatial Granite Club in Toronto, and for the same 13 years, staid old Hogtown didn't know it.

"The crowds in those early years were meager at best, and after a week's play, when the new champions were crowned, the write-up in the Toronto sports pages rated words that might be located eventually with a powerful magnifying glass.

"In 1940, yielding to vehement pressure of western delegates, it was decided to exhume the championship from its moldy repose in the Toronto graveyard and start it in circulation."

Actually, the Brier trustees had been considering moving the championship as early as 1936, but felt that establishing a foundation was necessary at first. As Watson pointed out, however, Toronto had become complacent with the Brier. The novelty of the opening years of the 1920s and 1930s had worn off, and the lackadaisical attitude of the Toronto press was growing more obvious. As well, it was becoming difficult to shoehorn any more people into the Granite Club. A much bigger facility, such as an arena, was clearly needed.

The idea of moving the Brier became the subject of many conversations among the curling fraternity, and it was eventually agreed, with permission from Macdonald Tobacco (which had to pick up considerably more expense) to take the show on the road. Walter Stewart's only stipulation was that the event would have to visit every province and be played in every provincial capital.

And so, at the official Brier banquet in 1939, to almost no one's surprise, it was announced that the championship would be held the next year at the Winnipeg Amphitheatre. This decision brought to a close the opening era of the Brier. From the pre-Brier tours of Manitoba teams to the inimitable styles of Gordon Hudson, Gordon Campbell and Ken Watson, from the creation of the DCA to the growing lists of new rules, the Brier had become the showpiece not just for curling but for all of Canadian sport. It was time to take the next step—and what a big step that would be.

3

Establishing Traditions

If curling has a center to its universe, it is undoubtedly Winnipeg. From the first time the granite slid down the ice in search of the button in that western city, Winnipeg has had a love affair with the roaring game that is unmatched.

It was fitting, then, that when the Brier trustees elected to move the big event, they selected Winnipeg as the first new host site. One reason for choosing this particular city was a standing invitation from the Manitoba Curling Association, and another was the fact that Manitoba teams had dominated play. It was obvious that the Brier would sell in Winnipeg and Macdonald wanted a big show.

From the moment the official announcement came down in Toronto, Winnipeg went mad awaiting the arrival of curling's national championship. A large committee was formed to administer the preparations and oversee the day-to-day activities. This group became the first Brier committee, an organization today with members numbering in the thousands. Most of the leaders of this 1940 committee belonged to the Manitoba Curling Association, which had gained a great deal of experience by organizing the Manitoba Bonspiel.

The committee, with full approval of the Brier trustees, added many new twists to the national championship. The first was the use of matched, neutral stones. Prior to this Brier, competitors were responsible for bringing their own rocks, although some borrowed stones from clubs around Toronto to avoid lugging them across the country.

The result, however, was a mish-mash of odd-looking and mis-matched rocks. Ken Watson went so far as to give some credit for his first Brier victory to special stones. In the book *The First Fifty*, he told author Doug Maxwell the story of his unusual granites. "The person who attracted us to the Brier was George Sherwood, whose trip east in 1926 filled us with envy. He told us stories of the games played, the fun of the trip and the start of the Brier. And he sold us his granites, which we used until 1940 when matched rocks came into use. When we came to sell the stones (to a little hamlet in Saskatchewan called Watson!) we discovered that the cup of those stones was five and a half inches in diameter instead of the normal five inches. I've always felt that the extra swing we got from those rocks helped us to 'bury them' as much as our sliding delivery."

By 1940, there was some recognition that differing stones could give one team an edge and so matched stones were provided. Not only did this policy mean fairness to all concerned, but it also started a revolution at curling clubs across the country. In fact, the Brier's decision to supply the stones led to curling clubs purchasing their own, and ended the long tradition of each curler bringing his or her own to each contest. While many clubs had had their own rocks for years, it was not the standard practice—until the 1940 Brier.

The stones in use in Winnipeg at that national championship had another feature—colored tops. Expecting large crowds, the championship was, for the first time, held in an arena, the Winnipeg Amphitheatre. Because organizers felt that people in the distant seats would have difficulty determining which stone belonged to which team, they differentiated the rocks by applying a lacquered paint to the tops. (In later years, clubs across Canada picked up this practice as well.) While there were a few instances of rocks picking up chips of paint, the idea was generally well received, especially by the large numbers of fans who streamed into the facility to witness the best curlers of the day.

While the Granite Club in Toronto had been a wonderful setting, it could accommodate only about 2,000 people comfortably. For the weekday rounds of the 1940 Brier, however, more than 3,000 curling enthusiasts sat spellbound as the play unfolded before them in the arena. Each day, a new attendance record was set and more and more people came to watch.

The fact that one of their own was in the running added to the numbers. Howard Wood, who had first ventured east on the 1925 pre-Brier tour and had won the Brier title in 1930 and 1932, had returned with perfect timing. His Winnipeg team ensured a large gate and a vocal audience.

During this era, Wood was as colorful as they came. He was always ready with a wave of his hand or a quick smile, and he loved to play the big shot. Later, in 1947, it was the Wood team that took home four new automobiles in the first carspiel.

At that time, it was virtually impossible to buy a new car, even if the money was available, because all the manufacturing was directed towards the war effort. But in the tiny town of Nipawin, Saskatchewan, organizers managed to procure four new automobiles as first prize for their bonspiel. Understandably, all the big teams came to play for this unheard-of prize, but one by one, they fell by the wayside. In the final, it was Howard Wood against Dalt Henderson. With his last rock to come, the score was tied and Wood was facing what appeared to be an impossible shot. Henderson had two stones, one on the front and back of the four-foot, and another out in the eight-foot. If Wood played a hit on the top stone in the four-foot, Henderson's second stone would be shot. If Wood played a double, he would likely roll away and Henderson's third stone would end up shot. But without a second thought, Wood put the broom down and began to walk to the other end to throw the ultimate shot.

The organizers of the carspiel were no slouches when it came to marketing. They had put the four autos on the rink, behind the hack from which Wood would throw his last brick. The cars were almost glistening under spotlights, and Wood couldn't help but stare at them as he made his way down the ice. Perhaps they spurred him on, because the legendary curler threw his stone, turned around and walked back towards the cars, opened the door to the one nearest him and sat down in the driver's seat—just in time to watch his rock make a delicate split of the two in the four-foot and stay for one point and the win.

This was the showman who made his way into the 1940 Brier. Despite his incredible curling talent, Wood's appearance was a bit of a surprise—especially to him. Just a few days before the entries closed for the Manitoba Bonspiel, Wood threw in a pickup team that included Roy Enman at lead, Howard Wood, Jr., at second and Ernie Pollard throwing third stones. It had been the elder Wood's intention just to keep his record of playing in the big spiel alive and maybe get in a few competitive games. But what transpired was curling's first Cinderella story.

The team won the Manitoba Bonspiel and went on to represent the buffalo province in front of the hometown folks at the Brier. Wood was already a grand figure in Winnipeg curling circles, and his friends were hoping that he and his underdog team could add to the fabled Manitoba curling heritage.

They didn't disappoint. Wood walked through the field with a perfect 9-0 record to grab Manitoba's ninth Canadian championship. He clinched it on the final night of play with a 17-11 win over Cliff Manahan's Alberta entry and earned a huge ovation by the 5,000 fans in the sold-out arena—at that time, the largest crowd ever to witness a curling game.

Many traditions were started, others were continued and still others ended at the 1940 event. Two traditions that changed were the opening and closing ceremonies. In Toronto, the teams had been led out onto the ice at the start of the competition and brought back for the prize presentation by Art Condie, a Brier official (later a director) and one of the first true characters of the competition. He was known for his quick wit as well as his practical jokes. One standard gag he practiced at almost every Brier came at the opening banquet, where the skips drew lots to determine their schedule. Condie would always pick on an unsuspecting rookie, and as the nervous curler rose from his table to walk to the front and take a number from the hat, Condie would sneak up near the table with a tray of silverware. When the curler had his back turned, Condie would drop the tray, and the stunned curler, thinking he had just knocked over the table, turned with a look of horror to the amusement of all in the room who were in on the joke.

At the opening and closing ceremonies, Condie had his shining moment. He didn't bleat away on bagpipes or a trumpet—he used a harmonica to lead the competitors onto the ice. His instrument of choice seems hilarious by today's standards, where full marching bands are the norm, but the players, most smirking, filed out onto the ice at the Granite Club as he played away on his tiny mouth organ.

In Winnipeg, Condie (who was listed in the program as the "Official Brier Musician") was replaced at the closing by the Queen's Own Cameron Highlanders, dressed in full regalia and pumping the pipes in fine Scottish tradition. Although Condie still performed his duties at the opening, the bagpapies became a custom of the Brier; with larger crowds in full arenas, no one could hear the mouth-organ king's performance, and he was gradually phased out.

Another practice established in 1940 that became standard in future years was the Brier church service. All the teams attended a dignified service, usually held in the local United Church in the host city. Many of the sermons took on curling themes with titles such as "The Stone You Threw" and "The Moving Rock." The latter, from the 1955 Brier, was given by Reverend H.A. Mutchmor, who said, "The game of curling is based on successful and sincere teamwork, but during our hours of business and pleasure, we must never forget the necessity for the closest kind of teamwork between God and ourselves in daily routine."

Other non-curling events were held right from the beginning. The trustees' opening dinner, which later became the opening lunch, was usually held on the first Sunday. At this event, the draw was decided by the skips pulling lots.

Tuesday evening was reserved for the official banquet. Aside from the curling, this celebration was the highlight of the Brier. A feature of the evening was always the guest speaker, who generally made Canada the theme of his talk. Cabinet ministers, military men, provincial premiers or media personalities often gave the speech.

In later years, David Stewart, the head of Macdonald Tobacco, would give an intensely patriotic commentary. For those in the audience for the first time, it was magical stuff that made the heart pound and set the internal flag waving. To the folks who attended many Briers—media, DCA officials and organizers—his talk was somewhat repetitious. The same speech came out—almost to the word—year after year, and many people had memorized a good portion of Stewart's utterances. But they still enjoyed his fervent commentary and had fun trying to mouth along silently with the tobacco king.

Stewart would often don the garb of some historical Canadian figure in honor of the banquet, and, at one memorable affair, showed up in the clothing of a 19th-century French-Canadian militiaman. Following the banquet, he ventured down the hall to make an appearance at the media party that traditionally followed the banquet. He knocked on the door and was met by radio broadcaster Jack Wells, who took one look at Stewart, turned back to his media pals and asked, "Anyone here order a pizza?"

The other great tradition established in 1940 was how the teams were selected. For the first time since 1927, all competing teams were decided by playdowns especially created for the Brier. In fact, Macdonald Tobacco had extended its patronage down to the provincial level in every province except New Brunswick, where Ganong, the confectionery company, continued to present the provincial championship.

This financial commitment was another indication of Macdonald's profound support of curling—and of its canny marketing sense. The nine provinces and Northern Ontario were all now competing for British Consols trophies, which also happened to be the name of a Macdonald's tobacco product. But the donated trophies and the financial support were exceptional, so the curlers may have overlooked the semi-commercialization of their events. They were pleased that such a large company had volunteered its support and were grateful for the assistance.

In 1941, the Brier returned to Toronto, where the first of many Calgary rinks took top spot. Howard Palmer emerged with an 8-1 record, a game up on Ontario. A year later, the teams traveled to Quebec City for that province's first national championship. Ken Watson won his second title with an 8-1 record, again one win better than Ontario.

During the more serious 1942 event, when much of the talk was of the battlefront, the Honorable Adélard Godbout, premier of Quebec, gave a reply at the annual banquet to the toast to Canada that resulted in a standing ovation. He reaffirmed Quebec's commitment to Canada and its war effort. Later, Godbout added much color to the event by introducing the teams in French.

At the annual trustees' meeting during this Brier, an invitation to hold the 1943 Brier in Saskatoon was approved. But it was later announced that the invitation was accepted "subject to any objection the government might raise in connection with travel restrictions on account of the war." That summer, representatives of Macdonald Tobacco met with federal officials and told them the company would suspend the annual playdowns if the government felt they would impede the war effort in any way. The government decided that this suspension was in the best interests of the nation, and so the Brier was put on hold and the bonspiel committee in Saskatoon was left waiting until the war ended.

While the national championship was missed, the provincial playdowns carried on and Macdonald continued its support at that level. Records in 1943 show that 92 prizes were purchased for the 10 provincial finals at a cost of $792.16, which included $170.16 for engraving and a 25 per cent luxury tax. Of interest is that the defending Canadian champion, Ken Watson, again won his Manitoba title in 1943. Had the national final gone ahead, and had he won it, he might have become the first four-time champion of the Brier in 1949, when he won the title again.

In 1946, when the Brier resumed, the feeling across the country was euphoric. Similarly to when the event had started in 1927, people were happy to be Canadian and proud to be involved with anything as patriotic as the Brier. The committee in Saskatoon had waited a long time to get their championship and made the most of it. Tommy Douglas, the premier of the province, opened the event, while a host of other dignitaries looked on.

Whether Douglas was aware of it or not, the Brier that year was the first "big event" Brier. For the first time, play was broadcast live from coast to coast on CBC radio, and the *Saskatoon Star-Phoenix* ran a special "Brier Edition" supplement to its regular paper. Huge crowds, which eventually exceeded 20,000, filed into the Saskatoon Arena to watch the games.

Much of the increased press coverage was thanks to Reg Geary, who worked for the advertising firm Harold F. Stanfield of Montreal, which handled Macdonald's affairs. He had made a cross-country tour of major media outlets to drum up support for the Brier, and the results had been impressive. A large press contingent descended on Saskatoon, including the people who would host the first live radio broadcasts of the championship. Doug Smith, who preceded Danny Gallivan as broadcaster of the Montreal Canadiens games, and Bill Good, who would go on to cover 45 Briers, handled the work with an original and entertaining style.

It was also the first Brier for young David Stewart, the heir to the Macdonald company.

Then just 26, Stewart had been sent to Saskatoon by his father to make the trophy presentation on the firm's behalf. Little did he know how long he would have to wait before finally putting the Brier Tankard into the hands of Alberta's Bill Rose.

It was a freezing day in the western city when the last draw was played, and after the final rocks had been thrown, three teams were atop the leader board with 7-2 records. Rose was joined by Manitoba's Leo Johnson and Northern Ontario's Tom Ramsay; all of them had won their final games.

Ramsay received a bye and looked on as Alberta beat Manitoba by a slim 8-7 margin. It was now after 10:00 p.m., and Alberta and Northern Ontario would take another four and a half hours to decide the nation's curling champions. In another nail-biter, Rose beat Ramsay 8-6 to take the crown.

The Saskatoon Amphitheatre was still packed, but not even the heat generated by the fans could thaw out young Stewart. To keep warm, he donned a raccoon coat before making the presentation, and that coat would become his trademark for the next 33 years.

Stewart's long love affair with the Brier was more with the people than the sport itself. A shy man (perhaps the result of growing up under his domineering father), he loved meeting the curlers, the media and the fans, and made many strong friendships during his years. But despite taking lessons from Ken Watson, he never seemed to gain a keen interest for the finer points of the roaring game. It was not uncommon for Stewart to take part in the opening ceremonies, disappear for a few days to some distant part of the country and then return in time to hand over the trophy to the winning rink.

He also had a love affair with old aircraft and, more often than not, his little mid-Brier sojourns would be in a rented aircraft of some historical distinction. (Stewart's attachment to vintage aircraft was so strong that he purchased the seat of an old plane and used it as the chair in his office.)

But Stewart's first love was for his country. He was one of the most knowledgeable people in the nation on Canadian history and geography, and could easily speak for hours on any part of the country or any significant moment in Canada's past. Similarly, he came to understand how important the Brier was to the sporting fabric of Canada. He knew it was the only event that brought all parts of the country together yet still retained a sort of sporting innocence that had been lost in football and hockey.

More than anything, Stewart was fascinated with how curling fascinated others. He was intrigued that people would travel from all across the country to attend the Brier, and was amazed that so many rituals had grown and become cherished parts of the event.

Over the years, he also gained a special fondness for the media. A sophisticated, undemonstrative and certainly an eccentric man, he seemed to loosen up in the company of journalists. Perhaps he felt comfortable because the ink-stained wretches of the day refused to bow down to him; despite his position, they treated him like one of the boys. For many years David and his wife, Lilianne, would host a press party in their suite on Thursday evening of the Brier. Because the curling was still continuing, it meant a late start and, more often than not, a very late finish. Mrs. Stewart, although married to one of the richest men in the country, took great pride in making her own pea soup for the event, and with an open bar, the party took off.

At one memorable soirée, recalled in *The First Fifty*, all the guests had left except for one Toronto reporter, the Stewarts and Frank O'Brien, who looked after many of the needs of the press. O'Brien suggested to the reporter that perhaps, seeing as it was 5:00 a.m., he might consider calling it a night. But Mrs. Stewart, ever the perfect hostess, said, "Frank, a guest is never reminded that he should go home. Mr. MacCarl will leave when he's ready."

In appreciation for the great party, the press would usually make a presentation to the Stewarts. More often than not, it was a painting. Jack Wells, one of the bon vivants of his day, would go into another room, grab whatever piece of artwork was on the wall and proudly hand it over with some sort of happy speech. Stewart was probably aware of the gag after a while, but always feigned shocked appreciation.

What Stewart and a lot of other Brier watchers never had to disguise was the thrill of watching the championship's next big names: Garnet Campbell, Matt Baldwin and a kid named Braun-stein. This trio would take curling into its next era.

4

Baldwin, Braunstein
and Campbell

Matt Baldwin, a native of Edmonton, arrived on the scene eight years after the Brier's war-time sabbatical had ended and in the middle of an incredible western domination of the national championship.

Six of the previous eight titles had gone to teams west of Ontario, and Baldwin was about to add to that total significantly.

In the 1950s, when Baldwin was making his mark, curling was a reserved game. Few competitors revealed any color or character, and the spirit of gentlemanly play ruled. If a great shot was made, a team acknowledged the accomplishment quietly, even if the crowd was cheering wildly. There was no high-fiving, no yells of "Great shot," no back-slapping. Such behavior might show up the opposition and that was just not done.

But Baldwin was different. A boisterous, confident, high-spirited man filled with energy, he had natural enthusiasm. For curling, he couldn't have arrived at a better time. While the Brier continued to be a success, the fans were aching for a charismatic hero. They found him in Matt Baldwin.

Baldwin had taken up curling in high school and had set his sights on the Brier from the start.

"I really didn't have my mind on anything else," he recalled. "It was the sport that took all my time and energy. At that time in my life, it was a very big deal for me."

After graduating from the University of Alberta in 1951 with a degree in petrochemical engineering, Baldwin took a serious run at competitive curling. In 1953, he won the Northern Alberta championship and lost the last game to go to the Brier in the province-wide playdowns. A year later, with third Glenn Gray, second Pete Ferry and lead Jim Collins, he won his first Purple Heart and played in the Brier in his hometown of Edmonton.

"When they piped the teams out onto the ice for the opening draw," Baldwin remembered, "I felt the hair on the back of my neck stand up. It was the biggest moment of my life. I knew this was where I belonged."

Perhaps he was still basking in the thrill of that moment when his first game began. Up against the famous Garnet Campbell family rink from Saskatchewan, Baldwin dropped three points in the opening end. It was an inauspicious start for a player who would go on to be one of the best curlers in Brier history. The Alberta rink managed to get back on track in that contest and prevailed 12-11.

The first indication that Baldwin and his team did not fit into the mold of the traditional Brier curlers came in the fifth round against Don Groom of Northern Ontario. In a tight contest, Baldwin made his last shot to squeak out a 6-5 win. When the final stone arrived at its intended target, Gray leaped into the air, let out an excited yelp and waved his broom. Baldwin raised a clenched fist as he came down the ice.

The crowd loved it and so did the press, which commented on the spirited Edmonton team the next day. But the Brier trustees were less than impressed. Baldwin remembered: "At the banquet that evening, one of the trustees came up to me and explained in a real reserved kind of way that what we'd done on the ice that afternoon simply wasn't acceptable. He asked us to try and control our emotions for the rest of the Brier."

But Baldwin was a showman. The bigger the crowd, the better he played. The higher the stakes, the more he gambled. He was part of the new breed of younger curlers arriving at the Brier, and he was intent on waking up the old game with his savvy.

The crowds ate it up. By the time the week was over, a record throng of some 32,000 had jammed the Edmonton Gardens to catch a glimpse of the hometown phenom. With every game, the young skip became bolder with his actions and he held the fans in the palm of his hand. He was a good slider and could sail out close to the hog line in the days before such a practice was common. The crowd began chanting, "Slide, slide" every time he stepped into the hack.

Baldwin, in fact, become renowned for his sliding. In a major Toronto bonspiel, the Tournament of Champions held in Maple Leaf Gardens, one hot dog player decided to excite the fans by sliding the entire length of the ice, and ended up stopping with the rock on the button. The crowd went wild at this sight, so much so that, the next day, the promoter of the event got four players to do the same thing before the start of the next round. One of the four was Baldwin. After the other three had traveled the entire length of the sheet with the rock, Baldwin pushed out of the hack and, because of his picture-perfect delivery, sailed down the sheet without a wobble. About halfway down, while in motion, he removed his hand from the stone, nonchalantly rubbed his nose and then replaced his hand to the rock, which was sliding along in front of him, still in position.

In the last round of the 1954 Brier, when Baldwin, sitting with an 8-1 record, was sure he had the game against New Brunswick and therefore the Brier, he submitted to the crowd's demand and slid halfway down the ice, finally releasing the rock, which ended up perfectly on the button. "It was the flukiest shot of my life," Baldwin admitted, "but everyone seemed to like it."

And while the officials went crazy trying to determine what to do, it didn't really matter, because the popular Alberta team had just won its first Brier with an impressive 9-1 record, losing a lone game to Ontario's Ross Tarlton, the oldest player in the field.

Not long after Baldwin received the Tankard, he added to his already growing legend by celebrating long into the night at the host hotel. "I just got plastered," he stated bluntly when asked about the evening. "There was a big party going on with jillions of people there. I think maybe the entire city of Edmonton was in that ballroom. I don't know when it ended, but it was a great party." From that point on, Baldwin became known as a man who never let curling stand in the way of a good Brier celebration.

His reputation was never proven more true than in 1956, when he returned to the national championship. The host city that year was Moncton, and in those days, the teams traveled by train. The special locomotive, later called the Friendship Train, would leave British Columbia and pick up teams along the way. Macdonald Tobacco had arranged for just about anything the curlers might desire on the train—as long as it was cigarettes or alcohol.

The players socialized with each other in the bar car, and in several of the big cities, the train stopped for receptions for all the provincial champions. It was a fun but none-too-healthy way to arrive at the Brier.

"By the time I got off the train in Moncton," Baldwin recalled, "I was shaking. We'd been drinking for five days straight."

But the party wasn't about to end. In those days, New Brunswick was a dry province, except in areas where special permits had been issued. Not expecting much, the Alberta boys went from their train to the hotel, only to find that their rooms weren't quite ready. So the four decided to check out the arena. Upon their arrival, they noticed a great deal of traffic at the Beaver Curling Club, right beside the rink.

"We walked in and there was a party going on—booze was flowing, slot machines were whirling and the dance floor was filled. I thought, 'Holy shit, this is going to be good,'" Baldwin remembered years later.

And it was—perhaps too good. Every night after the final draw, the Beaver Club held a dance that attracted huge crowds and ended when the last people locked the doors behind them, usually just as the sun was coming up.

Not all the teams went to those parties, not even all the Alberta players showed up, but if you wanted to find Matt Baldwin, there was only one place to look. He never went overboard, but he'd have a few drinks, maybe a dance or two, and laugh and joke well into the night.

Even though he finished with a 5-5 record, he said at the time that all the carrying on didn't affect his curling. In fact, Baldwin believed the odd nip or two—even the odd hangover—may have calmed his nerves. But he would later look back and realize his nights at the Beaver Club may have been a factor in his play.

So, while he didn't win the Brier that year, he most certainly won the party, and his popularity continued to grow.

Notwithstanding Baldwin's mediocre record in 1956 and the bad ice conditions, there was some exceptional curling that year.

Two fine teams concluded the round-robin tied in first spot with sparkling 8-2 records. They advanced to a memorable play-off that many regard as one of the finest curling games in Brier history.

Manitoba's Billy Walsh had won the Brier in 1952 and had returned for another try. Most players thought him to be as good a shooter as there was in those days, and he was known for being able to make a perfect draw anywhere, anytime.

Walsh's opposing skip was a talented all-around athlete. Ontario's Alf Phillips was better known as a diver than a curler. He had won the first gold medal ever presented in the Commonwealth (then called the Empire) Games in 1930 (a competition that had the athletes diving into the Hamilton harbor!), and had competed in two Olympic Games, finishing fourth in 1932, which is still the best finish ever recorded by a Canadian male in that event. Phillips had later turned his talents to curling and had become equally adept at that sport.

There was not much to pick between the two teams and few people were willing to wager on the outcome of the play-off. It was a close contest from the start, and it eventually went to an extra end—the only time this contingency occurred in the pre-play-off format days.

With only one Manitoba rock left to play in the 13th end, Ontario had a stone 90 per cent under cover on the four-foot circle. Walsh's only chance was to play a light tap, push the rock out and sit for shot. But to accomplish that, he would have to play his rock out into a heavy area of frost that was unpredictable. Sometimes the stone would never come off the frost and other times it would dive out of it on a sharp angle; no one could accurately predict what would happen. As well, light weight was almost impossible because the frost would slow the stone down quite easily.

"I thought we had the Brier won," Phillips admitted later. "I didn't think he had a shot there."

Almost everyone in the stands felt the same way. But Walsh delivered his stone, watched it get past the guard and catch just a piece of the Ontario rock, which spilled from the rings. At that point, the crowd went silent and every eye in the arena was transfixed on the shooter as it spun and spun and spun towards the boards—would it stop in the rings or roll out and force a 14th end? Just as the tension appeared unbearable, it stopped and grabbed a small bit of the 12-foot circle to give Walsh his second Brier victory.

Phillips, one of the country's great sportsmen, was the first to congratulate the new champion, telling Walsh it was the greatest shot he'd ever seen. One excited fan, who wanted to make certain that the moment was preserved forever, bounded onto the sheet, grabbed the rock and later had it mounted on a trophy for Walsh.

Baldwin came back in 1957 with some incredible shots of his own. The national championship was held that year in Kingston, and the historic city added another chapter to the Brier's annals. In the fifth round, Baldwin went head-to-head in another cliffhanger against the Campbell team. The winner of that contest, he knew, would gain a huge psychological edge over the rest of the field, who regarded the Campbells (winners in 1955) and Baldwin as the teams to beat.

But it was a different Baldwin who had arrived in Kingston. He had adopted a new strategy this time around—almost no partying.

"I wanted to correct what had gone wrong the last Brier," he said, somewhat sheepishly. "We put more energy into the curling than the parties, relatively speaking, of course."

The Campbells, meanwhile, were also looking for win number two. They were impressive in the early going, establishing a new scoring record in the second round when they hammered the New Brunswick team 30-3. (In 1957, teams were not allowed to concede their games, a rule that added to the embarrassment of the weaker entries.)

But against Baldwin, they were no match. The Alberta skip was featuring a new team of Gord Haynes, Art Kleinmeyer and Bill Price; however, he might just as easily have played with three novices because he was simply incredible. Almost single-handedly, he won the game 8-7 against the Saskatchewan rink, sailed through the rest of the field, and went undefeated to record his second title.

What Baldwin achieved was his most satisfying Brier win. When it was over, he knew that he had defeated a stellar field (including a young Don Duguid playing for Manitoba's Howard Wood, Jr.) under excellent conditions.

In 1958, the Brier went to Victoria and the talk of the town was whether Matt Baldwin, who had won Alberta with yet another lineup, could grab his third victory. The men of the media, with whom Baldwin had become good friends—because of their shared appreciation for the nightlife—built up the pressure by focusing on the Alberta mission. Could the Edmonton skip match the record of the great Ken Watson? Could he handle the attention and move into the record books?

Baldwin gave the press plenty to write about, not only by politely answering their questions but by checking out of the host hotel, the Empress. "All those ladies having tea are making so much noise we can't get any rest," Baldwin explained.

In truth, however, the Alberta team, which was made up of Bill Price, Gord Haynes and Jack Geddes, had walked into their rooms and found no televisions.

"I wanted television to relax in between games. I think we would have gone crazy without the television," said the gregarious skip. "So I phoned up a rental company and asked that two be delivered for the week. But when the rental company found out we were staying in the Empress, they said they couldn't deliver the sets because the hotel had a generator—direct current."

Not to be denied his TV, Baldwin and crew checked out and moved into a motel down the road that had sets. Their exodus didn't sit well with the Brier organizers, who wanted the Alberta rink staying in the host hotel. But Baldwin didn't care. He was happy with his television and told the trustees so.

Because the field that year was made up of lesser-known rinks, even more attention focused on Baldwin. Many of the big names, such as the Campbells, had failed to win their provincial titles. But one other team was causing plenty of commotion. The Manitoba entry of Terry Braunstein, brother Ron Braunstein, Ray Turnbull and John Hellemond had surprised curling's strongest province by winning the playdowns, despite the fact that all four were still considered minors. Terry Braunstein and Turnbull were 18, Ron Braunstein had just turned 17 and Hellemond was only 16.

As well, the foursome had only come together the night before the Manitoba Bonspiel.

"A few days earlier, our lead, Brian Longley, told us he was dropping out due to previous commitments. Most of the other curlers were already committed to other teams by this time, but I knew of one player who might fit in," Terry Braunstein recalled.

He didn't know how to get in touch with this player, however—all he knew was the kid's first name and the club he curled at.

"So I went on a stakeout at the club, hoping this guy would show up. He finally did, the night before the bonspiel began, and ended up playing with us."

When Braunstein filled in the lineup on the entry form, he wrote down Jack Hellemond. That name appeared on all the trophies the team won and on the official Brier records of 1958. Years later, Hellemond's brother, Andy, became a well-known NHL referee and was often seen on television.

"I noticed that the name on the back of his jersey was Van Hellemond," Braunstein stated. "I went and asked Jack why his brother was using the name Van Hellemond.

"'Because that's our name,' he replied. 'When you wrote down my name wrong years ago, I never bothered to correct you.'"

The four cocky kids came together, performed incredibly well and wound up winning one of the spots available in the provincial playdowns. Immediately, the Manitoba Curling Association called a meeting to determine if the youngsters should be allowed to play in that competition. While a lot of opinions on both sides were expressed, the eventual consensus was that it would be good for them to compete at that lofty level. Maybe they'd learn a thing or two that would help them when they grew up, the association said.

No one at that meeting ever expected them to win the province. But when Braunstein did just that, he set off another round of talks to decide whether or not the team should be allowed to play in the Brier.

Ironically, a year earlier at the Brier trustees' meeting, David Stewart had raised the point of an age limit. He asked the group what would happen if an underage team won a provincial championship. The question had arisen because a high school team from the Town of Mount Royal Curling Club in Quebec had gone as far as the provincial final before losing to Ken Weldon. The trustees admitted that nothing in the rules would prevent an underage squad from competing but, surprisingly, they did nothing to address the issue.

Back in Manitoba, Braunstein knew he could not be denied his rightful spot in the Brier field at this late hour. "If the MCA had allowed us to play in the provincial championship," he stated,

"they couldn't very well turn around and bar us from representing the province in Victoria." And so off they went to the
national final.

Their participation caused the Brier organizers more than a few
headaches. Liquor laws were quite stringent at that time, and many
social events connected with the Brier had to become dry affairs
because of the kids.

Although loose and fearless all through the provincial
playdowns, Braunstein's team was somewhat apprehensive when
it arrived in Victoria. The four were carrying a great deal of tradition on their backs, representing the province with the best Brier
record. To make things more stressful, they ended up with the
worst possible draw—a first-round bye and then a matchup
against Baldwin.

After anxiously sitting through the first draw, they walked onto
the ice to play the master. Braunstein was sure Baldwin was scared
of losing to the youngsters. "It was pretty obvious that no one
wanted to lose to us," he said. "I just got this feeling that Baldwin
was nervous in that game." Although Baldwin didn't like to lose to
anybody, he had some respect for the youthful curlers. "I knew if
they had won Manitoba, they must know something about the
game. You don't come out of there unless you can play."

He learned how much they knew very quickly. After two ends,
Braunstein had posted a 6-0 lead, shocking everyone in the arena.
Baldwin proved that experience did count for something, how-
ever, as he roared back to take the game 12-11.

Following that contest, Baldwin inadvertently created a mess
when a Canadian Press reporter asked him to comment on the
game and his youthful opposition. The skip stated that he was
impressed with the Manitoba team but that it had had luck on its
side early in the game. The reporter translated these words his own
way, and the next day's headline read, "Baldwin thinks kids
are lucky."

This statement drew the wrath of the Buffalo province. Baldwin
explained what had happened to Braunstein, who laughed the
matter off, but telegrams from Winnipeg and the surrounding area
flooded in.

"I remember one in particular," chuckled Baldwin, after the
fact. "It said, 'Not only are you a poor sport, Baldwin, but you're a

big prick.' I got a laugh out of that. At least I knew where they stood."

After that start and a few more games, the Manitoba team began to lose favor quickly back at home. The boys lost two of their first three and the province's headlines screamed, "Never send boys to do a man's job."

But Braunstein was not about to give up the dream just yet. One by one, his squad knocked off opposing rinks and ended up with an 8-3 record.

Meanwhile, Baldwin was putting together a fine showing of his own. He had seven wins by the time the final day of play arrived, and with two games remaining, the team could win the Brier outright by defeating Ontario and Nova Scotia.

But the popular skip had another problem. A terrible influenza had raced through the field and had hit Baldwin hard. In the morning game against Ontario, he had to bring a chair out onto the ice. To the crowd's delight and his discomfort, he would rise from the chair to call or play his shot, and then collapse back into it with a large thud. He also spent much of the game racing to the washroom. The Albertans lost the match 10-6.

Some accused Baldwin of going overboard with his performance that day, of playing to the crowd, but he says his behavior was genuine. In any case, the fans ate it up, wondering if he would fall flat on his nose at some point during the match.

After that game, Baldwin returned to his motel and fell into bed. The team spent a great deal of time debating what it should do. In the last round, the Albertans were to play Nova Scotia. A win would guarantee them a play-off; a loss might put them out. But, after looking at Baldwin, they elected to go with three players and let the skip sleep.

Baldwin had the radio on in the motel (there was no television coverage), listening to the updates. "If they had got down early," he admitted, "I was all set to get out of bed and get over there by the fifth end."

But he never had to get out of his pajamas. The three players hung on to beat the Nova Scotians 10-6 and forced a play-off with Braunstein and company.

The play-off game was a crowd pleaser. The underdog Braunstein rink, which had become a favorite of the spectators, up against the wily but ailing veteran Baldwin, who was in search of his third Brier win—no one could have written a better script.

Baldwin had recovered from the flu somewhat, but was still not 100 per cent. Adrenaline kicked in, however, and he was able to get himself into the game. After four ends, the Alberta team had posted a 6-1 lead, and although Braunstein was able to close the gap to 6-4, that was as close as he would come. The final score was 10-6, and Baldwin joined Ken Watson as the Brier's only three-time winning skip. He also became just the second player to win back-to-back titles, joining Gordon Hudson.

Unlike after his previous two wins, Baldwin's celebration this time was low-key. "I was still so sick, I didn't do too much. Although I did have a few drinks. That wasn't a particularly satis-fying win," Baldwin remembered. "I enjoyed the second win in Kingston much more. There was just something about that Brier that I didn't get a big bang out of winning, there was not that great a feeling."

Joining Watson in the three-win column was a triumph that would sink in later.

Baldwin made one more Brier appearance in 1971 in Quebec City. Again, however, illness took its toll; immediately after win-ning the Alberta title in Calgary, he came down with the flu and spent the two weeks prior to the competition in bed.

The championship was also marred by the horrendous rocks that the Dominion Curling Association had purchased a few years earlier. These stones were to be used solely for Canadian champi-onships, but they were resharpened with disastrous results that caused no end of problems for the curlers. (The DCA eventually abandoned the idea of having its own stones and the rocks were sold to a Southwestern Ontario club.)

Weather was also a problem at that Brier as a blizzard raged through the provincial capital, causing the first-ever cancellation of a Brier draw. The storm did, however, lead to another chapter in the history of Matt Baldwin.

On Friday evening, during the last round of play, with the weather outside still not cooperating, a power failure hit the Coli-sée. The entire arena was thrown into darkness for 15 minutes. When the power finally did come back on, the Baldwin team was nowhere to be seen. But on the sheet, where they had been playing against Quebec, eight Alberta rocks sat snugly in the four-foot. Baldwin and team emerged from the bar, where they had retreated, to accept the gales of good-natured laughter from the crowd for their prank. It became known as the Baldwin Blackout. Years later, you can still hear a team in trouble saying, "The only thing that can help us now is a Baldwin Blackout."

Although he finished with a 5-5 record that year, Baldwin was still the center of attention, as he had always been. He and his teammates were out of the running early on at that Brier, so they decided to enjoy it while they could. They checked out of their hotel room, checked into the largest suite in the Château Frontenac and began a week-long party that welcomed anyone who walked through the doors. The hosts left only when they had to play a game.

Few curlers could match Baldwin's colorful style or his presentation. He had made the Brier more than a competition—with his bon vivant attitude, he had made it a show. That he could curl with the world's best only added to his legacy. He may not have had quite as strong a team as some of the past and future greats, although they were far from weak. But more so than any other Brier competitor, Baldwin won those championships by virtue of his own shotmaking.

Individually, few players were as talented as he was. Several years later, an Edmonton television station organized a one-on-one competition with some of the top names in curling—Richardson, Campbell and others. Baldwin won the title for six consecutive years before the organizers politely asked him not to enter the following year because they wanted a different winner.

"If curling was an individual game," he proudly stated, "I'd kill anybody." Few who saw him play would doubt that.

As for Braunstein, he would return for another kick at the Brier can in 1965, a wiser and better player. There was also a change in his rink. Partway through the 1963-64 season, Van Hellemond injured his knee and was forced to retire from competitive play. The three remaining players decided to fill the hole on their team by asking Don Duguid, a close friend of Ray Turnbull's, to join them. Duguid had been to the Brier in 1957 as part of Howard Wood, Jr.'s team and was known as a strong shotmaker.

He agreed, and the team played together for the first time at the

1964 Manitoba Bonspiel. While the team didn't fare very well in
that event, the members elected to give the competitive circuit a try
full-time the following year. Practicing and competing together,
they knew there was some magic. The team played nine bonspiels
over the winter and won eight of them convincingly. They waltzed
through the provincial playdowns and reached the 1965 Brier,
scheduled for Saskatoon.

This team arrived in the wheat city with as much confidence as
any squad that ever came to a Brier. Terry Braunstein was more
aware of the game and a smarter player than in 1958. On the front
end, the gregarious Turnbull paired well with Ron Braunstein.
They were strong sweepers and good throwers. They could judge
weight with perfection and were excellent team players. The addition of Duguid made the unit complete.

The Saskatoon Brier was a popular one and large crowds
jammed every draw. What they saw was a Manitoba team rattling
off seven consecutive wins that kept it a game ahead of the pack. In
second place was the hometown Saskatoon rink, skipped by the
popular Harold Worth.

The crowd, with its boisterous cheering, had become a factor in
many games, but a few spectators were about to take things much
too far.

While playing their eighth game, the Manitoba team was sub-
jected to one of the darkest incidents in the history of the Brier. The
sheets of ice that year were very close to the boards and, consequently, to the stands. The crowds could practically reach out and
touch the players. Perhaps because Manitoba was one game ahead
of the hometown rink, perhaps for another reason, some fans
began to hurl anti-Semitic remarks at the Braunstein brothers. At
first, the two ignored the indignity, but when it continued end
after end, Ron Braunstein exploded.

Without warning, he jumped into the stands after one perpetra-
tor, followed closely by Turnbull, who was followed by his father
sitting nearby. Turnbull and his father are large, imposing men, and
when the two of them confronted the rude fan, he quickly left
the building.

Calm was soon restored, but the Manitoba team, obviously
upset at the incident, lost the game 12-6 and fell into a tie with
Saskatchewan.

The next day, Saskatchewan lost its second contest to the Nova Scotia team, while Braunstein handled Ontario 13-7. Those results set up numerous possibilities for the final draw, all of which could be negated if Manitoba beat British Columbia.

The game appeared to be going British Columbia's way, but two brilliant shots by Duguid in the eighth end led to a five-ender, and Manitoba prevailed 10-7. Eight years later, the "kids of '58" had their championship. The record crowds, now apparently free of anti-Semites, applauded approvingly as the still youthful rink was presented with the Brier Tankard by David Stewart.

It was also a popular win among the curling fraternity, whose members knew how hard the team had worked to reach its goal. Few curlers in the country held the game as close to their hearts as these four, and to see them succeed was a satisfying experience.

Indeed, Braunstein had proven right the members of the Manitoba Curling Association who, years earlier, had said that the underage team would learn something by playing in the provincial finals and the Brier. Braunstein and his teammates had learned many lessons on the ice, but even more off it. They learned that the Brier was much more than a series of curling games to declare a champion—that it was an event of great magnitude in the country. Their respect for the competition, as much as their curling talent, propelled them on to the 1965 title.

In this same era, a family rink from Saskatchewan clamored hard to win the Briers and finally did in 1955. Despite appearing in 10 championships, Garnet Campbell managed only one win, but his effect on the Brier was everlasting.

Campbell first played at the Canadian Championship in 1947 as a 16-year-old kid, skipping for his father, Sandy. Joined by Lloyd and Sam Campbell, it was the first time the famous Campbell family rink from Saskatchewan would play in the Brier, but certainly not the last.

Garnet Campbell was not a big man, but he possessed a huge heart. He played to win, but always as a gentleman. In 1947, the Campbells of Avonlea, Saskatchewan, finished third behind Manitoba's Jimmy Welsh and Frenchy D'Amour of British Columbia.

But seven years later, in 1954, he was back, this time with brother Don replacing Sandy. Four brothers on one team was a first for the Brier, and despite a stellar 8–2 record, the Campbells were still a game behind Baldwin.

In 1955, they finally hit pay dirt. The Brier was held in Regina, and many friends and supporters packed the arena hoping for a victory by the Campbells. Saskatchewan premier Tommy Douglas was so worked up about the competition, he predicted before the event started that the team would win.

At that time, Saskatchewan had never won the Brier, so the pressure was firmly on Campbell's shoulders. He responded by putting together a perfect record, 10–0.

It was a glorious moment in Regina when the team walked up to accept the trophy. To add to the occasion, Art Condie, director of playdowns, called Sandy Campbell to the mike to say a few words. The father of the team received a tremendous ovation from the crowd and his sons.

Garnet Campbell would go on to play seven more Briers, finishing second on four occasions, including 1971 when, as third for Bob Pickering, he lost a play-off to Don Duguid. In his 10 appearances, he put together an impressive record of 66 wins and 21 losses.

Few people embodied the spirit of the Brier as much as Garnet Campbell did. He played at every position but lead, supporting each and every team no matter where he was in the lineup. He was always quick to shake hands, win or lose, and that gesture made him popular as well.

Unfortunately, he had the misfortune of hitting his peak at the same time as people such as Matt Baldwin and the Richardsons. Otherwise, he might have had more than one title. But there is no disputing his and his family's place at the Brier table of honor.

5

The Richardsons

It is unlikely that while Garnet Campbell was winning the 1955 championship in Regina, he was aware of a couple of young men in the audience, sitting quietly with their parents, watching their first Brier. But the two fellows were glued to the inimitable Campbell.

At one point in the game, one of the young men leaned over to his mother and said, "You know, Mom, we're going to get into this."

The mother cast a sympathetic look at her 21-year-old son, who had been curling for only two years, and said gently, "I think you should have started earlier if you wanted to get in here."

"No, Mom, you'll see. It's not too late for us. We'll make it."

Those optimistic words were spoken by Garnet (Sam) Richardson, who, with his brother, Ernie, and cousins Arnold and Wes, did make it—in a big way.

In fact, what Arnold Palmer is to golf and Gordie Howe is to hockey, the Richardsons are to curling. In a world where sports superlatives have lost meaning, they are true icons, the greatest team ever to play the game.

Make it? They almost owned it. Never before had curling seen such mastery. Power, grace, control, balance—the Richardsons had it all and more. They were pure curling, playing to win but knowing how to lose. From 1959 to 1964, no one dominated the sport the way the Richardsons did. They won four Briers and almost claimed a fifth, establishing a record that has never come close to being equaled.

For several generations of curlers, these four men have been the heroes. Throughout the 1960s and 1970s, if a youngster was throwing stones alone in the early morning, you could be sure that he or she was playing an imaginary game against the Richardsons:

Last rock . . . Smith needs to draw the button to beat the Richardsons and take the Brier. Ernie Richardson has locked one on at the back of the button, swept there in a tremendous fury by Garnet and Wes. That means the Saskatchewan team is sitting two, thanks to that marvelous shot by Arnold earlier in the end . . . And now Smith has to go one better . . . The rock looks good . . . it's on line . . . YES!! Smith has made the shot and the Richardsons have finally lost. Smith has done the impossible and beaten the Richardsons to win the Brier.

While the Richardsons may not hold the same appeal for the junior curlers of the 1980s and 1990s, every player who has ever swept a rock knows who the Richardsons are. They are in the Canadian Sports Hall of Fame. They have been on the cover of *Maclean's.* They have had their own line of sweaters, boots, brooms and even socks. Ernie has been awarded the Order of Canada.

It has all been pretty heady stuff for four kids from the small burg of Stoughton, Saskatchewan. The four are the sons of three brothers, two of whom married sisters just to confuse the genealogical situation even further. Over the years, the family lines have been muddled by the media, but for the record, Ernie and Garnet (known as Sam) are brothers, while Arnold and Wes are cousins from separate families.

Perhaps the most amazing part of the Richardson dynasty is that the boys took up curling on a whim, almost by chance.

Ernie and Sam, sons of Melvin and Viola Richardson, grew up on a farm in the Dirty Thirties. Melvin eked out a living trucking anything and everything to Weyburn and Regina. In his spare time, he became a talented carpenter, and by 1945, when the situation in Stoughton didn't seem about to improve, he moved the family to Regina, sold his truck, bought a house and became a full-time carpenter.

It was not exactly a privileged childhood for Ernie and Sam.

"To make ends meet, Mom did washing, took in boarders and looked for anything else that would bring in a buck," stated Sam.

"Both of us worked after school to help out the family and there certainly wasn't any time for sports such as curling."

An entrepreneur, Mel worked for a while in the Wheat Pool as a carpenter, but then set out on his own to build houses. That business eventually turned into a construction company and things began to blossom for the Richardson family.

By this time, the boys were in high school. In Grade 10, Ernie quit and enlisted for a five-year stint in the air force, spending time on almost every base in eastern Canada. But the future skip decided he wasn't cut out to be a fly-boy and, in the early 1950s, bought his way out of the remainder of his enlistment with help from his father.

Sam, meanwhile, continued on in school and eventually joined his father as a carpenter, becoming a journeyman by the age of 20. He was not all that happy to see his brother returning to Saskatchewan because, with Ernie joining the construction firm, it meant Sam had to take a cut in pay.

It was not the first time the two brothers had disagreed. Growing up, they had fought like tigers. Ernie, the taller and stronger of the two, would usually lay out Sam, his younger by two years, in short order. But the feisty youngster always seemed able to get up and give it another go. Their fights often ended in a draw when Ernie, after knocking Sam down repeatedly, couldn't bring himself to hit his brother again.

In the booming post-war years, the house-building business was alive and well in Regina, and the Richardsons had plenty of work. On one project, the boys noticed a large building going up across the field, which turned out to be the Wheat City Curling Club. But although they saw it every day, they never gave it much thought.

A few weeks later, a group of Richardson builders went out for an after-work beer at a local hotel. A newcomer to the company, a carpenter from Portage la Prairie, Manitoba, asked what the other fellows did for fun in the winter. When the reply came, "Not much," he suggested they take up curling.

The new club was advertising for membership in the local paper, and soon after the new team was accepted. But before the first rock was thrown, the chap from Portage decided he didn't want to curl. That left Ernie, Sam and Arnold, who was also working at the construction company, as a threesome. They soon solved this problem when their cousin Norm Richardson, brother to Wes, agreed to be their skip. He had played before, although he talked a much better game than he played.

The four lined up for their inaugural season of curling—Norm skipping, Arnold at third and Ernie and Sam alternating at lead and second (neither one liked playing lead). All of the Richardsons were in excellent shape, Ernie and Arnold because of construction work, and Norm because he was in the navy (why he was stationed in Regina remains a mystery). They took to the game like termites to wood.

Because the winter of 1956 was mild and the Wheat City Club had natural ice, the squad played only about 17 games. But they were immediately hooked. "When we won a game—which wasn't that often—we [Ernie and Sam] would race home and wake up our parents just so they'd know how good their sons were," cackled Sam.

The second year, Norm was transferred closer to the water and Ernie told the other two he'd like a chance to skip. At six-foot-four, he was an imposing figure and no one dared disagree.

Over the next couple of years, the team had some limited success with a variety of players filling the lead position. They traveled around to bonspiels and usually came home with a prize, although winning was still a rarity. But through the experience, Ernie became a keen skip, always watching and learning from people such as Bill Clark and Garnet Campbell, two of the best in Regina in the early 1950s.

"I watched those guys every chance I could," Ernie admitted. "Campbell was more of a draw player while Clark used more of the hitting game, so I kind of got the best of both worlds."

Shortly after Campbell won the Brier, the Richardsons went up against him in a city bonspiel and lost when the veteran skip made a tremendous last rock.

"At the time, I thought we must be pretty good if we can lose on last rock to a guy who'd won the Brier," Ernie recalled. "But we still had a long, long way to go. We were still quite green even though we didn't know it. We thought we were hot stuff."

By the end of 1958, however, doubt was creeping into Ernie's mind. Although things had been going well, he felt the rest of the team was advancing faster than he was. He wanted to give up skipping and allow either Arnold or Sam to take the helm. Indeed, the team was making everything in front of their skip, but he was missing key shots, ones that would clinch games and bonspiels. To Ernie, those shots were life or death—they meant everything to him, and being unable to finish things off almost took him out of the game.

At the start of the 1958 season, Ernie went to Arnold and suggested that Arnold skip, but his cousin said no. "I knew he was the guy to be skipping," stated Arnold, the quietest of the four. "I just told him to not let big shots—or big misses—bother him so much. It was a game and if he missed, he missed. The team knew it wasn't because he wasn't trying."

With that advice, Ernie became a new player, overflowing with confidence. But one last piece of the puzzle was missing. All through Ernie's learning process, the lead position on the team was unsettled. Following Norm Richardson's departure and Ernie's move to skip, another friend from work, Wes Scott, took over at lead. After two years he left, and a plumber named Trev Fisher handled the duties. In the fall of 1958, looking for the perfect fit, the three turned to cousin Wes Richardson. He had been skipping a rink and having some success of his own. He certainly had the number of the other three, because he beat them more often than not. But, using his best negotiating skills, Ernie managed to persuade his cousin to drop his own team and play lead for the all-Richardson rink.

From the first moment they touched the ice together, it was clear this lineup was one that had it all. They enjoyed a triumphant bonspiel season, winning virtually every event they entered. After a march through the city playdowns, the squad went into the Southern Saskatchewan competition where the conditions were less than perfect.

"We played in Yorkton," recalled Ernie, "and the temperature was minus 30 degrees Fahrenheit outside the rink and minus 20 degrees inside. The frost on the rocks was so thick, we needed Chore Boys to clean them." Somehow, they knocked off the favored Clark in the last game and advanced to the provincial final.

That year, the event had been moved to the Regina Stadium to accommodate the crowds. The Richardsons knew the icemaker in charge and decided to practice at his club, to get a feel for the ice. While they were throwing rocks, the icemaker came out and told them the surface at the arena would be much quicker than anything they had ever played on before. It would be to their advantage to go there and test it, he told them.

That they did, and testing it gave them the advantage they needed. In the final against Gordon Grimes, the Richardsons used a delicate touch while Grimes, unused to the conditions, nearly drove his rocks through the end of the stadium. Although all 12 ends were played, the match was over in short order and the Richardsons were off to their first Brier.

On the Friendship Train to Quebec City for the 1959 Canadian championship, a number of other players told the Richardsons the young team was going to win. The boys had no idea what to make of this prediction. As Brier rookies, they had no expectations and didn't know the competition outside of the western entries, against which they had played in big bonspiels.

"I thought our goal should be just to put in a good performance," Ernie said. "I don't think we were thinking about winning at that point."

Together, the boys agreed to work towards the objective of respectability, carrying it as a common goal. The Richardsons' discipline has become famous among competitive curlers. Many a Brier hopeful has been knocked off stride by the outside events that always accompany a championship, but the Richardsons were always committed to giving their all.

Their approach was clear right from the start of their first Brier. After arriving at the Château Frontenac, the host hotel, the Richardsons' wives asked the boys what they were planning to do that evening. Sam, who was the team's front man, stated that they were going to relax and recover from the long train ride. Somewhat miffed, the wives informed their husbands that the Northern Ontario team and its spouses, whom they had met on the train, were going to attend a pre-Brier dance. Sam stood his ground and told the ladies that, if they wanted to go, perhaps they could tag along with the Northern Ontario group. So, while the team prepared for a grinding week of play, the women went out on the town.

The next day, the boys heard about a wonderful evening they

had missed. Many of the players were at the party and the Northern Ontario entry of Darwin Wark had danced the night away.

Two days later, the Saskatchewan team played the Wark squad in the first game of the Brier.

"It wasn't pretty," remembered Sam. "After three ends, we were up 6–0. In the fourth, Wark made a great shot to cut us out of six more."

By the end, the Richardsons had racked up a 17–8 victory, and when Sam met up with his wife after the game, she was saddened for the Wark rink.

"Gee, I felt sorry for our Northern Ontario friends," said Kay Richardson to her husband.

"Well, maybe they should have done a little less dancing," Sam replied with a mean smile. For the rest of the week, the team fulfilled its obligations, but put curling ahead of all else.

The social schedule in those days was certainly a busy one, and it is easy to see how teams became tired off the rink as well as on. In the 1959 Brier, there was a Saturday evening reception hosted by the Royal Bank, followed by a dinner hosted by the mayor. Sunday's events included the trustees' luncheon and an evening reception at the Jacques Cartier Curling Club. On Tuesday, the curlers' dinner was preceded by a reception thrown by the Bank of Montreal. There was a lunch on Wednesday courtesy of the Quebec Curling Association and a reception at night given by the Canadian Imperial Bank of Commerce. And so it went for eight straight days. Of course, there were also a few 12-end curling games to fit somewhere into that calendar of events.

But for Ernie and his team, the curling took precedence. And the games required some careful concentration—the ice in Quebec City was the opposite of what the team had played on in the Saskatchewan final.

"It was heavy and swingy and that favored us because we could throw it hard and control the big swing with our sweeping," Arnold said. "Other teams didn't fare as well. If a takeout was the slightest bit light, it would swoop across the sheet and could miss by three or four feet."

The conditions led to big ends and lopsided scores, not to mention some embarrassing misses. It was nothing to count 10 or 12 points and lose the game.

But the Richardsons continued to control the play, winning their first eight games with a dominating, hitting style of play. (In the eighth game, they defeated a B.C. team that had noted Canadian sports columnist Dick Beddoes as its lead.) The competition was front-page news back home, as the curling-mad fans in Saskatchewan followed their team in La Belle Province. Could the boys bring home the Wheat Province's second Canadian championship? Curlers were glued to the radio awaiting the results of every draw, hoping and cheering for the Richardsons.

While the big prize at the end of the competition was the Macdonald Tankard, there were other laurels waiting to be grabbed by the 1959 winner. Ken Watson had organized the first international matches between the Canadian and Scottish champions to be played right after the Brier. The first Scotch Cup, the forerunner of the world championship, created a buzz among the competitors.

There was also talk of the 1959 winner representing Canada in a demonstration of curling at the 1960 Olympic Games in Squaw Valley.

The excitement grew as news of these events spread, but it didn't derail the Richardsons. They stuck to their game plan and, while attending all the necessary events and social gatherings, were never the last ones to leave. They also rested at almost every opportunity. Well-known for playing at a quick pace, the team would often finish a 12-end game in two hours. As soon as they were off the ice, they would go back to their hotel, have a beer and a sandwich and listen to the remainder of the draw on the radio while stretched out on the beds. While they may have had only an hour to rest at a time, by the end of the week, when many other teams were sucking wind, the Richardsons were still full of energy.

In their ninth match, the Saskatchewan rink met up with the Quebec team, skipped by Jack Bergmann. The two squads had reversed records—Saskatchewan was 8-0 while the Quebec team was 0-8. With a win, the Richardsons could guarantee themselves no worse than a tie for first place. A loss could mean disaster because Alberta had only one defeat as well.

It seemed like a mismatch on the draw sheet, but on the ice it was one of the closest contests of the week. With nothing to lose, the Quebec team was relaxed and carefree. It didn't matter to them if they lost 100-0 and they chose to play aggressively against the leaders. The Richardsons, meanwhile, were a little complacent, perhaps casting their eyes ahead to their afternoon game against the tough Manitoba team. Before long, the Quebec squad had the Regina boys on the ropes, and with his last rock left to come, Ernie had to draw cold to the four-foot to win the game. He made it, and together the Richardsons vowed never to take any Brier team for granted again.

In the final round, however, despite their scare earlier in the day, they could not overcome Dr. Dick Bird's team. Putting on a masterful performance, Bird dropped the Richardsons 9-7, and when Herb Olson's Alberta team won its last game against Northern Ontario, a play-off between the two Prairie teams was required.

Following the loss to Manitoba, the most disappointed person in the Coliseum was Gaby Beauvant, who was the Richardsons' host driver for the week.

"He was so sure that we would clinch the title that afternoon, he had arranged a victory party for that evening," Ernie recalled. "When we came off the ice after losing, Gaby was literally crying at what had happened."

The team told him not to worry, just to push the start-time of the party back a few hours. Beauvant agreed but insisted that the team go out for a nice dinner before the play-off. That seemed an odd suggestion since a blizzard had been raging all day; the stands had been almost empty because few fans had ventured outside. But the enthusiastic driver, sensing the weather might become bad, had put chains on his tires early that morning and could plow through just about anything.

Accordingly, the Richardsons and a few of Beauvant's friends had a couple of drinks and then dined on shrimp cocktails and steaks. They chatted and laughed and generally enjoyed themselves, not worrying in the least about the upcoming contest.

Meanwhile, back in the Coliseum, Olson's team was staring at the walls and dining on a fine menu of hot dogs. They fretted and paced, especially when the gourmet-dining Richardsons arrived 10 minutes late for the start of the game.

"I always thought getting out made a big difference in that game," Ernie said. "I think Herbie must have been going nuts just staring at the walls, and meanwhile we were out at a fine restaurant."

The apparently cavalier style of the Richardsons and his long wait in the bowels of the Coliseum may have thrown Olson off his game, because the play-off was all but over mere moments after the two teams shook hands. Despite appearances, Ernie's boys were anything but laid-back.

"I don't remember us being worried about losing at all," Arnold reflected some time later. "I think we were more mad at ourselves for not winning it earlier. We were going to kick someone's butt and it turned out to be Herbie's."

By the fifth end, the Saskatchewan team had moved out to a 7-2 lead and they kept pouring it on. In the 10th, leading 11-6, Sam Richardson went to take a drink of water but couldn't get the water in his mouth because he was smiling so much. Like everyone else in the facility, he knew the team had won its first Brier.

Back in Regina, news of the victory was given the same prominence as the end of the war. "Curling Kings," screamed a headline in the *Leader-Post* in letters that covered half the front page. "The best in the Dominion" was the title of the lead editorial in the same paper. Radio stations led with the news of the win and carried on with reports on the new champions for the next week. Wherever people went in that city, the Richardsons were the first topic of conversation. Although one of the strongest curling provinces, Saskatchewan had only captured one previous Brier and the fans were devouring this new championship.

Unfortunately, the team was not due to come home until after the Scottish competition—another two weeks. And when they finally did arrive, bringing along the Scotch Cup title as well, they were minus their skip. Ernie stayed back in Ontario to be with his wife, who had gone into hospital following the Brier with a nerve problem.

But the other three Richardsons were feted like kings. At the airport, they waded through a huge mob of well-wishers before getting into convertibles for a parade through the downtown, complete with Mounties on horseback leading the way.

Little did these screaming supporters know that this was only the first of four such celebrations.

In 1960, the Richardsons continued their domination of the competitive circuit before winning another provincial championship. This time, they knew what to expect as they made their way to Fort William for the Canadian championship. And so did everyone else.

After the Richardsons walloped Manitoba 17–5 and Northern Ontario 19–3 on the opening day, the *Globe* offered an analysis that must have expressed the thoughts of everyone in the competition: "The 1960 Canadian Curling Championships are only one day old and already the question uppermost in the minds of observers here is: 'Can anyone stop the Richardsons?'"

The one-sided scores indicated not only the Richardsons' curling ability but also their facility handling corn. Before the competition, Curlmaster Broom Company had obtained the right to have the players use their BlackJack brooms exclusively. These brooms were notorious shedders, and in the hands of the best sweepers in the country, they soon filled the ice with loose corn and other debris.

"The ice was like a cornfield," Arnold remembered. "It was really a mess." Although the ice was quick and had a good curl to it, the chaff was everywhere. After the fifth end of every contest, the ice would be swept—although some wags suggested a hay baler might have worked better.

Once again, however, this situation favored the Richardsons, who were extremely talented sweepers. Wes was as strong as a bull and a master at slinging the corn. Sam was also no slouch when it came to sweeping, and together the two would go up and down the sheet, end after end, tiring out the people who were watching them perform.

They were also excellent judges of weight and could tell Ernie or Arnold just how the sheet was running at any particular time. They would tell Ernie, "It's like the second end at Yorkton." Ernie would be able to recall that situation from memory and translate the information into just the right weight.

Of their four wins, the 1960 championship may have been the Richardsons' strongest performance. They were so dominant that, by mid-week, it was a question not of whether they would win but of when. Playing so well, the four relaxed more than they had the previous year, taking in nightly performances by an up-and-coming Bobby Curtola at the Fort William Curling Club.

In the seventh round, the Saskatchewan rink found itself up against Ontario's Jake Edwards, a wily veteran out of Kingston. If the Richardsons were the world's fastest rink, Edwards may have been the slowest. He took a methodical approach to the game and analyzed every shot; on average, an Edwards game would last 40 minutes longer than a Richardson match. Because the Saskatchewan players were still following their regimen of returning to the hotel for a rest in between games, they had banked a physical edge by the week's end that kept them ahead of the fading Ontario four.

But, in the head-to-head tilt, the slow play confounded Ernie, whose normally razor-sharp concentration began to wander a bit in the long, drawn-out affair.

Perhaps he played better the slower the game, but whatever the case, Edwards was simply unbeatable that day. His third, Bob Elliot, was also making everything. A normally nervous player, Elliot would slip behind the boards after every few ends and have a quick shot to calm him down.

The Kingston crew snoozed its way to an 11-6 upset over the Richardsons, preventing the celebration from beginning too early.

Following that defeat, however, the Richardsons did not stumble again. In fact, with wins over Manitoba, Northern Ontario and Nova Scotia, they had captured the Brier with one draw left to play, a draw in which they had a bye.

While they waited for the other 10 teams to finish out the now meaningless round-robin, the Richardsons sat in the bar, rejoicing in their second win.

When it came time to make the presentations—about four hours later—the four Regina men walked down the sheet to the applause of the Fort William fans. Many in the stands may have thought it was a great show of team solidarity that Ernie, Arnold, Sam and Wes held hands as they moved down the ice.

"The truth was, the four us were well into it and we needed to hang on to each other to avoid falling down," Ernie laughed.

The team recovered in time to travel to Scotland and win the second Scotch Cup. Once again, Regina went mad for its curling champions and planned an even bigger celebration. However, with the Scottish trip, the organizers were having trouble finding out when the Richardsons were going to arrive back home. They finally made contact with the team when it reached Toronto, and were horrified to learn that the boys were scheduled to arrive three days *before* the big party had been planned. That would not do—Regina couldn't have its favorite sons back home prior to the big bash. And so the instructions went down the wire for the Richardsons to stay put, and despite having been away for the better part of five weeks, Ernie, Arnold, Sam and Wes shacked up in the Royal York Hotel for a few nights, courtesy of the Scotch Whiskey Company, which had learned of their predicament, and awaited the call to come home.

When they were allowed back in Regina, there was another huge celebration. But this time, the tributes and notoriety spread out beyond the city limits. Curling was booming across the country, especially in urban centers such as Toronto, where a flurry of curling clubs went up in the late 1950s and early 1960s. In an attempt to tap into this lucrative market, advertising firms were after the stars of the game, and none were more appealing than the Richardsons.

Before long, there were Ernie Richardson sweaters, Ernie Richardson curling boots, Ernie Richardson brooms, gloves, socks . . . the list went on. Ernie's picture was soon appearing in catalogues and newspaper ads. He would make public appearances at retail outlets to promote his wares.

Although every item carried Ernie's name, a four-way split was worked out for all the team members. At the start, the money allowed the boys to go on a vacation with their wives. Later, this advertising income grew, and while it never became a fortune, the earnings from the sweaters, the most popular of the items, amounted to about $100,000.

In 1961, the great Richardson train was derailed. Despite the fact that the team played even better on the competitive circuit than it had the previous two years, it never made it out of the city playdowns. At the time, there were 250 teams playing down to get out of Regina, and the odds never favored any team, even the two-time defending champion Richardson rink. In the end, it was their former mentor, Bill Clark, who knocked them off, stealing a point in the final end to sideline the great rink.

"It was a tough loss for us," Ernie said. "I think, though, that we realized the fact that we weren't going to win every game and this was just part of curling.

"There were a few people who asked us, 'What went wrong?'

But most of those were folks who didn't know anything about curling."

Sam, however, remembered that even some relatives thought the end might be in sight.

"At a family gathering just after we got knocked off, one of the parents suggested we should retire, but that drew all sorts of hoots from us."

As Ernie remembers, the loss in 1961 actually hardened the team's resolve. "It made us come back even stronger the next year, committed again to winning the Brier. We wanted it even more."

True to his word, Ernie and the Richardsons were back in the national championship in 1962, up against a tremendous field that included Manitoba's Norm Houck and Hec Gervais, the 275-pound potato farmer from St. Albert, Alberta, who had claimed the title in 1961.

Also in the field in Kitchener-Waterloo was an Ontario team that caused some controversy. With curling clubs springing up all over southwestern Ontario, many Westerners had ventured east to take up jobs in the clubs, which were operated as businesses rather than community gathering spots. Three of these people, who worked in Toronto as curling club managers, won the Ontario provincial title. Bayne Secord, twice the Canadian Schoolboy champion, Vern Larson and Russ Lindberg were all from small towns in Saskatchewan and lived in Toronto for eight months each winter to operate the Tam O'Shanter Curling Club. After the season ended, they went home and farmed. Along with Dave McDonough, they had rolled through Ontario, winning 27 straight games, and had a perfect 7-0 mark in the provincial final. Along the way, they had gone 130 ends without giving up a score of more than two.

But complaints rolled in quickly. Other provincial associations cried that Saskatchewan really had two entries. Even the Ontario Curling Association wasn't on the team's side, stating that the three players from Saskatchewan were professionals who should be banned from the Brier, which was solely for amateurs. The Ontario association lobbied the DCA to pass legislation that would prevent future transient teams from representing another province.

Later, at its annual meeting, the national association decided that all reps must be bona fide residents of the province they are representing by August 1 of the previous year. That rule effectively put Secord and the like out of business, but another motion put on the table would have far greater effects on the Brier field. The OCA called for a Brier ban on any curler who accepted a bonspiel prize of more than $150.

Almost every successful curler at the time would have been guilty of such an offense, especially the Richardsons, who had won cars and other big-ticket items with their curling prowess. The motion also stirred an East-West split, as the spiels that offered large prizes were held out west. Events in the East still presented winners with medals and small trophies.

Nothing but discussion was heard at that meeting and the whole affair was tabled for the following year. But this motion would cause a great deal of controversy down the road.

The Richardson rink didn't get involved in the furor over either issue. It was too busy worrying about its opening record. It had lost two of its first five games—to Nova Scotia and British Columbia—and was already in danger of falling out of the race for its third championship.

After losing their fifth-round contest to Nova Scotia, Ernie was quite down. The leaders, Gervais and Houck, were only a game up on them at 4-1, but the sullen skip was worried, and although he didn't say anything, his mood filled the car on the way back to the hotel.

Trying to lift his team's spirits, Sam chirped in optimistically, "It's okay, Ernie, we only have to win seven straight and we haven't played anybody yet."

"If we haven't played anybody," the skipper growled, "how come we have two losses?"

The car went silent, and when the team arrived back at the hotel, Ernie didn't follow the team's regular routine of resting in the room.

"I remember I went to the barber shop in the hotel and got a haircut, shave and anything else that would keep me in the chair," he said quietly. "I don't know why, but I just wanted to be by myself and think."

Ernie needed to regroup his thoughts and regain his focus. If the Richardsons were to win a third Brier championship, it would be largely up to him. And in that chair, he made up his mind that Sam had been right. Five more wins would get them a play-off. Two wins there would give them the Brier. If it could be done, surely the Richardsons were the team to do it.

That night, the Saskatchewan rink put in its best performance of the week and beat Houck 7-5. The next morning, they played Gervais, the team Ernie knew he'd have to beat if he was going to complete his mission.

That game is still considered one of the classics of all Brier matchups. The Richardsons got ahead early, but the friendly giant from Alberta, who had a touch that belied his massive size, came roaring back. Only a magnificent last rock by Ernie allowed his team to win by a score of 9-8.

"That was a turning point for us," Arnold stated frankly. "We got some zip back in our game after that."

With their confidence recharged, the Richardsons quickly reeled off wins against Newfoundland, New Brunswick and Quebec to end the round-robin at 8-2.

That record was good enough to tie the team for first with Houck and Gervais, and the first part of their mission was complete.

There is an old adage that says, to be good, you have to be lucky. Ernie Richardson was certainly lucky. If there was a break to be had, you could count on Ernie to get it. When it came to the play-off format for this three-way tie, his luck held. The round-robin records were not considered when deciding who would get the bye to the final. If they had, the Richardsons, having beaten both Gervais and Houck, would have moved on. Instead, organizers decided on a pea draw to determine who got the bye, with the other two teams playing a semifinal. Guess who won the draw?

"But I told the press afterwards that I felt we should have received the bye in the first place because we'd beaten the other two," said Ernie. "I told them that I thought we deserved to be in the final."

That statement was probably as much gamesmanship as anything else and it rankled both Houck and Gervais, who felt the Richardsons had received enough breaks over the years. But either way, the Saskatchewan rink was in the final. It had effectively won another game—six in a row. It had gone from being almost knocked out to one win away from a third title. And the mood of the team members had gone from downcast to exuberant. They were ready to take on either Alberta or Manitoba and kick some butt.

Many fans and media had predicted at the Brier's outset that Gervais would walk away with the title that year. After getting out to a strong start, however, he had stumbled and had never looked good through the second half of the week. Part of the problem may have been several warnings the big man had received from the DCA regarding his slide. Gervais had taken the slide to extremes and was charged three times with going over the hog line. He was told he would incur a penalty if it happened again. From that point on, the Alberta skip wasn't the same. Whether he altered his delivery to meet the demands of the DCA or simply fell into a streak of bad luck is not clear. Whatever the cause, he was winning games but he didn't dominate, and only narrowly beat the Northern Ontario team in the last round to make the play-off. In the semi, Gervais continued this pattern, managing to hold on to beat Houck. He took one point in the last end for an emotional 8-6 win.

Despite that victory win over Houck on Friday, when he arrived for the Saturday morning final, Gervais was still not himself. And at that time in his career, he was having all kinds of problems with the Richardsons. The final proved to be no different.

"We always had poor old Hector's number in those days," Sam said. "I don't think he ever beat us when we were winning Briers. Then it turned around, later, and we couldn't beat him, but in those days it was really funny."

After five ends, Ernie and the boys had taken a commanding 8-2 lead and cruised to a 14-7 win and their third Brier title.

Once again, the Richardsons had won the big games, a knack they displayed throughout their reign as the world's best. The tougher the match, the better they played. When it came to clutch contests, few teams were better.

With their third title, the Richardsons had also joined curling's elite. This was a select club, but the team wasn't satisfied with its membership there yet—it wanted more. And most observers believed the players could do it. They had the makeup, the desire, to win five or six Briers.

Individually, there were better curlers than each of the Richardsons, but no team was superior. Collectively, they meshed into a single entity that dominated in every aspect of the game.

Ernie's strength was his ability to focus. He was single-minded, and when he began a task, he shut everything else out until that task was completed. He was a tremendous gambler who knew the proper time to take a chance. He was also an excellent pool player and had an eye for angles, so necessary in curling during that period when there were plenty of rocks in play.

He was also a fair man who loved to win, but could accept losing. The game was everything to him, and he didn't have time for anyone who didn't adhere to the traditions or gentlemanly manner of the sport.

"In the '59 Brier," Sam offered, "[New Brunswick skip Dick] McCully had hurt his back and asked Ernie if it would be okay if he sat in a chair between shots, à la Matt Baldwin. Although it was against the rules, Ernie said, 'I don't care if the third throws all eight rocks and the front end sweeps all eight, let's just play.'"

Arnold Richardson may have been the most talented thrower on the team. He had a textbook delivery with perfect balance that allowed him to make virtually anything. It was a rare occasion when he didn't come up big in a significant game. Despite his great skill, he never boasted. In fact, he rarely talked at all, preferring to let his curling speak for itself. Ernie would joke that sometimes the other players would have to kick Arnold to get a word out of him. At one Brier party, where there were lots of different conversations going on around the room, Ernie suddenly stood up and shouted, "Quiet, everybody . . . Arnold's going to say something."

Arnold was also the perfect wedge between the two brothers on the team. Although Sam and Ernie had only two fights during the 15 years they curled together, it was Arnold who broke them up.

Sam was the consummate second player, strong on hits, capable on draws and an incredible sweeper. He also had a knack for making his best shot after his opposition second had missed. Sam was also the team's joker. "You never were quite sure what was going to come out of his mouth," Arnold said. "He loved to talk," remembered Ernie. "It's hard to believe but he was really quite shy when he was a kid, that is, until he discovered beer."

Sam was the cheerleader on the team, always reminding the boys that they were still in the game no matter how far behind they might be. He was the guts of the team, a fighter, a go-getter, a never-say-die kind of guy.

Wes was the most competitive of the four, always pushing himself to win. He was excellent at drawing stones out to the very edges of the circles, something that required a special touch in the days of bad ice conditions. He was also a relentless sweeper and an impeccable judge of weight. If he had a weak point, it was that his emotions sometimes clouded his view. In difficult situations, he would often get tense and lose perspective. But Sam was always there to bring Wes back in line.

"Sometimes," Sam admitted, "I would find an attractive girl in the audience and ask her to go up to Wes and say she thought he was the best looking of the four of us. That usually took his mind off things long enough to allow him to cool down."

These were the four players who began 1963 in search of a fourth Brier title, something no one had ever accomplished. But shortly after the season started, Wes developed back problems. At a couple of early spiels, he was hobbled by severe pain and couldn't even finish the competition. He consulted a doctor and the news was bad—he would need surgery to fuse two vertebrae. That meant he couldn't make the run for the fourth Brier title and the team would need a replacement.

The story many people heard, however, was not one of back problems, but of cracking morale. Rumors of dissension abounded. Wes had been dropped, the gossip went, because of a split with the other three. Slowly, news filtered out that maybe the team was coming apart. But the truth was on the operating table in Regina. Physically, Wes was simply not able to play.

While the loss of their lead saddened the other three, the upside was that, with three Brier wins under their belts, it wasn't difficult to find someone who was willing to take Wes's place. In fact, curlers were lining up to fill the void.

The team selected a close friend and ardent curler, Mel Perry, to handle the duties. He fit into the team perfectly, bringing with him a cool demeanor that hid his intensity. "Many people thought he was too nonchalant," Ernie said, "but deep down, he was into every game."

Once again, the boys won the Saskatchewan title, and this time it was off to Brandon, Manitoba, for a try for number four. "We felt if we could get back to the Brier, we'd win it a fourth time," Arnold said. "We weren't really cocky, just confident."

By this time, the media representation had grown much larger and it included a number of regulars. Bill Good, Jack Wells, Jack Matheson, Don Fleming, Neil MacCarl and Doug Maxwell were fixtures on the bench, and along with a crew of newcomers, they were priming the pump for the Richardsons' attempt at Brier history.

While several teams posed the most serious threats to the Saskatchewan team's fourth Brier title, the ice was a close second. Sheets A and B presented some of the most unusual conditions ever seen at a Brier. A two-foot dip in the ice ran completely across the eight-foot on A and halfway across B. Because of the uneven floor underneath, Sheet B also had almost no ice in one corner of the away end.

Luckily, the other sheets were much better, but games on A or B were full of surprises. Alberta skip Jimmy Shields was the player most affected. He had a short slide that only took him to the dip in Sheet A, so while his rock was traveling up one side of the dip, his foot was going down the other—most other players were able to slide through it. But for the talented Shields, these were difficult conditions to get a decent release.

The strangest situation, however, came in a game between the Richardsons and British Columbia, Glen Harper, the B.C. skip, had a stone sitting in the four-foot, and Ernie was attempting to hit it and spill his shooter from the rings in order to blank the end. When the Saskatchewan skip hit the B.C. rock on an angle, it spun back towards the dip, moving through the dish and up to the top. Then, to everyone's amazement, the rock came back down the dip and slid out the front of the house.

"The fans were laughing," Sam recalled. "So were we—no one could believe it."

That game proved to be the Richardsons' only loss of the week and the team finished with a 9-1 record, one better than Alberta's

Jimmy Shields, whom the Saskatchewan team had beaten in a key game earlier in the schedule. They had done it again.

Brier number four was perhaps even more sweet than the previous three. The Richardsons had established a record that even they felt would stand up for a long time. They've been right so far. In accepting the Tankard from David Stewart, Ernie told the crowd, "This has been the greatest week of my life." No one doubted him for a minute.

While much has been made of the four titles, it has often been overlooked that the Saskatchewan dynamos came very close to making it five. In 1964, with Wes back at the lead position, the Richardsons again won the Saskatchewan title and traveled to Charlottetown for the 1964 championship. There was a lot of attention on the defending champions, and Ernie dutifully performed interviews with every little radio station in Atlantic Canada. Also drawing some notice was Bruce Hudson, son of Gordon Hudson, who was skipping the Manitoba entry in his first Brier appearance.

But both of these stories took a back seat to the simmering battle over amateur versus professional status, which had started in 1962. After that Brier's debate, the Ontario Curling Association had gone to Brandon in 1963 and tabled what it called "Rules of Eligibility." The three-point amendment to the rulebook, which later became known as the Code of Ethics, would preclude any curler who had earned money playing the game from participating in the Brier. It stated that the following players would be ineligible: 1. Any curler who gives instruction by article, books or in person for financial gain; 2. Any curler who uses his name for the commercial sponsoring of any article or service; 3. Any curler who accepts a bonspiel prize in excess of $150.

While no one ever discussed this fact, it was clear that the rule was targeted at western curlers in general, and the Richardsons in particular.

Led by the OCA, the amateur faction arrived in Charlottetown ready to kick out the players they deemed to be pros. It suggested that the "professional" curlers were ruining the game and taking an unfair advantage over the true amateurs. As well, the faction said, with curling heading into the Olympics (although this event was considered a certainty in the 1960s, it is not scheduled to happen until 1998), it would be necessary to make adjustments now.

Out west, there was outrage at the thought of banning players such as the Richardsons, Gervais or Shields. If a guy could make a buck or two throwing a rock, thinking went, then why not let him? The growth of big bonspiels had certainly helped curling along, and if that was to end, then the game would surely shrivel away.

In the *Regina Leader-Post*, John Robertson summed up the feeling in western Canada: "It costs him [Ernie Richardson] considerably more to curl than he gleans out of the game each year in prizes and endorsements, but this, apparently, is of no consequence."

At the DCA's annual meeting, there was much debate pitting East against West and the traditionalists against the progressives. When the vote was called, things looked tight, but one of the last speakers may have swayed the balance. The Saskatchewan delegate that year was Ted Culliton, who was a curler and also the chief justice of the province. A brilliant orator, he spoke to the assembly for 15 minutes, shooting down all three clauses with brilliant logic and emotion. He concluded with a strong punch:

"If your rules (as suggested) had been in effect in August 1963, insofar as our province is concerned, neither the finest in the south nor in the north would have been eligible for competition. More than that, there would have been 10 to 12 strong rinks who were important factors in our playdowns, who would not have been entitled to play. With what result? It would have spelled the death knell of the Saskatchewan Curling Association and would have set back curling so that we'd have no organization at all.

"I'm going to say this in conclusion—I don't want to take up too much time so that discussion can take place—but the Brier has developed as one of the three leading sporting events in Canada. You have the Stanley Cup, you have the Grey Cup, you have the Brier.

"The Brier is the top prize in curling in Canada and the one prize to which every curler in Canada aspires. And here we are, having taken a good many years to build the Brier into that position, to go along and pass a bunch of rules that have no foundation in principle, and which are not needed; to spend our time fighting windmills; to try and destroy what has been accomplished over 28 years.

"As far as we're concerned in our association, we don't think there's any requirement for these rules. We think that in the final analysis [they] will be detrimental to curling. We don't subscribe to the puritanical view that some of you do in respect to curling. We think [curling] is on a sound basis. We think anything in this respect would be detrimental and detract from the Brier. It would no longer be the competition that it is, and so far as we're concerned, I'm going to move, Mr. Chairman, that this report be tabled."

His motion now on the floor, the members of the DCA voted 24–19 to kill the Code of Ethics by tabling it. Quite obviously, Judge Culliton's speech had been the deciding factor, although some felt that there was confusion in the vote and that a few voters believed they were voting in favor of the code by supporting Culliton's motion to table it. In any case, it was as good as dead and the issue has not been raised since.

Out on the ice, the Richardsons were anything but dead. They rattled off wins in their first six games before stumbling to Northern Ontario when Arnold played what some fans felt was his poorest Brier game. They rebounded to defeat New Brunswick and had a 7-1 record, tying them for the lead with Lyall Dagg's entry from the Vancouver Curling Club. British Columbia had won its first seven games but then lost to Quebec. It appeared that the 10th-round match between the two teams would decide the championship.

The night before the big match, the Richardsons did something that may have helped to decide the winner of this important game.

Their regular driver had taken ill and Doug Cameron, a former competitor at the Brier and perhaps Prince Edward Island's best player, offered to fill in. On the Thursday evening, he invited the Richardsons over for what they presumed would be a quiet dinner.

"When we got there, I think half of Charlottetown was in the Cameron house," Sam recalled.

The party carried on and the boys had a few beers before sitting down to a late seafood dinner. The burly Richardsons tucked into the lobster in a big way. Each player had two or three of the crustaceans before Cameron finally drove them back to their hotel.

In bed that night, the lobsters took their toll. The rich, buttery seafood rolled around in the stomachs of the meat–and–potatoes boys, keeping them awake most of the night.

"Every time I rolled over, Wes rolled over," Sam said. "I don't think any of us slept a wink."

The next morning, instead of being prepared for the big game with Dagg, the Regina team was dragging. Right from the start, it was clear the boys were not sharp. On Ernie's first stone, he called the front end to sweep. They pounded the rock halfway down the sheet, stopping in time to watch it sail through the house. They wrecked on guards—a rarity for the Richardsons, who viewed wrecking on come-around shots as the worst possible outcome.

On and on it went, and coupled with Dagg's brilliant performance, it was no contest. British Columbia won the game 8-3.

For the Richardsons, destiny was now in the hands of others. The only way the team could get back in was if the hometown Prince Edward Island team could knock off Dagg in the last round, while the Saskatchewan team beat Nova Scotia.

In their traditional speedy manner, the Richardsons defeated Ian Baird's Kentville four and then watched to see the outcome of the P.E.I.–B.C. match. The game was a close one, and at the conclusion of 12 ends, everything was square at eight, with Charlottetown skip Art Burke holding the advantage of last rock.

When Burke came to throw his first stone, British Columbia was lying one. The Island skip attempted to play a draw down to that stone and the crowd agreed with the shot selection. As he sat in the hack, there was plenty of cheering, the fans hoping their boy would make good to force a play-off game between Dagg and Richardson. Perhaps pumped up too much, Burke came heavy and the rock slid through the rings. Dagg threw another one in and Burke now needed to draw the four-foot for the win.

Again the crowd cheered and again Burke pumped his rock heavy and wide and watched in agony as it sailed through the house. With that shot, Dagg was crowned as the Brier champion and the Richardsons' reign officially ended.

The Regina four would never make it back to the Brier, despite a few more efforts. After losing in the provincial final to Bob Pickering in 1968, the team disbanded. Their place in the Brier's history is carved in stone, however. In five Briers, they won four and finished second once. In that stretch, they lost only seven games (five of which were on unpredictable outside sheets) and created a new style of play that emphasized hitting without losing the strategic importance of drawing. They were the first curlers to land significant endorsement deals and to benefit off the ice from being the best in their sport.

Perhaps most importantly, the Richardsons came to exemplify the true competitive curling team. They were players who knew their positions and worked at all aspects of them. The four may have been the first rink to be more than the sum of its parts. Everything went together—sweeping, shooting, strategy and attitude. But what may have been the decisive edge for the Richardsons was their hunger to win. The bigger the game, the more they wanted it. The tougher the shot, the better they played it. The Richardsons were always able to take their game up one more notch, and make that clutch shot when it had to be made.

They were champions, and they brought the sport and the Brier to a new level.

6

The Owl and Company

J ust before the start of the 1963 Brier in Brandon, when the Richardsons were shooting for their fourth Canadian championship, Sam Richardson entered a crowded elevator in the host hotel and boasted to those on board, "Only thing we have to worry about is Alberta. If we can beat them, we'll win it."

Tucked into the back of the same elevator was a 27-year-old with thick-framed glasses and closely cropped hair. He could have been a bellboy, on his way to deliver room service.

Two days later, the same young man was throwing third stones for the Alberta rink in his first Brier. To this day, he isn't sure if Richardson had spotted him and wanted to make him nervous, or if Sam was just being Sam. But the remark stuck in his head for the rest of that week, and when the Richardsons won a hard-fought 11th-round game over his Calgary team to assure itself of a fourth Brier win, he decided that, as long as he was wearing the colors of Alberta, no one would beat him again.

From 1963 to the close of the sixties, very few teams could touch him. The owlish-looking curler headed up a squad that inherited the mantle from the Saskatchewan dynasty as the world's best team.

Ron Northcott, the Owl, may have looked more like a high school science teacher than a great athlete, but the game has likely never seen a more tenacious player. Along with his front end of Fred Storey and Bernie Sparkes, and a rotating roster of thirds,

Northcott won three Briers in a four-year span. Not only did his team win, it dominated. At their peak, the players were capturing countless bonspiels and ripping through Brier fields like a hot knife through butter. As the Richardsons had been before them, the Northcott four were a step above the rest of the teams of their era. Curling was in their blood—they lived for the competition and thrived on clutch situations.

For Northcott, Sparkes and Storey, much of that desire had been fostered in the tiny Prairie communities in which they grew up. All three had those small-town instincts that pushed them just a little harder every step of the way.

Living in the community of Vulcan, Alberta, in the late 1940s, Ron Northcott didn't have many options when it came to winter sports. "There was a hockey rink and a curling rink," Northcott remembered. "When the hockey rink was full we went over to the curling rink to give that a try. After a while, though, we just went right by the hockey rink and straight to curling."

In 1952, Northcott received his first taste of the Brier, second-hand. Local curler Art Simpson led his team from the Bassano Curling Club to the Canadian competition and returned with enough stories to amaze and encourage a wide-eyed youngster. "I thought it would be just great to play in the Brier against all the great teams, in front of the large crowds," Northcott said years later, the enthusiasm still rippling through his voice.

The next year, he got his inaugural dose of national competition when he skipped a team in the Canadian Schoolboy Championships. His competitive spark had begun to rage like a gas fire; his talent was obvious, his desire even stronger. At every moment, Northcott was practicing and dreaming.

Meanwhile, in Empress, Alberta, Fred Storey was also catching the curling bug. In 1948, the same year he started playing, he won his district high school championship, eventually rising to become runner-up in the Canadian Schoolboy three years later. Like Northcott, he curled at every opportunity and practiced when he couldn't persuade his friends to play a game.

Not far away, in Claresholm, Bernie Sparkes was following a similar path. His father was the icemaker at the local club and Bernie would tag along whenever his dad went to work. Hour after hour, the younger Sparkes would practice his shotmaking skills while his father tinkered with the surface. Like his future teammates, Sparkes also skipped an Alberta entry at the national Schoolboy, a few years later in 1957.

By 1960, the three were living in Calgary. Storey had already played in his first Brier, as lead for Stu Beagle. That team posted an 8-2 record, good for second place behind the Richardsons. Three years later, Storey was lead on the rink skipped by Jimmy Shields that had Northcott as third. Again, he was 8-2 and again he was second to the Richardsons.

After that Brier, Shields took a sabbatical from competitive curling and Northcott assumed the skipping duties with Mike Chernoff at third and Ron Baker at second. The boys won Alberta and traveled to Charlottetown for the 1964 Brier, finishing with a mediocre 5-5 mark.

That team spent another uneventful season together, missing out on the provincial title. In the off-season they disbanded, although Northcott and Storey remained committed to curling together.

At the start of the 1965-66 season, Northcott and Storey were entered in the Canadian Open Carspiel in Edmonton, one of the major events on the competitive schedule. Due to some conflicts, however, the other two players listed were not able to join them.

"I called a friend of mine, Ron Borgstrom, to see if he could play," Northcott recalled. "He couldn't play but he told me I should call Bernie Sparkes and George Fink because they were in the same situation."

At first, Northcott balked. He had played against Sparkes for many years, including in Schoolboy days when the two were adversaries. He thought that an accomplished curler such as Bernie would want to play skip, and he certainly did not want to move back to vice. However, as the start of the spiel drew closer, Northcott was running out of options. He called Sparkes, who readily agreed to play front end, and the four came together.

Right from the start, there was a sense of greatness. The team won the bonspiel handily. As they were driving the four new cars back home, they pulled in at a rest stop on the outskirts of Calgary. Northcott, who had been mulling things over in his mind along the journey, thanked the other three for their efforts and then proposed they enter the playdowns together. The other three quickly agreed.

They eased through the Alberta playdowns and soon found themselves heading to the 1966 Brier in Halifax.

By this time, some things about the Canadian championship were evolving from the traditional to the practical. It was the last year for the Friendship Train, which had become only ceremonial as all but the Atlantic teams flew to Montreal and boarded the train there for the journey to Halifax. It was also the first Brier at which officials discussed shortening games from 12 ends to 10, although it would be a few more years before that recommendation would be accepted.

Other conventions were maintained, however, such as the parade of teams around the city. Haligonians lined the streets to watch as the players, outfitted in their team uniforms, weaved their way through the streets and were eventually piped into the arena by the 1st Battalion of the Black Watch.

The annual opening banquet was also a memorable one, with Dr. J.B. Hardie, a professor at Pine Hill Divinity College in Halifax, serving as the guest speaker. Dr. Hardie told the curlers and others in attendance that there must have been curling in ancient times because of all the references to the roaring game in the Bible.

"He that is without sin among you, let him cast the first stone," he quoted. He followed this with the passage from Judges about the tribe of Benjamin: "Among all this people there were 700 chosen men, every one of whom could cast a stone to a hair's breadth." Even the name of the competition must have come from the Bible, Dr. Hardie said: "Pluck out the Briar from among the rocks."

He concluded his speech by saying, "The only thing I have not been able to discover in the Old Testament is any reference to Macdonald Tobacco."

When the curling finally began, it became obvious that this was an evenly matched Brier. By the end of the fourth round, every team had lost at least one game, and at the start of the last round, there was a good chance of a three-way tie between Northcott, Joe Gurowka of Ontario and Saskatchewan's Bob Pickering.

Unfortunately, Pickering, perhaps the best curler never to win a Brier, was upset by the host Nova Scotian team, sending Northcott and Gurowka to a play-off for the title. As the Toronto rink staked itself a 4–1 lead after five ends, that game appeared to be going to Ontario. But Northcott was not about to give up.

"All year, I had told the guys that if we could stay close after six ends, then we wouldn't lose very many games," Northcott revealed. "We were such great finishers that if it got to that situation, the other team was going to have to beat us. We weren't going to miss."

That credo was as much a testament to the team's notorious slow starts as to its strong finishing kick. And in those days, because ice conditions were less than perfect, it was possible to survive the odd miss. "I even remember in one playdown game to get to the 1966 Brier," said Sparkes, with a light chuckle, "that Ron had missed his first 10 shots but we ended up winning 10-5. He just never missed anything after that."

And so, with some determination, the Calgary rink moved to within one point after six ends of the Brier play-off and then tied it after seven. The teams exchanged singles until the 11th, when Northcott had a chance to hit and roll from the rings to retain last rock in the last end. But his shooter grabbed just a sliver of the 12-foot, which meant a tie game coming home, with Ontario having the advantage of last rock.

In the final end, Northcott, with the assistance of a guard on the center of the sheet, made what many feel is one of the finest clutch shots in Brier history. With exacting weight, he came down, took out an Ontario stone at the side of the four-foot and rolled completely under cover at the top of the same circle.

"I couldn't see anything of his stone," Gurowka said in a reflective moment years after the game. "All I had was to draw the cold four-foot." But to get there, he would have to venture out onto an unpredictable piece of the ice. If he was at all wide, the rock might not curl. If he was narrow, it could swoop across the sheet. On a normal sheet of ice, the Ontario skip likely would have made his stone nine times out of 10, but the ice was only passable at best, as it was in many Briers at that time. Down the center it ran fine, but out at the sides it turned hairy. And that was where Gurowka had to go.

The front end of Ken Ingo and Don Mackey put the brooms on Gurowka's rock, as much out of anxiety as anything else. Whether that affected it or whether the stone was hot from the start isn't clear, but by the time it was two thirds of the way down the ice, the rock was obviously heavy. Even if the weight had been right, it certainly wasn't going to curl enough to reach the four-foot. It hit the house and kept right on sliding past the Alberta shot stone and out the back.

It took a few seconds for a stunned Northcott to realize the implications of the miss—he had won the Brier. "It's a different feeling when you win after the other team misses," Northcott said. "It's not like when you make a big shot. You're just kind of standing there watching, helpless really, and you don't think the guy is going to miss. But after growing up as we did and starting to curl as young as we did, it's sort of always a dream just to go to the Brier. To win it is unreal."

Although the team members had a small celebration that night, it wasn't until they were on the plane home that the realization of what they had accomplished began to sink in. Their awareness was helped by a fun-loving Alberta curling administrator named Ray Kingsmith, who had taken over the duties of flight attendant from the regular staff and was pouring liberal drinks while sashaying up and down the aisles to the uproarious laughter of the curler-filled plane.

After a week of celebrations back in Calgary, the Northcott team experienced something that afflicts all championship teams —letdown. It is only logical that such a high will be followed by a low, a sadness brought on by the fact that for another year, curling is over.

"There was a period of depression after it," remembered Sparkes. "You go all season long and you're so keyed up for every game. You get to the Brier and then, all of a sudden, there's nothing. Nothing to replace that adrenaline rush you get all winter. I went through it every spring. It's even more so if you win because you've accomplished the goal, reached the top of the mountain, if you will. Now there's nothing to look forward to."

Call it the post-Brier syndrome or the rock-throwin' blues, but more than one championship team has succumbed to this off-season funk.

Luckily for the Northcott four, they were able to pull out of it before the 1967 season. In fact, the team enjoyed one of its best years on the competitive pre-Brier circuit, faring well in every spiel it entered. It easily won Alberta again and went off to play the Brier and celebrate the nation's centennial in Ottawa.

While everything ended up in spectacular fashion, the 1967 Canadian championship had a number of peculiarities. First, all things being equal, the '67 Brier likely wouldn't have been held in Ottawa if it hadn't been the centennial year.

Two years earlier, in the presentations to the trustees and decision-makers, several groups representing cities made their pitch to become the 1967 host site. Far and away the best of those presentations was made by a crew from Toronto. Not since the days of the Granite Club had the Brier come to Ontario's capital. Many believed Hogtown had grown too big for such an event, fearing that the Brier might get lost among other spectacles. But a group headed by Doug Maxwell pulled out all the stops to get a return engagement for the Brier's birthplace. They were so impressive that, after everything was said and done, several officials let it slip that Toronto would have won if it had been any other year.

For 1967, however, the Ottawa organizers would have been successful if they had stuck a picture of the parliament buildings up on the wall and stood on their heads in the corner. The trustees simply decided that, during Canada's 100th birthday, the Brier should be in the capital.

And it was, in the end, a marvelous championship, although it began under a cloud of sadness.

On the Sunday before the start of play, the Right Honorable Georges Vanier, Governor General of Canada, passed away. A number of changes were hastily made to the schedule. The parade through the streets was canceled, as were several events planned for the Monday, Tuesday and Wednesday evenings. The opening banquet, usually held Tuesday evening, was moved to Thursday, and some of the draws were rearranged.

Nevertheless, enthusiasm for the Brier was not dampened, and when the itineraries were sorted out and the curling began, spirits lifted. The ice in the arena (which was actually in Hull, Quebec) was easily the best ever produced, and the field was quite deep. But all eyes were on the defending champions from Alberta: Northcott was the favorite, and after winning his first six games, he appeared ready for the repeat.

But one team begged to differ. Telling anyone who would listen that they were going to take the title were four of the brashest, cockiest kids ever to slip on curling boots. The host Ontario squad—Alf Phillips, Jr., John Ross, Ron Manning and Keith Reilly—was full of swagger and had just enough bravado to think itself unbeatable.

For all four, curling was almost a way of life. All came from notable curling families in the Toronto area and Phillips' father, Alf Sr., had come within one shot of winning the 1956 Brier.

They grew up playing with and against each other in junior curling and on teams with their fathers. In 1963, they finally united with Ross at skip. From that point until the start of the 1966-67 season, the team was almost unbeatable in bonspiels around southwestern Ontario. But for some reason, they couldn't win the provincial title. They were second twice, but something was holding them back.

"After finishing second again in '66," Ross recalled, "I went to Alf and said that I thought we should switch. He agreed and the rest, as they say, is history."

The young men, all 29 at the time, hammered the opposition to win the Ontario title, and by the time they made it to Ottawa, they were quite proud of themselves. They arrived early in the nation's capital to warm up for the Brier; Phillips had arranged a few games against local Ottawa teams at the Rideau Curling Club. Large gatherings of club members turned out to watch the team that would represent Ontario the next week in the big show.

"We got creamed by those club teams," recalled Reilly with an embarrassed laugh. "All the people behind the glass couldn't believe we were the Ontario champions. I'm sure they were thinking that it was going to be a long week."

At that time, Ontario was not exactly a power in curling. Its last Brier victory had come in 1939, and with the exception of Phillips, Sr., Gurowka a year earlier and a few other close calls, the Ontario teams had been mediocre. With Phillips, Jr., big things were expected, but after the club games, many believed the team would be another in the long list of also-rans. The boys were worried, too. While none of them would admit it out loud, each was beginning to have doubts.

Except for Ron Manning, that is. Manning, the cannonball-shaped second nicknamed Moon, was still spouting off that Ontario would not be beaten. He also bellowed that he would be the best second in the competition. With every boast, punctuated with a raucous laugh, he upped the ante just a bit for his team.

When they hit the ice for the first game, the Ontario four were up against Manitoba's Bruce Hudson, a formidable opponent. While they managed to play somewhat better than at the Rideau Club, they were defeated 9-7.

But then something changed. The four lads from Toronto regrouped and set their minds to the task at hand. Combining fine play with an active social life, they managed to reel off eight consecutive wins before getting the bye in the second-to-last round.

What had made the Toronto team successful in the first place— and what it had reverted to after its opening loss—was more than an obvious talent at throwing rocks. It was brilliant strategy.

"Nobody ever played corner guards before us," Ross said. "The opposition had no idea what we were doing. In those days, the way you got a big end was to freeze on an opposition rock in the house. We had a special signal on the team and when we gave it, it meant we would play a short rock, although we pretended we were playing a freeze and had just thrown it short. The other guys wouldn't know what was going on and with our next shot, we'd draw around and lock it on."

While it became a common strategy in later years, no one at that time could understand what the Phillips team was doing placing stones out in front of the rings way over to the side of the sheet. The key to making this strategy work was the talented front end of Reilly and Manning. They rarely missed, and in those days, when it was still possible to get to the Brier with a weak lead and second, they were the edge. They combined a wonderful touch with tough sweeping, and the confidence they instilled in Phillips and Ross was immeasurable.

When the Ontario team returned from its bye for the final game, the entire field had tightened up. If Ontario and Saskatchewan lost, and Alberta and Manitoba won, all four rinks would have 8-2 records, and the fans who were packed into the arena— many had made the short trip up from Toronto because their boys were now in the hunt—would have an evening of entertaining play-off curling.

But that never happened. Saskatchewan was edged in a tight

game by Manitoba and Alberta's Northcott was upset by Nova Scotia, allowing Ontario to determine its own fate.

Although the Toronto team was down 6-0 to Prince Edward Island after just three ends, it rallied to tie the game after 10 and then, following a score of three in the 11th, ran the opposition out of rocks in the last frame.

Phillips' win triggered a spontaneous and unforgettable celebration.

"It may be the only Brier that was never really finished," Ross remembered. "When we ran P.E.I. out of rocks to win it all, everyone from Toronto poured out onto the ice while all the other games were still going on. I don't know it they ever finished those other games."

Although the records show all five games were completed, those in attendance and those on the ice would disagree. With so many people on the ice and the games no longer relevant to the outcome of the championship, several matchups were abandoned.

While the Phillips rink has been remembered as the team that ended Ontario's long Brier drought, what it became most famous for occurred a few weeks later, during the Scotch Cup in Perth, Scotland.

Near the end of the round-robin, the Canadian team was in the running along with Scotland and the United States. Despite a late-night sampling of the sponsor Scotch Whiskey Association's products, Phillips hammered a hapless Norwegian team in an early morning contest. In the afternoon, a showdown for first place was looming between Canada and the United States, and the Phillips team decided to return to the hotel for a short nap. They emerged from the rink and found two buses waiting to transport the teams, but no drivers. Phillips boarded one and, finding it running, summoned Reilly to join him. The skip then began a short tour of Perth that ended when he parked the bus on top of a guard rail.

"Originally, we had intended just to hide it," remembered Reilly. "But we got stuck on a roundabout and couldn't get off. We tried to pick up some passengers to help us, but once they got a look at who was driving, no one wanted to get on."

The Canadian press played up the incident as an international embarrassment, but after the initial shock wore off, it became a big laugh for everyone involved. The team went on to lose the Scotch Cup semifinal to Chuck Hay of Scotland.

A year later, the Phillips team lost out in its local playdowns but, along the way, found itself in a battle that would affect curling in Ontario and, indirectly, across Canada. Early in the fall, the rink played in the CBC Curling Classic, a made-for-television bonspiel that was taped for broadcast on Saturday afternoons throughout the winter. The top teams in the country were brought together for the event and the prizes were lucrative. Phillips and his team placed well and won four snowmobiles. Back in Ontario, that win meant trouble.

Although the Ontario Curling Association had lost in its attempt to have the Code of Ethics passed nationally, the intent of the legislation had been put in place in Ontario. It stated, among other things, that curling professionals would not be eligible to represent the province at the Brier or any other national championship. Under the rules, a "professional" was anyone who had won more than $150 in a bonspiel.

Well aware of the draconian regulations, the Phillips rink delayed accepting their snowmobiles and entered the Ontario playdowns. When Ray Grant, another top Ontario team, knocked them out along the way, the four huddled. Their chances of repeating had ended, but their opportunity to take a stand had not. They felt the Code of Ethics was wrong; if Ontario was to have any hope of being competitive on the national level, teams had to play in big events where cash and cars were awarded as prizes. With the team's profile still high, it decided to put the OCA to the test.

"They [the OCA] wanted us to sign a form saying we wouldn't take the prizes," Ross said. "But we wouldn't do it."

The team wrote to the Ontario Curling Association, announcing that they would now be accepting the snowmobiles. The OCA wrote back and warned them of the consequences. While Ross, Manning and Reilly were willing to stand tough, they advised their skip to take a softer route. Phillips had signed on to be the manager of the Parkway Curling Club and was thus in violation of another clause in the Code of Ethics. Another strike against him, such as accepting the snowmobile, may have jeopardized his curling career even further. So the team arranged for a Toronto service club to buy his snowmobile for a raffle and then announce that it had been donated by Phillips.

The OCA let the skip off the hook, but the other three were defiant.

"Here we were—Ontario's only Brier champions in almost 30 years—and the OCA wasn't going to let us play because we'd been successful," said Ross, still shaking his head in disbelief almost 30 years after the incident.

Most curlers across the province were outraged at how the association was treating the team, but a number of influential players were in favor of allowing amateurs to represent Ontario in the Brier. The issue split the province's curling fraternity even as it had divided the national body in Charlottetown four years earlier. When the vote finally came at the OCA's annual meeting, the team was banned. The decision disappointed many but surprised few. The real question was how long the OCA could hold up under public pressure. The Phillips team was popular in the powerful Toronto curling community. High-profile players were on its side, the media supported it, and the rest of Canada's curlers, who couldn't believe the treatment that Ontario's heroes were receiving, were allies as well.

Eventually, under the barrage of pressure, the OCA relented, but not until the following year. By that time, the Phillips rink had run its course and was in the process of disbanding. Although it had won the battle for the next wave of Ontario curlers, such as Paul Savage and Ed Werenich, the team had paid a price by missing its competitive peak.

Whether Phillips could have played an important part in the Canadian scene during those missed years is moot. But if he and his team had been eligible, they would have faced an ever-strengthening Ron Northcott rink.

After losing to the Ontario four in 1967, Northcott had to deal not only with the loss when his team had played so well but also with the departure of his vice, George Fink, who moved to Regina. After scouting out several replacements, Northcott, Sparkes and Storey had trouble finding anyone they felt would fit the team's makeup. After some discussion, they decided to try enticing Jimmy Shields to come out of retirement and play for them. He had quit the competitive circuit not long after skipping Northcott and Storey in the 1963 Brier, and he was reluctant to suit up again. After some gentle arm-twisting didn't work, the three pleaded with him to come back.

"We actually only convinced him the day before the entries closed," said Sparkes. "I don't really think he was too keen on the whole idea."

The new team went to work, winning numerous bonspiels and eventually capturing another Alberta championship. That sent them off to the 1968 Brier in Kelowna, British Columbia, where they found horrendous ice conditions, caused largely by the balmy 50 degree Fahrenheit weather outside and the large crowds inside.

"Down the center of the sheet the rocks reacted normally, but three feet on either side of the center line, it was no man's land," said Northcott. "A stone out there had to be 15 to 20 feet heavier to make it to the rings. And you had no idea how it would curl."

The unpredictable, frosty ice was especially tough on the pre-tournament favorite, Bob "Pee Wee" Pickering of Saskatchewan. Pickering's delivery had an extremely high backswing that saw the rock go above his head at the peak. The combination of that delivery and the ice spelled disaster for the talented skip, who could hardly get the rock to the other end of the sheet. All eyes quickly shifted to the flawless style of Northcott and his Alberta team.

The Calgary four were hot from the start, winning their first six games—including a 17-6 thumping of Pickering—before getting a bye. In the seventh round, they defeated British Columbia before they were finally upset by Ontario's Don Gilbert. But a win against Manitoba set up the finale against Northern Ontario. A win and Northcott had his second Brier. A loss would likely throw him into a play-off with Pickering, who had two losses.

The Alberta–Northern Ontario match was an exciting game. Halfway through, the score was tied at six, and after eight it was all square at eight points each. Northcott was doing his best to main-tain his team's practice of coming on strong in the second half of the game, but Northern Ontario wasn't letting up. And the Alberta skip had something else to worry about. Up in the crowd, a loudmouth kept trying to get his attention. End after end, whether he was holding the broom or coming to shoot, the fan would yell his name and wave in an attempt to get Northcott to look up. But fortunately the steely concentration of the Owl held tight. It turned out that the fan was holding up a Kelowna newspaper that had already printed its front-page headline for the next day: "Northcott Wins Brier," it screamed.

"Thank God I didn't see that before the end of the game," said a relieved Northcott later. "I don't know what I would have done had I seen it, but if we didn't win that game, we were going into a play-off. That might have jinxed everything."

But the folks who run the printing presses in the Okanagan city must have known something, because Northcott got three in the 10th end and then stole two more in the 11th before finally running his opposition out of stones in 12. Northcott had won his second Brier.

It was a special victory for the man from Vulcan because he had his longtime friend Shields playing with him. But that relationship, from a curling standpoint at least, was about to end.

Shortly after claiming the Brier, the Alberta rink represented Canada in the first Air Canada Silver Broom, the new world championship. Backed by the airline, the global competition was expanding and taking on a bigger profile worthy of a world championship. And, for the first time, it was being held in Canada, in Pointe Claire, Quebec.

Shields hated flying and dreaded the five-hour flight to Montreal. It was white knuckles from takeoff to landing, but somehow he survived and set his mind on winning a world championship. Shortly after arriving, the team was invited to a reception, and Northcott told his players to have a good time, but to remember that this was the last drink they were going to have until after the Silver Broom. The stakes were just too high, he told them, and they'd have to save their frivolity until after the competition.

But Shields couldn't stand it. Whether his nerves were shot from the flight or whether he was tense because of the importance of the event, he needed something to relax him. Unknown to the skip, the third arranged for the team's driver to bring him a spiked soft drink several times during each game. Northcott was oblivious and so, with a small glow on, Shields performed brilliantly and the team won the first Silver Broom.

But that was his swan song.

"On the flight home, Jimmy announced that he was once again retiring," Northcott said. "I think he knew it was a long road back to winning another Canadian championship, but he figured this team would have a good chance. And with the Silver Broom in Scotland, the thought of having to fly across the Atlantic was enough to make him hang it up."

And so Northcott, despite winning two Briers in three years, was again looking for a new third player. The replacement was Dave Gerlach, who had played against the Northcott team a number of times and had recently moved to Calgary. Gerlach fit the team's mix, so once again the crew was up and running.

True to form, the team won the Alberta championship and advanced to the 1969 Brier in Oshawa, Ontario. This time it was clear who was the favorite. Northcott faced an increasing barrage of media people asking what it would be like to win a third title and join the likes of Ken Watson and Matt Baldwin. Ever the diplomat, Northcott dutifully answered every question and conducted every radio and television interview.

Two days before the start of the competition, the Alberta players were relaxing with some cohorts in their hotel room. The mood was upbeat and the beer was flowing. Ray Kingsmith, the man who had taken over as flight attendant on the way home from the first Northcott Brier win, was one of the best when it came to telling a story, and on this particular day he had command of the room. With a drink in one hand and a cigarette in the other, he was telling a long and spell-binding joke, but at one point, while emphasizing a sentence with a wave of his hand, he stuck his cigarette in Gerlach's eye.

The laughter ended abruptly as Gerlach fell to the floor. Immediately, they summoned a doctor, who shipped the new third off to a specialist. There, Gerlach learned that, although he couldn't see out of the eye, there was no permanent damage. The sight would return.

Relieved at the news, the Alberta players now faced a new dilemma.

"It was a day before the start of the Brier and we weren't sure if Dave would be able to play. The rules at that time said whoever we got to replace him had to be a member of our club back in Calgary and who had not entered the playdowns at any level."

There was only one candidate—Jimmy Shields. The question then became not who, but how: how were they going to get him on a plane to Toronto? While Northcott dealt with that issue, Gerlach took some medication for his ailing eye and prayed for an overnight recovery.

The next day, Gerlach went out to the rink and found that his sight was returning. He managed to throw some rocks and judge the line without any trouble. He decided to play. Somewhere in Calgary, Shields let out a big sigh of relief.

If that incident had been a stroke of bad luck, it was balanced by a chance meeting with a former trainer of the Winnipeg Blue Bombers. A curling fan, the trainer offered his services to the Northcott team and it quickly accepted. He set up a table in the hotel room, and after each day's play, the team members got a rubdown that helped take them through the long week. For Sparkes and Storey especially, the massage after a long day of sweeping proved invaluable.

"It was the only Brier that I ever finished feeling really great," Sparkes said.

As play got under way, many observers felt Alberta would walk away with the championship. Few gave much chance to Kevin Smale and his B.C. rink from Prince George. Playing in his first Brier, however, Smale managed to win his first eight games, while Northcott rattled off seven consecutive wins before the two teams met head-on.

The Thursday evening draw was standing room only in the Oshawa Civic Auditorium. Everyone knew the consequences of the game, including the players. Alberta simply had to win. In the end, Northcott hung on for a 9-8 victory and moved into sole possession of first place.

Sitting on an undefeated record with Ontario and Saskatchewan left to play, Northcott could smell his third victory. Ontario had been playing poorly despite the support of the fans. Ken Buchan of London had won only one—a 9-8 extra-end decision over Quebec, in the same draw as the Alberta and British Columbia game. At 1-8, Buchan's totals suggested that he wouldn't put up much of a fight, and Northcott's team may have been looking past the Ontario game to its match with Saskatchewan's Bob Pickering. To the surprise of many, however, Buchan played one of his finest games of the week, storming out to a 9-6 lead after 10 ends. It seemed he was about to hand Northcott his first loss and allow the B.C. team back into the picture. But in the 11th, reality struck as Alberta grabbed four and then scored a single in the 12th to post an 11-9 win.

That victory set up another Pickering-Northcott match. With British Columbia finishing at 9-1 and having a last-round bye, the Albertans had to win the final game to avoid a play-off. They got off to a fast start, leading 4-0 at the end of three, but by the eighth end, they only had a one-point lead.

In the ninth, Northcott made a sensational raise for three points that Pickering matched in the next end with a marvelous takeout. The Saskatchewan skip stole one in the 11th and the two came home tied.

With only the final two rocks of the game remaining, everything was clear except for a stone in front of the 12-foot. With his last shot, Pickering drew partially behind cover, right into the top of the four-foot.

Now Northcott would be tested. Unlike his first Brier win, where the opposition had missed the final rock, and his second, where he had the game well in hand in the last end, Northcott had to make his final shot to win the Brier. Despite the consequences, the Owl's expression never changed. As he did in every end of every game he played, he stood quietly, without any trace of emotion, and sized the situation up.

He elected to play a tap-back with weight just heavier than a draw. As he made his way down the ice to throw the stone, he thought about the shot but nothing else. "You don't allow yourself to think about the consequences," he would say later. "You don't go down and think, 'Gee, if I make this, we win the Brier and if I miss, we lose.' You'd probably miss them all if you thought that way. You just go down with the overall feeling that you're going to win."

The power of positive thinking worked for Northcott. His final shot landed right on target, his shooter spilling just into the eight-foot to count one.

As the team hugged in celebration, the crowd gave them a standing ovation, as much for the shot as for the undefeated record and a third Brier win.

For British Columbia, however, it was a tough result. At 9-1, they had every right to expect a play-off at worst. But this year, their record was just not good enough.

Although Northcott's rink tried to come back and win a fourth Brier, it never succeeded. The following year, they were beaten in the Alberta final by Hec Gervais. In 1971, Sparkes moved to British Columbia where he competed in another eight Briers. Northcott went to the provincial finals four more times and into the championship game once more before finally deciding to call it a career.

But what a career it was. No matter who played vice, all Northcott teams played with passion. They were ready to take on anyone at any time. Northcott, Sparkes and Storey all shared that small-town background that had instilled in them a genuine love and respect for the game, which carried them through many battles. No matter who came out on top, curling won, and the three players would walk off the ice with smiles. Like the Richardsons before them, they also had a tremendous front end, one that could seemingly sweep forever. As Northcott pointed out, "Anyone who said sweeping never made a difference to a rock never had the good fortune of playing with those two."

And Northcott was no slouch when it came to playing the game. He was a brilliant strategist and he read ice better than any curler of his generation. He also became a skip who never missed the big shot.

With its trio of vices—Fink, Shields and Gerlach—this was a dominant and devastating lineup, one that will be remembered for a long time.

7

The Seventies

As the sixties became the seventies, Manitoba was in a Brier drought. At least, for the winningest province in the national championship's history, it was a dry spell. The last Manitoba win had come in 1965, when Terry Braunstein had accomplished the task. Before that, it was Billy Walsh in 1956. By Manitoba standards, this record was a disaster. But one young curler with a link to the previous two wins was about to change all that.

In 1956, Don Duguid, 21, had lost the provincial final to Walsh while playing third for Howard Wood, Jr. In 1965, he was the third on Braunstein's Brier-winning team. Although pegged as a future star, it seemed that the 1965 win might be the end of Duguid's Brier career. Despite a few more efforts, he was unable to make it back to the big show.

In 1966, 1967 and 1968, he was still part of the Braunstein team and had come very close to winning the provincial title, but always fell just short. In 1969, after the Braunstein crew disbanded, he skipped his own squad but kept losing to what he called "lucky" teams, opponents he felt he should have thrashed.

"I got really frustrated," recalled Duguid. "I knew we had a good team and were playing games we should have been winning easily, but for some reason, we'd lose. The other team would get a wick or catch a hair and stop on the button. It didn't matter what we did, we just couldn't win."

And so the hunt became too much for him and he decided that,

The Macdonald's Brier Tankard. For 50 years, this trophy was presented to the championship team. It is now enshrined in the Curling Hall of Fame and Museum of Canada in Baie D'Urfe, Quebec. *Courtesy Warren Hansen*

T. Howard Stewart was one of the leaders in getting Quebec players to switch from irons to granites. Note the broom and curling attire of the day. *Alexandra Studios/Courtesy Doug Maxwell*

The first Brier champions, from Nova Scotia (left to right): J.E. Donahue, C.L. Torey, J.A. MacInnes and Professor Murray Macneill. *Canada's Sports Hall of Fame/Courtesy Doug Maxwell*

The famous Campbells were among the early family rinks to play in the Brier. (Left to right): Lloyd, Sandy, Glen and Garnet are shown here in the 1947 championship in Saint John. *L.H. Shaw,* Regina Leader-Post/*Courtesy Doug Maxwell*

Known as Mr. Curling, Ken Watson (far right) won the championship three times. This team, the 1949 champions, features (left to right) Charles Read, Lyle Dyker and Grant Watson. *Powell Photos/Courtesy Doug Maxwell*

Garnet Campbell went on to play in 10 Briers, winning just once. Here he calls the line while Matt Baldwin (right) and Glenn Gray look on during play in the 1954 Brier. *King Studios/Courtesy Doug Maxwell*

Following a dramatic extra-end playoff game in the 1956 Brier in Moncton, Billy Walsh of Manitoba (left) is congratulated by Ontario's Alf Phillips. The game was decided on a thrilling last shot made by Walsh. *Les McAuley Photo/Courtesy Doug Maxwell*

The Richardsons are the Brier's only four-time champions. (Left to right): Ernie, Arnold, Sam and Wes. *Courtesy of the* Kitchener-Waterloo Record *and Doug Maxwell*

Terry Braunstein almost won the 1958 Brier at the age of 18. In 1965, he came back to win it all. *Courtesy Warren Hansen*

David Stewart, known affectionately as the Man in the Coonskin Coat, presented the Tankard for more than 30 years. Here he hands the famous trophy to Ernie Richardson in 1962. *Courtesy of the* Kitchener-Waterloo Record *and Doug Maxwell*

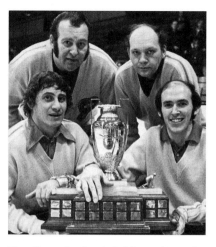

Hec Gervais (back left), perhaps the biggest man to win the Brier, possessed a delicate touch. Here, his team of Ron Anton (back right), Warren Hansen (front left) and Darrel Sutton celebrates a win in the Alberta final before going on to capture the 1974 Brier in London. *Courtesy Warren Hansen*

Ron Northcott (top) led his team to three Brier wins, all with different third players. This team, the 1969 winners, featured Dave Gerlach (second from top) with the consistent front end of Bernie Sparkes (third from top) and Fred Storey. Sparkes has appeared in a record 12 Briers. *Courtesy Warren Hansen*

Jack MacDuff completed the impossible dream when he led his unheralded Newfoundland team to that province's only Brier win in 1976. The victory set off a province-wide celebration and MacDuff ended up having his curling shoes bronzed. *Michael Burns photo*

In 1977, Jim Ursel skipped the only Brier winners ever to come from the province of Quebec. The competition took place in front of a home-town crowd at the Olympic Velodrome. *Michael Burns photo*

Al Hackner, left, and Rick Folk share a joke before facing off in the first regularly scheduled Brier playoff in 1980. Folk humbled Hackner but both would go on to take the Brier crown twice. *Michael Burns photo/Courtesy Labatt's*

At the final Macdonald Tobacco–sponsored Brier in Ottawa in 1979, every living Brier-winning skip was brought together for this unique photo. (Left to right, front row): Gordon Campbell, Ken Watson, Ab Gowanlock, Billy Rose, Jimmy Welsh, Theo "Frenchy" D'Amour, Tom Ramsay; (second row) Don Oyler, Matt Baldwin, Garnet Campbell, Ernie Richardson, Hector Gervais, Terry Braunstein, Ron Northcott, Alf Phillips Jr.; (back row) Don Duguid, Orest Meleschuk, Harvey Mazinke, Bill Tetley, Jack MacDuff, Jim Ursel, Ed Lukowich, Barry Fry. *Michael Burns photo*

Although he only played in one national men's final (losing the semi-final to Al Hackner in 1980), Paul Gowsell's antics have left him a prominent place in Brier history. *Michael Burns photo/Courtesy Labatt's*

Pat Ryan and his Ryan's Express used a devastating defence to win consecutive Brier championships in 1988 and 1989. He also won the 1994 Brier playing third for Rick Folk. *Michael Burns photo/Courtesy Labatt's*

Kevin Martin (rear) and Kevin Park were an explosive pair who battled as much off the ice as on. Here they are shown in the 1991 final, which they won, as Saskatchewan third Brian McCusker calls the sweep. *Michael Burns photo/Courtesy Labatt's*

Many predicted the egos of the Dream Team would lead it to break up soon after it was formed in 1982. But this photo shows otherwise. Sid Oland of Labatt's (middle) presents the Tankard to (left to right) Ed Werenich, Paul Savage, John Kawaja and Neil Harrison. *Michael Burns photo/Courtesy Labatt's*

No one screams harder or more often than Russ
Howard, Brier winner in 1986 and 1993. In contrast, a low-key Vic Peters (rear), champion in
1992, rarely raises his voice. *Michael Burns
photo/Courtesy Labatt's*

The Labatt Tankard was first presented in 1980 when the
beer giant took over sponsorship of the Brier. The original
cost to manufacture the mug was well over budget at
$35,000, but in 1994 it was insured for $350,000. *Michael
Burns photo/Courtesy Labatt's*

rather than face another season of humiliating losses, he would give up the game, at least on a competitive basis.

At the start of the 1970 season, Duguid kept true to his word and declined several offers to play on competitive teams. But then Rod Hunter came calling.

Hunter was known around Winnipeg as the Arrow because of his flawless delivery. There was never a wobble or a drift to it—it was perfect every time, curling poetry in motion.

Hunter had dedicated years to perfecting his delivery. He applied that same dedication to recruiting Duguid to skip his team, which had Jim Pettapiece and Bryan Wood on the front end. Hunter's brother, John, had left the skip's position the previous year.

"Rod was a pretty persuasive guy," Duguid remembered. "So I agreed to play with the team for one bonspiel in Transcona, but I told them it was a one-time thing."

He believed he was not committing himself to anything but a weekend of curling.

But during that weekend, a feeling developed; a wave came over the four players. They knew this team was special, even if they didn't say anything at the time. They walked over the opposition on that magical weekend and easily won the bonspiel.

Despite the obvious, however, Duguid wasn't ready to jump back into the competitive fires just yet. He would only go as far as committing to one more bonspiel. But when the team captured that one, the players agreed to go into the playdowns together.

They made short work of the Manitoba championship, and then had the distinction of playing in the Brier in Winnipeg.

"Everyone was telling us how lucky we were to be playing the Brier in our hometown," said Duguid. "But I was just absolutely shitting myself. I knew if we went 0-5 they would be throwing bottles at us."

Duguid was especially nervous because his skipping experiences had been limited. Fortunately, he had been teaching curling in a traveling school run by his boyhood friend Ray Turnbull, and because he was responsible for the strategy sessions, he had been forced to analyze one situation after another.

Of his throwing ability, there was no doubt. His unique delivery, grooved over years of practice, was well suited to his compact and stout body type. He came out low to the ice, balanced

on his toe and released the rock with gentle forward movement
of the arm. The slide allowed him to develop a touch that few
could rival.

Duguid had spent long hours perfecting his style. "My father
used to take the winters off and make the ice at the CPR Curling
Club," he recalled. "I used to go along with him and throw rocks
on the sheets where he wasn't working. Later, he would moon-
light selling beer out of the basement and I'd work on the ice. But
I loved to practice. I'd even sneak in the building late at night and
throw in the dark."

In the first game, Duguid had additional pressure. He was facing Hec Gervais, former Brier champion and a man Duguid had
watched intently over the years. He had learned a great deal by
analyzing the strategy of the potato farmer from Alberta, and his
knowledge would be put to the test as he began the 1970 Brier.

Unfortunately, the ice in that opening round had almost
turned to water. Players had to throw as hard as possible just to
get the rock to the other end; takeouts were virtually non-
existent.

But, in the last end, Duguid forced Gervais to throw an out-
turn shot with his last rock. That was the Alberta skip's weaker
handle, and the move paid off. Manitoba had its first win by a
10-9 margin.

Although both squads were certainly aware that their show-
down was a big game, it is doubtful that they realized just how
important it would be. By the start of the last draw, Manitoba
had an 8-1 record, having been beaten only by British Columbia's Lyall Dagg. Alberta was at 7-2, its other loss coming at the
hands of Saskatchewan's Bob Pickering. A win by Manitoba over
Saskatchewan would clinch the Brier. A loss coupled with an
Alberta win would mean a play-off.

With fans anticipating a tremendous finish, the Winnipeg
Arena filled. As game-time rolled around, local radio stations
were warning people to stay away from the arena, as it was filled
to capacity.

Duguid began the game by scoring two points in the first end,
which would be as big a lead as he would have until the conclusion. In the final end, the game was tied when Pickering made a
hit-and-stay with his final rock. Duguid now had an open hit for

the championship, and as he slid back down to the hack to prepare his stone, the crowd fell silent. Despite the relative simplicity of the shot, no one was ready to hand Manitoba the Tankard until the skip had finished. But by the time Duguid's final stone was halfway down the sheet, everyone saw that it would find the mark, and the crowd erupted into a deafening cheer.

The hometown win triggered a celebration that Winnipeg curlers will never forget. Back at the host hotel, things were just getting rolling at 1:00 a.m. and lasted well into the wee hours.

The next morning, Duguid was awakened at the crack of noon by a call from Thelma Wood, Bryan's wife, inquiring as to the whereabouts of her husband. She reported that he hadn't come home and she was trying to find out where he was.

Duguid had no idea but said he would make some calls. About a half hour later, Duguid's phone rang again and a grizzled voice came down the wire.

"Dugie?" inquired the voice.

"Yes. Is that you, Woody?" Duguid answered.

"It's me," Wood replied.

"Bryan, where are you? Thelma's looking for you and we have to go to a reception at the club at 6:00 p.m."

"Well, Dugie, I don't know where I am and I don't have any money."

By now, it was obvious that Wood was still celebrating, but Duguid became a little worried that his lead would not make it to a planned reception for the new champions at the Winnipeg Granite Club, their home rink.

"Woody, go and ask someone where you are," Duguid instructed his teammate.

Wood did as he was told, and when he came back on the line, the answer he gave stunned his skip.

"I'm in Kenora, Dugie. I guess I went for a drive and ended up here."

After the parties had ended, and the summer began, Duguid once again considered hanging up the slider. He had a growing family and an increasing number of business commitments that were begging for more time. Some curlers suggested that he never really enjoyed skipping.

"I don't think he ever got comfortable calling the game and

throwing the last shot," said Terry Braunstein. "Before a lot of the major games, he used to go into the toilet and barf. It was because he was so intense, so into the game."

But Duguid remembered differently. "I was so relaxed a lot of the time, I'd fall asleep before games. I don't think I was ever nervous."

Nevertheless, there were good enough reasons for Duguid to consider dropping curling, but what brought him back was his pride. Despite the glowing record, Duguid had to put up with an off-season full of people suggesting that their win was merely a fluke, an odd occurrence. It would never happen again, the nay-sayers said boldly.

"We knew that wasn't true," Duguid said. "We knew we were just a solid team and so we went back to prove it to everyone else."

This time, the team played the full circuit and were just as impressive. "We won the Tournament of Champions in Toronto, we won cars out west, we beat Northcott, Gervais, Merv Mann . . . anyone," Duguid said. "It became almost automatic."

In 1971, the Brier went to Quebec City where one of the biggest opponents was Mother Nature. As had happened the last time the Brier had visited the Quebec capital, a huge blizzard raged on the Thursday of Brier week, forcing the cancellation of one round and leaving teams to shuttle from the rink back to the hotel on snowmobiles. It also caused the famous Baldwin Black-out, where a power outage left the arena in darkness for an uncomfortable 15 minutes. Add to the situation the awful rocks used—they were sharp and inconsistent, which played havoc with fine deliveries—and the 1971 Brier was not one of the more memorable championships.

Still, the Manitoba rink came out flying, playing as well as it had all year. The team was firing on all cylinders and enjoying their regular routine.

At one point in the week, Hunter came up to the hotel room shared by Duguid and Pettapiece with a shocked look on his face.

"I just walked by the bar. Woody's in there and he's pissed," Hunter announced, in despair.

"So what," Duguid replied, not surprised. "He's curling 98 per cent. When he starts slipping to 75, I'll tell him."

By the time the blizzard hit, the Manitoba team had established itself as the four to beat, but it was tied for first with the unheralded Bill Tetley of Thunder Bay, who had knocked off the Winnipeggers on Thursday morning.

Tetley's Northern Ontario rink had run its record to 6-1, losing only an early contest to Bob Pickering's Saskatchewan team. When Pickering beat Duguid 9-8 in 13 ends, Tetley was in the driver's seat. He had only to defeat lowly Prince Edward Island to claim the title, but Kip Ready's Charlottetown team jumped up and bit Tetley's boys 9-4. That win meant a three-way play-off between Northern Ontario, Manitoba and Saskatchewan.

Lots were drawn to determine position, and Duguid managed to get the bye. While Tetley ground out a 10-9 win over Pickering, the Winnipeg boys relaxed. The rest obviously paid off as Duguid led his team to a commanding 11-6 victory over the Northern Ontario rink to become only the third repeat Brier winner. No one was calling this win a fluke.

But, by the time he reached the Silver Broom, Duguid had lost the thrill of winning.

"In the final game of the world championship against Scotland," the diminutive skip admitted, "I was holding the broom and I began to wonder, 'What am I doing here? Why am I chasing after this brass ring that's taken so much of my time?' I realized that if I'd put as much energy into business as I had into curling, I would have made a ton of money. Everything was curling, curling, curling. It was time to get outside that and see the real world."

And so, shortly after polishing off Scotland for his second world championship, Duguid retired again. A year later, he signed on with the CBC and became the country's most well-known curling commentator.

How good could the team have been if it had stayed together? Certainly, if it had kept up its pace, it had every chance to win again. But predicting what might have been is an inexact science. Problems could have arisen. In fact, the team members later went through bitter times, and friendships were strained over some shoe endorsements. Some people suggest that personality conflict was what actually led to the team's demise.

However, most curling fans will remember Duguid's four on the ice and they will always hold a special spot in Brier history.

In 1972, the Brier was hosted by St. John's, Newfoundland, which fulfilled the dream of Walter Stewart, who wanted the event held in every provincial capital.

The teams were treated to some typical Newfoundland weather on the first day, when fog prevented the planes carrying the teams from landing. After two nights in Montreal, the field finally arrived to a noisy celebration in the streets of St. John's. This was certainly going to be a party.

While Newfoundland was a new host, the winning province that year was familiar. Manitoba claimed its 19th title when Orest Meleschuk, one of the gruffest, toughest curlers to pick up a broom, stormed through to take the title.

Meleschuk posted a 9-1 record, losing only to Quebec's Bill Kent. He delighted the fans with his intense play, which included a lot of broom slamming and loud yelling. Those who were close enough to hear him talking also received a lesson in cussing.

Meleschuk could talk a blue streak and had become known for this talent in curling circles. The *CBC Curling Classic* television show was the first to broadcast the voices of the curlers as they decided on their shots, and with Meleschuk, the audio department had its work cut out for it preparing the taped show for broadcast.

Live television was another matter. In Sudbury, one winter, the local television station decided to broadcast the final of a big cashspiel in which Meleschuk was playing. At one point, when the big skip found himself in a tight situation, he asked his vice at the time, John Usackis, and the entire television audience, "What the fuck are we going to do here, John, eh? What the fuck are we going to do? What the fuck are we going to do?"

Despite his brilliant curling in that 1972 Brier, Meleschuk will always be remembered for his world championship win, which came under unusual circumstances.

Meleschuk had walked through the round-robin undefeated and ended up playing the American team of Bob Labonte in the final. Despite having thrashed the U.S. side in their first meeting, the Canadians were in trouble in the final, trailing 9-7 after eight ends. The ninth was blanked, and in the 10th and final end, the Canadians finally got something going. When Labonte came to throw his last brick, he was staring at three Meleschuk counters. But he calmly called for and made a splendid double, and rolled half-buried. The Americans were now sitting first and third shot, with a Canadian stone second.

Meleschuk had to make a hit and stay to force an extra end. He made the hit but rolled out to the eight-foot where American third Frank Aasand swept it, hoping to push it out to third shot. When Aasand stopped, he glanced over at the Canadian rock, then back at the American, and then raised his broom.

That was the signal for a celebration. Labonte ran towards the house and began jumping up and down, but slipped and, incredibly, kicked the Canadian rock. In all the confusion, Canadian third Dave Romano had not had a chance to examine the two stones, and chief umpire Doug Maxwell did not see the incident (he was standing right behind Labonte). Maxwell asked Aasand if he had burned the stone but did not ask Labonte. (In fairness to Maxwell, it was a madhouse on the ice with photographers swarming and no one quite sure what was happening.) When Aasand replied that he had not, Maxwell called for a measure of the rocks, and 10 minutes later, it was determined that Canada had scored two. (Even if Maxwell had asked Labonte and he had admitted to burning the stone, the result would have been the same.)

In the final end, Meleschuk made a sensational draw to the button behind a guard with his last rock, and Labonte came heavy with a hack-weight hit attempt. Canada had won but Meleschuk would be forever branded with his "booted" world title.

The 1973 Brier returned to the West and Edmonton. It was a memorable championship, but not for the right reasons. While putting curling ice in arenas is a difficult task at the best of times, the surface in Edmonton was likely the worst ever manufactured. It didn't take long for the players to begin referring to the competition as the "Bad Ice Brier." It quickly became a contest of who could throw the rock down the ice the hardest, because that was the only way to reach the house on certain parts of every sheet.

The frost build-up became so thick that it looked like a car windshield after an ice storm. If a stone could avoid the frost, it might get stuck in the tiny pools of water that haphazardly dotted the ice.

Thankfully, the trustees and CCA had earlier approved a change to the rules of play, allowing teams to concede a game anytime after 10 ends had been completed. The change came as a result of some embarrassing scores, particularly from the Atlantic provinces, which were often not the equal of their western counterparts. Extending games to their finish had been a humbling experience for players on the wrong end of scores such as 30–3.

Not surprisingly, luck played a big part in deciding the winner of the 1973 championship. Harvey Mazinke and his team from Saskatchewan played excellently, but they certainly weren't the favorites going in.

Danny Fink had taken over skipping duties of Duguid's old team, Mel Watchorn of Alberta was an experienced player, and a young Paul Savage from Toronto was the new kid on the Brier block. All three were ranked above Mazinke, but all three were noted for being better on quick, swingy ice.

Mazinke was able to adapt to the conditions and reeled off a 9–1 record. The rest of the field wallowed in a quagmire of mediocrity, as evidenced by the fact that Nova Scotia's Peter Hope and Toronto's Savage were tied for second at an unimpressive 6–4, the lowest record ever to claim second place.

The following year, the Brier returned to Ontario and was hosted by London. The ice improved, the curling became better and the championship came down to the final draw. While the games were unfolding in dramatic fashion, there was another memorable occasion that involved many of the competitors. At midweek, a select group of teams and other notables received invitations from the Pro Glove Company to the unveiling of their model for the next curling season. The company was headed by Alf Phillips, Jr., the 1967 Brier winner, and Peter Birchard, a no–nonsense entrepreneur who was the unofficial leader of a group known in Toronto as the Curling Mafia. They were influential people who also ranked among the best players in that part of the country.

Together, the fun-loving duo had procured a suite in a local hotel for their launch. One by one, the guests arrived and were greeted with a cocktail and a handshake. Although no one may have noticed immediately, as they milled around and shared a joke or two, the entire guest list was male.

Phillips called for the attention of the room and thanked the group for attending.

"And now, gentlemen," he said in his distinctive voice, "I'd like to unveil the new Pro Glove."

With those words, the bathroom door swung open and out walked three women, sporting deerskin curling gloves and absolutely nothing else. As the attendees hooted and hollered, Phillips continued, unfazed.

"Notice the fine stitching and the double-reinforced Velcro closure," he continued. "These gloves will stand up to the toughest test . . ." And on it went. Needless to say, the launch of the Pro Glove was the talk of the Brier for the rest of the week.

Back on the ice, the round-robin was going as predicted with two provincial entries staying on top of the leader board. The combatants in this head-to-head race to the wire were Hec Gervais of Alberta and Larry McGrath of Saskatchewan. After their opening round match, which Gervais won 8-4, the two teams appeared to be on a collision course for the title.

After a second-round loss to Quebec's Jim Ursel, McGrath won six straight. Gervais, meanwhile, moved his record to 7-1 before losing to Ontario's Savage.

That left Alberta at 7-2 with a bye in the second-to-last round, while Saskatchewan was at 6-2 with games against Newfoundland and Ontario remaining. The final day of play would not be one for the faint of heart. Most spectators were predicting a play-off.

Gervais, the favorite, had been around curling circles a long time, winning more than his share of prizes. But he had also suffered some humiliating defeats. In 1964, he had missed a chance to go to the Brier when he fanned an open hit with his last rock by four feet. Some observers felt he should have won a half-dozen more provincial titles than the four he did.

"He was an incredible guy back then," remembered Warren Hansen, second on that 1974 team. "When he decided that he wanted to win, no one could beat him. Unfortunately, he wasn't always in that mode. You could tell he was ready to win when he was growling and mean."

Heading into the Alberta playdowns in 1974, the Gervais team had not been playing well. In fact, it had been getting kicked all over the province. But when the Brier trail started, Gervais went through a metamorphosis that turned him back into the curler who had won the 1961 championship.

"I remember one of the first playdown games," Hansen said. "We had been playing so badly up to that point that we kind of wondered what we were doing there. I was standing at the hog line looking around at the other sheets and this voice bellowed down at us, 'We're curling on this sheet.' It was Hector and I knew then that things were about to change."

And change they did. The Albertans ran off a great record that took them one game away from clinching a Brier title.

There are many curlers who might not be able to sleep the night before a big contest, especially with the Brier on the line. Some might choose to prepare themselves with a quiet evening, lots of rest and perhaps some analysis of the opposition's strengths and weaknesses.

Not Hec Gervais.

At 2:00 a.m. the morning of his championship game, the big skip was sitting in Birchard's room, drinking rye with him and Ontario skip Paul Savage. The three of them went at it hammer and tong until they had finished the bottle on the table. Savage, who was out of the running but could play a spoiler role because of his game against Saskatchewan, began to stumble out of the room. But Gervais was on a roll.

"Birchard," he demanded, "I know you've got another bottle of rye in here. Let's have it."

Birchard tried to reason with the Alberta skip.

"Come on, Hec," he pleaded. "You've got a Brier to win tomorrow."

Gervais was belligerent. "I know you've got another bottle in here."

Finally, however, Birchard managed to convince Gervais that it was in the Alberta skip's best interests to go to bed and rest up for the game the next afternoon.

It was not an uncommon incident for the big man. As Hansen remembered, "We had to sort of corral him a lot of the time. We'd try to make a pact with him to save the celebrations until after the bonspiel. But I must say he did play pretty well with a hangover."

The final day of the 1974 Brier probably proved Hansen right. Saskatchewan won its morning game against Newfoundland, setting up the last draw. If both Alberta and Saskatchewan won, a play-off would be necessary. If only one team managed a win, it would be the champion.

As play unfolded, Alberta and Quebec were locked in a low-scoring struggle, while Ontario and Saskatchewan were in a different sort of battle. Ontario third Bob Thompson was from Saskatchewan and knew and loathed the St. John brothers, Rod, Wayne and Ron, who made up the rest of McGrath's team. They had been enemies back in Kindersley and were not about to start getting along at this point.

All through the game, the St. John boys accused Thompson of palming, leaving his bare hand down on the ice to melt it and possibly affect the next rock to travel that same path. Thompson made equally preposterous accusations against the three brothers and the war of words escalated. The Ontario vice was probably upset at the fact that, two days earlier, due to strong personality conflicts with his teammates, Savage had told him that the Brier would be the last competition that Thompson would curl as a member of the Toronto team. He had been cut, and the team's second, Ron Green, was counting down his rocks out loud.

"Okay, Thompson, you've got 10 rocks left as a member of this team," he would say.

As with so many curling teams, togetherness is easy when they are winning. When they are losing, however, tensions rise after a long season of close contact. Savage, Green and Werenich had been willing to put up with Thompson en route to the Brier, but when it became clear they wouldn't get their hands on the Tankard, the frustration boiled over, and suddenly, the Saskatchewan import wasn't such a great guy anymore.

While the players fired barbs at each other, the skips, two of the best-natured and friendly players ever to grace the Brier, kept apologizing for their teams. It was not, they agreed, the best way to play a game of such importance.

In the other game, Gervais and his team of Ron Anton, Warren Hansen and Darryl Sutton were grinding it out. Ursel, the Quebec skip who hailed from Manitoba, was a crafty player who was not about to hand the Tankard to Gervais without a fight. Gervais, however, probably hated to lose more than any curler who ever played. He was an intense man who, despite his size, had an incredible touch, even on heavy ice. He was now in position to win his second Brier and he and the team were working hard. Sensing the kill, he eked out a 4-2 victory over Ursel.

On the other sheet, there was still an end and a half to go. Things were looking good for Gervais as Savage took a three-point lead into the final end. That lead, however, was only just enough; the pudgy Ontario skip was forced to throw his final stone in order to defeat the scrappy McGrath and assure Gervais of the Canadian title. It had been 13 years coming, but the Alberta skip was a two-time winner.

The 1975 Brier went east, to Fredericton, and saw the field expand to 12 teams as the Territories made its debut. Don Twa of Whitehorse, a cigar-chomping robust man, had the honor of skipping the entry from the first non-provincial rink since the days of the Montreal and Toronto city teams.

He proved that he belonged, ending up an impressive 8-3, tied for second. The team was in the thick of the action right up to the last round.

The eventual champions were also from the north, but not quite as far up as Whitehorse. The Northern Ontario team, skipped by Bill Tetley, won only the second championship for that jurisdiction with a 9-2 win-loss mark.

It had been a long and confusing trail for the team from Thunder Bay. Tetley, playing in his third Brier, had begun the season curling with Tom Tod, Peter Hnatiw and Bill Hodgson. Just before the local playdowns began, Hodgson injured his wrist and was replaced by a 21-year-old wunderkind named Rick Lang. They advanced to the provincial final and Hodgson returned. But then Tod got sick. Once again, Lang got the call, this time to play vice. Although they played well enough to win Northern Ontario, for the young third the situation was as clear as mud.

"After four games of the provincials," Lang remembered, "we were 4-0 [in the five-game round-robin] and everyone else had two losses, so we'd won. But I still wasn't quite sure if I was going to the Brier or not because I was just a fill-in."

While the other three celebrated at a banquet held in the champions' honor, Lang remained quiet and confused. Sensing something was wrong with his third, Tetley approached him. "You don't seem very excited about all this."

"I'm not sure how to feel," Lang replied. "I don't know what your plans are."

Tetley wasn't certain either. In fact, he hadn't even thought about it. But a week later, Lang's phone rang and he was told to start packing. Although to this day the situation remains quite touchy between all the parties involved, Tetley told Lang he was replacing Tod.

The Brier that year was as evenly matched as any held. No one seemed ready to leap out and take the reins, but by midweek, the Tetley team was 4–1.

"I remember being conscious of getting to the halfway point and being 4–1 and leading," Lang reminisced. "I thought that was incredible. Here I was, 21 years old, and winning the Brier."

Their fine play continued as they managed to sneak out win after win. Tetley, in particular, was putting on a show, especially in the later ends of games.

"For the first eight ends of every game, he was just average," Lang recalled. "And then, in the last four ends, he would turn into this magical guy who would never miss. He made absolutely everything and we won about five games when the other guy missed his last shot."

The team from the Fort William Curling Club stole six of their eventual nine wins. They never had what could be called an easy game. Each was a nail-biter, including the last.

Going into the final round, the field was closely bunched. A two-, three- or even four-way play-off was possible. But if Northern Ontario could defeat Newfoundland in the last round, it would win.

The night before the big match, nerves were troubling all four Thunder Bay players. "My roomie [lead Hnatiw] and I went to bed about 1:30 a.m," Tetley told the *Ontario Curling Report*. "About an hour later, I heard him thrashing around and found out he was awake. I rapped on the wall because the other guys [Lang and Hodgson] were in the next room and they rapped back immediately. So we got up and sat around talking until about 4:00 a.m."

Newfoundland was skipped by Bob Cole, known as *Hockey Night In Canada*'s play-by-play man. Although he didn't play that well, he did enjoy a bit of celebrity status because of his television work. Earlier in the week, Tetley had pointed out Cole to Lang, telling Lang who the Newfoundland skip was.

"I didn't believe him," Lang recalled. "So I went over and asked Bob who he was. I think he was a little upset that I didn't know."

Cole was an ardent curler competing in his second Brier, but it was not his year. He had only one win in his first 10 games and nobody expected him to test the leading Northern Ontario team. However, after three ends, Cole had moved in front 4-0, thanks, in part, to some heavy draws by Tetley. After five, however, Tetley had managed to work back to take a one-point lead, 5-4. By the time they reached the last end, Tetley was up one with last-rock advantage.

With skip rocks left to play, Cole drew to the back of the eight-foot, and Tetley came down to him. Cole then drew on top of that and sat two, his shooter just at the back of the four-foot, and another on the other side of the eight-foot.

Tetley then made a tremendous final brick. "Never in my life have I had to make a pressure shot like that," he told the *Ontario Curling Report*. "That was it. I threw a draw on my first to get my weight down, because the ice was faster than it had been all week. All I wanted to do on my second was a draw and not play to the backing."

The last stone finished full in the four-foot, just barely touching the Newfoundland shot.

In a bit of irony, Neil MacCarl of the *Toronto Star* had a few comments about the winning team's vice: "If there was one possible weak spot, it was third Lang's inexperience in the rings when Tetley was shooting," he wrote. "An example was in a last-rock loss to New Brunswick when skip Clark made a great double takeout and stayed for a pair. Tetley had tried to tap his own rock in for shot but was light and came to it. But if Lang had called off the sweepers, it might have been a perfect guard and no double would have been possible."

Perhaps spurred on by the commentary, Lang went on to become probably the greatest third player in the history of the Brier.

The year 1976 provided one of the most unforgettable Canadian championships on record. It was the greatest underdog victory in Brier history as Newfoundland won its only title. And as the story unfolded in Regina that year, it became a heartwarming tale of four overachievers who put on a performance that defied all the odds.

The skip of that championship team was a transplanted Nova Scotian named Jack MacDuff who had an exceptional talent when it came to throwing the rock, and a charismatic personality that endeared him to everyone who met him that week.

MacDuff had grown up in Lunenburg, Nova Scotia, where he began his serious sports participation with hockey. By the time he reached high school, despite being an avid hockey player, he was encouraged to give curling a try by a teacher named Dougald Burke. It didn't take long for MacDuff to catch curling fever, and under the tutelage of Burke, he began to develop some solid skills.

A typical weekend for the young curler was to play hockey early in the morning and then make the short journey over to the curling club, put on his father's curling boots and throw rocks. He would play for hours on end, usually one-on-one against a friend. When he couldn't persuade anyone else to go out, he would play entire 12-end games against the Richardsons, throwing every rock, hanging every end.

"It was the Richardsons from Saskatchewan against Jack Mac-Duff of Nova Scotia," remembered MacDuff years after his championship season.

By the time he was in his second year of high school, he was skipping his own team, which was made up of boys in Grade 12. He was nervous about skipping and told Burke he didn't think he should. Burke disagreed.

"He told me that I was cut out to be a skip," said MacDuff.

In 1966, the Brier was held in Halifax and MacDuff's father took him to watch. Jack was thrilled by the sights and sounds of the big event, and watched the big names such as Northcott and Gurowka as they competed.

When he had finished high school, the curling bug had left him, and by the time he went to Acadia University, he fully intended to continue only with hockey. But a chance meeting with Al Ledgerwood, a competitive curler from Prince Edward Island who was also enrolled at Acadia, changed his mind. Ledgerwood persuaded Jack to skip the varsity team. As the squad played and won many events, MacDuff began to make a name for himself throughout Nova Scotia.

A few years later, while visiting his brother in Newfoundland, MacDuff had another chance meeting that would forever change his life. He was driving around one day and decided to drop in on another Acadia friend, Roy Durant, and when they arrived, they met Roy's brother, Fred, a noted curler who had played against MacDuff.

"Fred knew I was leaving Acadia and asked me if I'd ever consider going to Memorial [University]," MacDuff related. "I said no but I might do so. He said that if I'd come and curl with him, he'd get me in."

At the time, Fred Durant was executive assistant to Fred Rowe, the Newfoundland Minister of Finance. Durant took down Mac-Duff's name and birthdate—but no marks—and, as things worked in the province at that time, MacDuff was enrolled in the university a few weeks later.

MacDuff, once again excited about curling, had a second motive for the switch. "The real reason I went over there," he admitted, "was that I thought I could curl with Fred for a year and then maybe get on with Bob Cole or Lester Bowering. I went there for university but if it hadn't been for curling, I doubt very much that I would have gone."

While the mission may have been made with the future in mind, it paid immediate results. The team won the provincial championship and had the distinction of playing in the first Brier held in Newfoundland.

Getting to the Brier was the most incredible feeling MacDuff had ever experienced, and receiving his Purple Heart meant the world.

"You just wanted to take that thing and smack it on your face," said MacDuff, who drew pictures of the crest and sent them home to his parents. "You wanted to put stitches in it and cut eye holes in it and wear it around. In the summer, I wanted to put it on one of my golf shirts and wear it around. You wanted to call yourself 'Jack MacDuff, PH' for Purple Heart. I walked a little higher after getting that."

While curling that year at the St. John's Curling Club, MacDuff had seen many of the old-timers out on the ice wearing their hearts and he had a great respect for them. It was as if these older players belonged to an exclusive club, a club that MacDuff dearly wanted to join.

"Even though some of those guys went 0-10, they wore the Purple Heart out. Every time they played, they had it on. That's what made it special."

With their crests securely sewn to their sweaters, the team from Memorial was set. But if Ernie Richardson had all the luck in the world when he curled, the Newfoundland teams had none—except for bad luck, that is. In the draw to decide the schedule, Durant picked the worst possible position—first-round bye, second round against Manitoba.

While the opening round was being played, the Newfoundland team could do nothing but sit in the stands and watch, growing more anxious with every passing hour. MacDuff was especially nervous, watching the likes of Bernie Sparkes, Mel Watchorn and Orest Meleschuk. After a few ends, he left his seat and sought refuge underneath the stands. The team's driver, Roger Mabey, found MacDuff pacing about, looking as if he was about to blow up with tension.

"Are you all right, Jack?" Mabey queried.

"Roger," said MacDuff, shaking like a leaf, "do you think I can miss every shot tomorrow?"

As much as he wanted to play in the Brier, he was dreading it, questioning whether he deserved a spot in this elite field. For MacDuff, the dream had become reality, but he wasn't quite sure he wanted to wake up.

"When you played on The Rock," MacDuff said, a hint of the Newfoundland accent he picked up still peppering his speech, "that's all you played. You didn't get to see all the other teams. You never saw the big names so when you did play them, it was intimidating."

Although he didn't miss every shot in that first game, the team's overall performance was about on par with previous Newfoundland entries. They finished at 3-7. But by the time they were 0-4, MacDuff had decided just to drink in as much of the atmosphere and history of the event as possible. He went to as many functions as he could, introduced himself to hundreds of people and curled as well as he was able.

"I didn't want to miss a thing," he enthused. "I stayed up late and talked to everyone. I just lived it to the hilt because I didn't know if I was going to get back there again. I can't imagine that I could have had a better time."

The following year, MacDuff quit curling to concentrate on school. Despite numerous pleas, he resisted the temptation to jump right back in, knowing that, as good as the previous year had been, an education was more important. The most persistent suitor was Cole, who would not take no for an answer. Finally, MacDuff made a deal with the gregarious broadcaster.

"I told him that if my marks were good enough at Christmas, I'd curl in the new year," said MacDuff.

So, shortly after Christmas, Cole went over to Memorial, used his influence to find out the hotshot curler's marks, and upon finding they were acceptable, phoned MacDuff and told him to be ready to go in January.

For the next three years, MacDuff and Cole played together and spent a great deal of time together. But they could never get to the Brier. They came only as close as last rock of the provincial final.

In 1975–76, MacDuff decided to strike out on his own. He lined up the best team he could, learning that many top players had wondered why he had waited so long to assume the skipping duties. It was obvious to everyone but MacDuff that he was the hottest player in the province.

"Jack," said Ken Templeton, with whom MacDuff had curled over the years, "I don't care who else we curl with, but I want to play with you because you have the best shot in the province of getting to the Brier."

Templeton joined Toby McDonald and Doug Hudson on the team, and together they set their sights on the Canadian championship. MacDuff was initially nervous about skipping, not having held that position for some time. But he got reassurance from two old friends.

"I ran into Mr. Burke, who congratulated me on getting to the Brier once," MacDuff said. "But he reminded me, just like he'd done in high school, that my real position was at skip. That meant a lot."

And Cole also added his blessing, telling the young curler,

"You'll find out if you're cut out to be a skip when you go to throw the last rock."

The team did not have an auspicious start. In their club, they were regularly beaten by lesser teams. Doubt began to creep back into MacDuff's mind as the losses continued.

"I think maybe I just thought we could show up and win," MacDuff remembered. "Then we started having meetings before every game and analyzing the opposition. We sat down and talked about our games and then we started winning. We became a team."

Preparation and fundamentals win games, even for the best of teams, and the Newfoundland group quickly began to realize that fact. Their reputation as good players didn't mean a thing once they stepped onto the ice.

When it came time for the playdowns, the boys were peaking. "We told ourselves, we only had to go to the provincials, win five, go the Brier, win 10, to the worlds, win 10, and then we could retire," MacDuff laughed.

Little did he realize how close he would come to living that dream. He won the five at the provincials and set off for the Brier in Regina as the Newfoundland representative, not looking for 10 wins, but hoping for five, which would make them one of the best Newfie teams in Brier history.

"Before we left," MacDuff remembered, "I asked [five-time Brier competitor] Bill Piercey how he thought we'd do. He said, 'It doesn't matter if you win two games or you don't win any, you aren't going to win the thing so go and have a good time.'"

In Regina, preparations to welcome MacDuff and the other teams to the big show were coming together. At one meeting, the host drivers had assembled to decide who would drive which teams. Sam Richardson had agreed to be a driver, and as the meeting came to order, he stood up and in his usually boisterous manner said he would drive Bernie Sparkes, the B.C. representative. From the front of the room came a dissenting voice. "Fuck you, Sam," the chief organizer said. "You've won this thing too many times already. You're getting Newfoundland."

And so, when MacDuff's team arrived at the airport, it was greeted by Richardson. MacDuff almost fell over, he was so thrilled.

"Hi," the young skip said as he greeted the legendary second. "I've curled against you before."

"Yes," said Richardson, "in the 1973 Canadian Mixed, right?"

"Yeah," MacDuff replied, "but I also curled a thousand games against you when I was growing up in Lunenburg."

With that, an incredible relationship began. Richardson became more than a driver to the Newfs; he was a friend, scout, confidant, coach and manager. The first step in this relationship came as they sat in the car on their way to the hotel. MacDuff turned to Richardson and said, "Sam, I want you to run our show just like the Richardsons. Exactly."

Richardson's first job came at the hotel. The players began to pair off with their wives to pick up keys to the hotel rooms. Sam simply told them no way. Skip and vice in one room, he said, lead and second in the other. Not only were their wives told to stay down the hall, but they were not allowed in the curlers' rooms an hour before the game.

"We were just mesmerized by him," MacDuff related, with a smile. "Thursday night, we had a big party back in our room and that was fine. Friday night, we had an even bigger one—the music was going and the Screech was flowing. But on Saturday night, no one came back, even though we had agreed to have another party. I went to Sam and said, 'Gee, where do you think everyone is?' And he said, 'Jackie boy, I told 'em all to go away. I said come back next Saturday if you want to have a party.'"

Although they were having fun, the players were still nervous about the curling, especially MacDuff. He did not want to embarrass the team and he had doubts about whether he would even make a shot.

When the first rock of the first end was thrown by Templeton— an in-turn hit—it came a little inside. MacDuff, resplendent in red and white golf shoes that had been transformed into curling shoes, let out a tentative call for sweeping that may not have been heard even if the game had been played in the St. John's Curling Club, and certainly wasn't audible in a standing-room-only arena.

The rock missed, and McDonald came down to his skip to advise him of the problem.

"Jack," he said, "you have to yell louder."

"Okay," the skip answered, "but there's 5,000 people in here and about half of them know the game better than me. If I yell sweep, they're going to yell whoa."

They won that game and ended up with a split of their first four contests. In the fifth round, they faced the veteran Jim Ursel of Quebec, among the field's favorites. In a close match, the Newfies managed to steal a win when the usually dependable Ursel jammed his final rock. That was a turning point—and an omen.

"If he doesn't miss," MacDuff theorized, "we could easily go 2-9."

Now the boys were a game out of first place and well on their way to reaching their five-win goal. Thanks to Richardson's management, the team was on a roll. "By the time they beat Ursel," Richardson remembered, "they were flying so high they weren't even walking on the ice."

Big Sam had implemented the same practices as his team had used and they had a great deal to do with the team's early performance. In between games, it was back to the hotel for a beer and a sandwich, and a quick rest. In the evenings, it was one beer and then to bed. It was a tough regimen for a usually wild bunch of Newfies, but there was no doubting its effectiveness.

"He knew how to keep us relaxed," MacDuff said. "He kept us away from everybody and focused. We didn't even realize at the time what he was doing."

And there was plenty of psychological help as well. On their way to the game against Manitoba's Clare DeBlonde, Richardson planted a seed.

"Jackie boy, if you don't beat Clare, he's going all the way," Richardson said. MacDuff took up the challenge and beat the Manitoba team.

While driving to the game against Alberta's Wayne Sokolosky, MacDuff asked Richardson how his team had done against the Alberta rinks.

"We were 7-0, Jackie boy, 7-0," came the reply.

"Sam," MacDuff questioned, "how could you be 7-0 when you only played in five Briers?"

"Two play-offs, Jackie boy, two play-offs."

The car burst into astonished laughter at Richardson's quick memory, and Sam's words fueled the team on. The match against Sokolosky was vital, and many Newfoundlanders were keeping a

close tab on how their squad was doing. Lester Bowering, one of
the province's top curlers, was one of those following the competition. He was serving an administrative role in Regina and was
stuck in a meeting while the big contest was being played. During
a break, he phoned down to the front desk and tried to get an
update.

"Excuse me, ma'am," he said to the receptionist. "I wonder if
you could go over to the television in the lobby and tell me the
score in the Alberta-Newfoundland game."

The clerk obliged and returned to the phone to report that it was
6–1 for Newfoundland after four ends.

"Okay," a disbelieving Bowering replied. "Now, could you
please go over and tell me the score in the game between Newfoundland and Alberta?"

Once again, the clerk walked over.

"As I said, sir, it's 6–1 for Newfoundland after four ends."

Bowering, still not ready to accept this answer, begged her to
check one more time.

"Sir," the haughty reply came, "it's N-F-L-D, 6, A-L-T-A, 1,
after four E-N-D-S."

Although it was true, everyone was having trouble believing it
—even the team. But they beat Alberta and they were winning
the Brier.

"Everything was just going our way," MacDuff related. "I felt
that I could throw it left-handed between my legs and I would
have made the shot. That's how confident I'd become." The ice was
incredibly quick in Regina, quicker than anything most of the
players had ever curled on. More than one game was lost when a
last-rock routine draw sailed through the rings. But MacDuff was
able to pick up on the quickness of the ice to gain belief in his
ability to deal with it.

The crowd began to sense something special was happening
and, with the hometown team out of the running, adopted the
Newfies as its own. Huge cheers would go up when the team came
out to practice, and during the games, the fans were even more
boisterous in their support.

Back home, things were almost out of control. All of Newfoundland was on edge. When MacDuff went to 6-2, St. John's
mayor Dorothy Wyatt called and told the team, "If you do hap-

pen to win, there will be the biggest parade this town has ever seen."

Premier Frank Moores also called MacDuff. "A lot of people here don't know a thing about curling, but they're going crazy anyway."

Telegrams came in by the hundreds and the team gave each and every one a special treatment. "We were rooming just down the hall from them," recalled Rick Lang, who skipped the Northern Ontario team in 1976, "and on Friday night, they called us down for a minute. Their entire room was wallpapered with telegrams. There wasn't an inch on the wall that didn't have a telegram. I've never seen anything like it."

And they kept coming. Every day, the bellboys would carry telegrams up by the armload as the team captured the imagination of the entire province.

Richardson was the biggest cheerleader. He kept yapping at them, pumping them up. He was relentless in his approach and the team accepted it. They also took all the luck they could get. More often than not, they were the beneficiaries of bad crucial shots from opposing teams.

On Friday afternoon, Saskatchewan's Roger Anholt was heavy with his final stone in an extra end, allowing the Newfoundlanders to steal a point and the victory. The luck factor wasn't lost on the winning team.

"I'm going right out to buy a lottery ticket," McDonald said, after claiming that win.

On Friday night, the MacDuff team defeated Howie Brazeau of the Territories by a 9-1 margin and moved to one win away from capturing the Brier. Once again, Sam took charge, taking the boys back to the hotel, giving them each one bottle of beer and then sending them to bed.

"I remember lying there trying to get to sleep and I just couldn't," MacDuff commented. "As a child, I had dreamed about winning the Brier. All of a sudden I realize I only have to win one game to win the thing. It was kind of a scary thought."

The Saturday afternoon match was against Joe Gurowka, the same player MacDuff had seen in the Brier final against Ron Northcott in Halifax years before. The previous night, Gurowka had thrown a game scored at a perfect 100 per cent, certainly a curling rarity. (Gurowka was calling the game but throwing third stones. Bob Charlebois threw the skip's rocks for Ontario.) A win, and the title was Newfoundland's. A loss would mean a play-off against DeBlonde, if he won his last. On their way to the rink, MacDuff couldn't offer much of a pep talk to his team, but he at least summed up their position.

"Boys," he told them, "I know one thing for sure. We'll never, ever be in this position again in our lifetime. We'll never get this close again."

The Newfoundland team began the match confidently, scoring a single when their skip made a graceful double. After a blank in the second, MacDuff stole one in the third and moved the score to 3-1 after six ends.

MacDuff scored two in the eighth to get it to 5-3 and picked up a steal in the ninth when Charlebois rolled out on a hit attempt. In the 10th, the game was sealed. Drawing against three Newfoundland counters, Charlebois' rock failed to reach the rings. With the score 9-3, Gurowka offered to concede and held out his hand. But before MacDuff could take it, Doug Maxwell of the CBC raced out onto the ice, telling the teams, "You have to keep playing, this game is on television and we've got another hour to go."

"To this day," MacDuff said, "I can't imagine why I wouldn't have shook hands and got out of there. I don't know why we agreed but it was, 'Okay, yes sir, Mr. Maxwell, we'll play.' "

And so on it went for two more ends. In the final frame, Mac-Duff called his boys together and told them to concentrate and not to miss. And they didn't. Hudson, who had not been very happy with his performance that week, took consolation in throwing the final rock that clinched the victory and the first Brier win for Newfoundland.

That opened the floodgates on a celebration that Brier fans had never seen before. Family and friends poured out onto the ice for a group hug, and in the stands, a huge ovation rang through the rafters.

For Richardson, it was as if he had done it all over again. "Jack always tells me I won five Briers," he said. And while his name might not be on the Tankard, he did get a reward. Just before play began, Richardson bought a ticket on Newfoundland to win in a pari-mutuel run by the organizers. Only one other person bought a ticket, so the large purse was split just two ways. The other ticket? It was held by MacDuff.

Back home, Newfoundlanders went wild. Right from the airport, when the team returned, enormous numbers of fans swelled, hoping to catch a glimpse of their new heroes. During the huge motorcade, people lined up six and seven deep along the entire route. There were civic receptions, provincial receptions and curling club receptions. MacDuff's famous curling shoes were bronzed and put in the showcase of the St. John's Curling Club. He even received a congratulatory card from out west that was simply addressed to "Jack MacDuff, Newfoundland."

"I don't actually think it hit us for a while," MacDuff said. "It took a little bit to understand it all."

Even though the bubble burst at the world championships, where the team managed only a 2–9 record, it didn't matter. Mac-Duff and company had their Brier title, which no one would ever take away from them. And it is safe to say that few curlers have ever treasured their victory in the Canadian championship the way MacDuff cherished his. He respected it, loved it and esteemed it. He knew and continues to understand the importance of the Brier, and feels honored to be among the men who have held the Tankard high.

MacDuff proved a fundamental Brier truth: with enough hard work and faith, anyone can win.

A year later, the Brier moved to Montreal and another historic competition was played out as Quebec won its first title. Montreal was still basking in the afterglow of the 1976 Olympics and sports were on the mind of every resident. But whether that enthusiasm would translate into appreciation for the Brier was not known. Curling had not gained mass appeal in the francophone province. The French had never taken to curling in large numbers, and despite its large population, Quebec was a small force in the Canadian curling community.

But organizers, under the chairmanship of Tom Fisher, did manage to put on a tremendous show and attract good crowds. The competition was held in the Olympic Velodrome, certainly a unique location for the Brier. One of the early problems for the curlers was the roof. The stylized, translucent covering overhead made for a bright interior, but it also allowed the sun's rays to affect the ice surface. The result was afternoon draws where the ice was heavy and swingy, and evening rounds where the ice was quick and straight. The players were required constantly to adjust both the speed and the ice being given, depending on what time of day they were playing.

One of the reasons for the good traffic through the turnstiles was the home-province team skipped by Jim Ursel. A native Winnipegger, Ursel had played in four Briers previously and had reached a play-off in 1962, when he was third for Norm Houck of Manitoba.

Along with his team of Art Lobel, Don Aitken and Brian Ross, Ursel had a following as the province's best squad. In 1976, the team had posted a 7-4 record and tied for third place. A year before that, with Howie Atkinson at lead, Ursel had managed a 6-5 mark highlighted by some agonizing losses.

In a game against Manitoba's Rod Hunter, the Quebec team had a rock buried in the four-foot. Hunter attempted to draw down to it, but just ticked the guard, his shooter spilling out into the eight-foot. Ursel elected to play the hit on the Manitoba stone but came wide, wicked Hunter's rock, rolled across the house and took out his own shot rock, the shooter rolling out as well. Hunter easily drew for two to take a 7-5 win. In another match against Harvey Mazinke's Saskatchewan crew, Ursel learned the hard way that the rings were actually a half-inch too large—a rock that was clearly on came up short when the measure was put to it.

In 1977, however, Ursel and company were a little more confident. They had won the CBC Curling Classic earlier that year, beating a good field. And no one questioned Ursel's capability at the helm. He was a brilliant hitter, and his draw game wasn't bad either. On the strategy side, he was also one of the best. He knew when to stick with a plan and when to bail out; consequently, he rarely gave up a big end. He wasn't flamboyant, but he got the job done.

The rest of the team was also solid. At lead was the easy-going Ross, a strong sweeper with a calm, cool demeanor. He would never challenge a call, never question the strategy. He was just there to do his work.

He was the perfect foil for Aitken, the team's second. Aitken was more intense and competitive. He hated losing and was always into the game. Around Quebec, Aitken was considered the prodigy who had arrived. He had taken to curling in the Town of Mount Royal, one of Canada's early planned communities where sports facilities were abundant. After just a few years of playing, he had nearly won the Canadian Schoolboy title. He was in his fifth Brier (and would go on to play in nine) and may have been the consummate second. Also a strong sweeper, he combined a talented touch with a strong hitting game.

Lobel, the Jimmy Cagney look–alike, was also in his fifth championship. Along with Aitken, he had been Brier runner–up on Bill Kent's Quebec team in 1972. He was a talented shotmaker who rarely missed big shots, and made the most of routine ones as well. Going into the Brier, however, Lobel had been saddled with an ailing back. A week before play began, he was at the orthopedic surgeon, begging for help. The doctor gave him an epidural, which eased the pain but didn't help his mobility. For seven days, Lobel stayed in bed, not moving, hoping a miracle would allow him to play.

"I was really looking forward to playing in the Brier because it was in our hometown and I thought we had a good chance," Lobel remembered. "But I wasn't sure if I was going to make it, the way my back was."

A day before play began, Lobel went to the Velodrome and threw rocks. The pain was still there, but he was able to play through it. Ever the team player, he decided to let his team vote on whether or not to get a replacement. The decision was unanimous —Lobel would play.

That decision led to one of the strangest Brier incidents on record. Because his back would not allow him to sweep, Lobel spent the entire time he was not throwing at the end with Ursel. It was like team skipping. This arrangement also meant only one sweeper, with Ross and Aitken handling all the work on the first four stones solo.

"That was certainly a strange situation," Ross said. "I remember getting a lot of strange looks from the other teams who were trying to figure out what was going on. But we had played together all year and we weren't about to get a new player at that point."

The unusual system seemed to work. Through the first four

games, Quebec was undefeated. They finally lost to Alberta's Tom Reed by giving up three consecutive steals of one point each. The chief competition, though, came from Roy Vinthers of British Columbia, who was undefeated in his first eight. It looked as though the rest of the field was playing for second.

But the never-say-die Quebeckers kept playing. In one of the biggest wins of the week, Ursel beat Ontario's Paul Savage in the 10th draw when both teams were tied for second. This crucial match was played in the afternoon, when the ice was heavy. Savage, who had Ed Werenich and the intimidating front end of Ron Green and Reid Ferguson, which could sweep any duo under the table, relied heavily on the finesse game.

"I think the soft ice helped us in that game," recalled Lobel. "They were trying to finesse things while we were throwing the high, hard ones. Their game just didn't work."

Not only did Ursel have the ice on his side but he also had the help of the draw. British Columbia had the unfortunate schedule of first- and last-round byes, meaning a grinding itinerary of 11 consecutive games. Down the stretch, the western team's fatigue began to show.

First, Vinthers lost an extra-end contest to Alberta 7–6. The next morning, Ursel handed him his second defeat with a 9–6 decision going in favor of the Quebeckers. In their final game on Friday evening, Vinthers and his team were beaten for the third consecutive time, losing to Newfoundland 5–3.

While Newfoundland was winning that match, Ursel was knocking off Manitoba's John Usackis to move to 8–2. A win over Nova Scotia in the last round would give Quebec its first Brier championship.

With the title riding on the line, even the ailing Lobel picked up a broom to share the sweeping duties. "I figured if I hurt myself then and we won, I had two or three weeks to recover before the world championships," he said. "I thought I'd take a chance."

A huge crowd of more than 7,000 jammed the former bicycle track to cheer on Quebec. And it worked. With Ursel up three coming home, Nova Scotia skip Bob Fitzner came up light on his first rock and handed Quebec the championship. A huge ovation burst out as Quebec, after 48 years of trying, won its first Brier.

For a short time, the celebration reigned in Montreal. But after a while, the victory became almost bittersweet. In comparison to Newfoundland's outpouring of affection a year earlier, Quebec's reaction was subdued.

"I think there's something significant for having won it for Quebec," Lobel related, with a wistful tone. "On the other hand, I think that, for the teams that win for some of the other provinces, it probably means a little more for them because the support is there. In Manitoba or Saskatchewan, when teams won, they won a lot. They were encouraged to go to the big spiels, had their ways paid and they got sponsorships. We got nothing but an invitation to play in Switzerland. I still feel good about it, but at the same time, we didn't get the recognition others do."

Lobel's lament is one many Quebec curlers have expressed. While the core curling community is as strong as anywhere in the country, outside of that, support falls away rather quickly. French Canadians have now begun to infiltrate the ranks, but in those days, there was a clear division along linguistic lines.

Nevertheless, the Quebec victory was definitely a high point. Unfortunately, the 1977 Brier will also be remembered for a stunning blow that took everybody by surprise. David Stewart announced that, after 50 years of support, Macdonald Tobacco would be ending its alliance with curling in 1979. That decision marked the end of an era and shocked curlers across the country. It would have a profound effect upon the future of the sport.

8

Changing of the Guard

A lthough there had been some media speculation concerning the end of Macdonald Tobacco's sponsorship just before the 1977 Brier, the announcement was difficult to believe. Macdonald and the Brier had become inseparable, or so it seemed.

But at the opening banquet in Montreal, David Stewart dropped the bombshell. The Canadian Curling Association had no forewarning, and when the news came down that 1979 would be the final year of Macdonald Tobacco's assistance, members and minions scurried about, asking who would pick up future tabs and pointing fingers at the reason for Macdonald's departure.

Meanwhile, Macdonald was pointing fingers of its own. In addition to rising transportation and hotel costs, David Stewart said, the federal government's tobacco advertising restrictions had played a part in the final decision.

"The Brier was never intended as a piece of advertising," he said to reporters at a press conference the next day. "But over the last 10 years, the government has put a gun to our heads and said we would have to police ourselves.

"We got out of advertising on radio and television but never considered the Brier as a part of other avenues. Now, however, we have an audit, on not what we call advertising, but what the people call advertising—and that includes the Brier.

"I don't think there will be a change in the government point of view," Stewart added with remorse. "There will never be a reversal back to freedom in advertising. It has got to the point where in two years' time, we will have to hang up our broom."

Stewart's announcement sent a chill throughout the '77 Brier. While Jim Ursel was winging his way to victory, the CCA executives were in a nervous fret. Not only did they now have to begin looking for a new sponsor, but for the first time since the Brier began, they would have to take complete control of the event. Macdonald would no longer be appointing trustees or directors to make the important decisions.

"I think we were in a state of shock," said one prominent CCA member at the time. "I don't think anyone had the foggiest clue of what the hell we were going to do. Everyone was zipping around yelling the sky is falling instead of realizing that we had a very marketable commodity."

Even during those dark hours, however, play got under way. During the first round, Doug Maxwell, then working for the CBC, was at his customary seat on the media bench when his phone rang. The caller was Dick Bradbeer, then director of national promotions for Labatt's. Just a year earlier, the brewery had set up its first national sales office and was looking at getting involved with national events to promote its suds. Bradbeer had heard the news of Macdonald's departure and his ears pricked up like radar detectors. Curling, he thought, was the perfect vehicle for a beer company.

"I thought the Brier fit because it had television opportunities and it started from a grassroots level," the affable Bradbeer reflected. Not to mention, of course, the fact that curlers and beer go together like salt and pepper.

Maxwell told Bradbeer that he would pass the information on to the CCA folks and have them contact Labatt's when something concrete was in place. Little did the big curling promoter know that by passing on his information to CCA President Herb Milhem, he would be asked to join a search committee to hunt out a new sponsor.

That committee was made up of five people: Maxwell, CCA vice presidents Cliff Thompson and Frank Stent, Don Anderson of St. Thomas, Ontario, and former champion Harvey Mazinke. It quickly drew up a presentation package that was fired out to any company with a few extra bucks.

Serious offers came in from Canada Packers and the Royal Bank, but no organization was as committed as Labatt's. Maxwell's oratory skills in the meetings probably didn't hurt either.

While the committee was entertaining offers, it also had to decide how it would package the sponsorship. It wasn't sure what the going rate for Briers was because none of the members were privy to what Macdonald had spent each year.

But in addition to asking the sponsor to pick up all the costs, the CCA decided to leverage the television rights, which it controlled, as part of the deal. It set the fee for that add-on at $35,000, escalating $5,000 every year of the five-year agreement. At the time, no one in sports marketing believed any company would accept that kind of contract. As Montreal Olympic organizers had learned, television rights weren't sold off that way in the 1970s. But Labatt's was more than willing to put its name on the line, realizing just how sweet a deal it was getting. The CCA had been negotiating with all the sophistication of an inexperienced card player holding a royal flush—it was obvious the curling association desperately desired the brewery's sponsorship.

However, there was one stumbling block to overcome before the brewery could sign on the dotted line. Seagram's was sponsoring the Canadian Mixed championships and had an ironclad exclusivity clause in its contract. This clause virtually prevented any other beverage company from dealing with the CCA.

But the association knew a good sponsor when it saw one, and Labatt's was about as good as they come. So the committee went to Seagram's and told them straight up: "We're going with Labatt's; stick around if you want."

Seagram's did, and in Vancouver the next year, CCA president Herb Milhem and Don Macdougall, president of Labatt's, inked the deal.

Labatt's was thrilled with the package, especially because it felt that it had come out the winner in the agreement. "We ended up getting the deal for less than the CCA wanted," Bradbeer remembered, "because it became pretty obvious in the negotiations just how badly they wanted us."

For Labatt's, getting the rights may have been the easy part of the deal. Putting on the Canadian curling championship, however, was something it knew absolutely nothing about.

"We were neophytes when it came to curling," Bradbeer admitted. "We had been looking at the thing to sell beer."

But the company learned quickly, if not always easily.

Bradbeer's first step was to bring Grant Waterman from Toronto, where he was Ontario promotions coordinator, to the head office in London, Ontario, to assume the position of national promotions manager. He was given most of the responsibility for getting the Brier up and running.

"I didn't know the game and I wasn't a curler so I didn't know the whole process," Waterman related. "But I quickly came to understand that it was one big political scenario. There were a lot of egos and personalities involved."

Undoing what had been done in the Macdonald years was difficult. As they had always stated, the tobacco people had run things not as a form of advertising, but as a help to curlers. Labatt's was not about to make the Brier a charity event. It wanted to sell beer.

"I was dismayed at the internal bickering among the curling cliques," Waterman remembered. "I had an interesting time trying to put the people and personalities in place so as not to offend anyone."

A couple of the early ideas for establishing a Labatt's presence were flops, roundly unwelcomed by the curling fraternity. "One of the first things we did was to look at a new name," Bradbeer said. "We felt Brier didn't mean anything to anyone, and our plan was to keep the name for a few years and then gradually change it to something that reflected the brewery."

That idea sailed like a lead balloon and Labatt's quickly backed off. It was trying to establish a good rapport with the curlers and had not made a brilliant beginning. Many players began to wonder if getting Labatt's on board had been such a good idea.

Waterman decided that the best way to put a finger on the pulse of the curling community was to meet some of the rock-throwing brethren. He began a cross-country tour to visit the presidents of every provincial curling association. "We went out and told them that we were going to do things a bit differently," he said. "We wanted to make the Brier a bigger event and it was to our benefit to have them onside. So we told them that we weren't here just to hand out silver trays, we wanted to make this thing first class. In retrospect, it was probably a very smart thing to do."

The tour may also have made bringing in a new trophy somewhat easier but, internally at least, no less challenging. In meetings, Waterman and Bradbeer decided that creating a new tankard would be a way to begin establishing a new identity for what was now to be called the Labatt Brier.

"We said, 'In our wildest dreams, how much do you think we could spend on a trophy?'" said the quick-talking, fun-loving Waterman. "We started at $5,000 but eventually settled at $10,000. We thought we should be able to get something pretty good for that price."

Bradbeer asked Waterman to get the job done and left Labatt's for a short period of time to work on an election campaign. When he returned six weeks later, drawings for the new tankard were finished, and Bradbeer was pleased that his co-worker had gotten such a beautiful tankard for such a reasonable price.

The new trophy would be exquisitely formed, resembling a large two-handled stein. The brilliant gold color and the Labatt Brier logo on the front would make it one of the most noteworthy trophies in Canadian sport.

Little by little, news of the designer mug began to leak out and the press were anxious to see the trophy. But Waterman managed to fend off all the nosy reporters and photographers—and even other Labatt's staff—until a promotional event for the 1980 Labatt Brier in Calgary, where the brewery's sponsorship would begin. There, in front of a large gathering, the Tankard was unveiled.

Sid Oland, vice president of Labatt's, was on hand for the ceremony and, like the rest of the onlookers, was thrilled with the new Labatt Tankard.

"Grant, you've done a really good job with that," a delighted Oland exclaimed. "How much did the trophy cost?"

"Well, about $35,000," Waterman said quietly.

Oland's face turned ashen. "$35,000? Are you out of your head? I thought the budget was $10,000."

"That's what it cost for the case," Waterman explained. "We can't have this thing getting banged up."

Once the initial shock had subsided, all parties agreed the trophy was worth the cost. (In 1993, it was insured for $350,000.) But the Labatt Tankard was just one item in an increasingly expensive arrangement. For the first year, Labatt's had budgeted $350,000 for the Brier. It believed that amount would get things up and running to an appropriate level. When the final numbers were tallied, however, the expenses totaled a whopping $1.7 million.

The curlers accepted the Labatt Tankard and didn't seem to mind giving up the Macdonald trophy. The Purple Heart crest, however, was another matter. With an eye to promoting itself, Labatt's had introduced a new oval-shaped crest for provincial winners that had graphics of both the Purple Heart and the Labatt Tankard on it. Labatt's felt the new crest was a progressive step.

"We weren't really keen on keeping the Purple Heart," Bradbeer admitted. "Again, we wanted something more Labatt's-oriented."

But the curlers were outraged. The January edition of the *Ontario Curling Report* hammered home the fraternity's sentiments in a front-page editorial:

> The Heart is symbolic of the Brier; it represents curling supremacy. After the Brier, all that remains are the fine memories and the Heart.
>
> Every competitive male curler dreams of playing in the Brier. The Brier is the pot of gold at the end of the rainbow. The Brier is the Stanley Cup, the Super Bowl, the end all, be all.
>
> Now the new sponsors of the Brier have created a new symbol that they are incorporating into a crest. The new crest does not resemble the Heart, although they have tried to keep the coveted Heart by placing its design in the center of this new symbol. This new creation destroys the image that has been established from 50 years of annual competition. Every curler in Canada identifies with the Purple Heart; it is the symbol of excellence.
>
> Labatt's sponsorship is a welcome addition to the game. However, curling has established legends built around the Heart. You can do anything with the design of the Heart, but don't mess with the winner, the Heart of the game.

The front page also printed an open letter to Labatt's president Peter Widdrington from one of Ontario's finest curlers never to make it to the Brier. John Cushing eloquently expressed the

players' hurt at losing the emblem, even though Cushing didn't
have a Purple Heart of his own:

Dear Mr. Widdrington:

In three articles recently published in various curling circu-
lars, the enclosed picture apparently represents the new crest
for future provincial winners of the Labatt's Tankard.

Our purpose in writing is to present why the change to the
new crest is damaging to the game of curling and to the reputation of Labatt's, either of which, we are sure, is not the
intention of Labatt's sponsorship. Your designer has grossly
misunderstood curlers when he tries to incorporate the heart
symbol into the tankard crest, rather than incorporating the
tankard into the traditional Purple Heart crest.

Curling is a game based on tradition. For 50 years, curlers
have strived to wear the famed Purple Heart, symbolic of a
provincial curling championship. Unlike other sports where
big prize money is the attraction of the participants, the provincial curling championship has the Purple Heart, which
every curler knows cannot be bought with prize money. To
take away the Purple Heart is to take away what curlers want
most in the game.

The implications of retaining the Purple Heart to Labatt's
are twofold. First, the Labatt's name and Labatt's products
will hold the respect of curlers, and secondly, every winner
will wear their Labatt's Purple Heart with pride. Without the
Purple Heart, Labatt's is risking some serious negative
publicity.

Labatt's has taken away the most cherished prize in curling.
Please reconsider your change in crests and have a heart.

Bradbeer said the *Ontario Curling Report* articles hit a nerve.
"When we saw that newspaper, we realized just how important the
Purple Heart was," he said. "It wasn't that we were being stubborn, it was another case of not realizing the importance the
curlers put on it."

By the time the masses gathered at the inaugural Labatt's Brier
in Calgary, emotions were heating up. Cushing's letter had arrived
with more than 200 signatures on it. Similar sentiments were
being expressed in all corners.

Not all the people involved, however, were aware of just how big an issue the Purple Heart was. "I was surprised at all the fuss," Waterman remembered. "A day earlier, I had spoken to Harvey Mazinke [a CCA executive at the time] and he told me everything would be fine. He said that as long as we had the Purple Heart in there it was okay. And we did."

But at the closing banquet, Oland did something without telling any of his Labatt's co-workers. He stood up in front of a packed hall and announced that the Purple Heart was coming back.

"Somehow, the degree of emotion involved with the Heart was not made clear to us," Oland told the *Ontario Curling Report* later. "We saw no reason not to respect the feelings of the curlers."

The curlers rejoiced, and every player in the 1980 Brier was given a collector's edition crest, issued only once. (Later, they all received Purple Hearts.)

What Labatt's had learned was that the Purple Heart and the Brier name, along with many other symbols of the game, had long since ceased to be associated with Macdonald Tobacco. Most of the competitors had no idea how the Brier got its name or what the purple crest on their sweater symbolized. As far as they and 99 per cent of the fans looking on knew, these were traditional curling emblems. Labatt's, in its wisdom, agreed.

But the new sponsor did institute some changes to the competition, and its work with the media was a good example. Macdonald had associated with a media old guard, fellows who had been around for a long time. They treated these reporters with the utmost respect and gave them plenty of assistance. If, for example, one reporter was a little short when it came time to pay his hotel bill, a Macdonald rep would make up the difference and nothing more was said.

While the majority of the press corps were hardworking and devoted to their task, a number of hangers-on had found their way onto the bench. Just by attending a few Briers and getting a media friend to sign an accreditation form, they became part of the press, although they never seemed to do any actual work. Under Macdonald, they were tolerated. But Waterman wanted to change all that.

"Many of the guys who had been around for a long time thought it was a bit of a joyride," Waterman recalled. "When I took over the media bench, I felt the guys who were working should sit up front and I had to kick a lot of the old cronies into the back. Why, for example, was [former Brier chairman and pin manufacturer] Laurie Artiss sitting in the front row while [the *Toronto Star's*] Peter Krivel was way up in the back? I think I ruffled a few feathers but things had to change. I turfed a lot of the old guard into the back rows and moved the working guys up front. That just seemed to make sense."

Labatt's also changed the draw. Unlike in the Macdonald years when the draw was made by the competing skips just before the start of play, Labatt's decided to have it a year in advance, so that it could be used for promotional purposes.

The 1980 Brier was also the first to use a play-off system. If curling was going to be successful as a television sport, clearly the final game would have to be vital. Under the old round-robin system, on many occasions when viewers turned on their televisions, the championship had already been decided.

Many credit Labatt's for the play-off system, but that was not the case.

"The play-off format wasn't a condition of the contract," stated Bradbeer. "That came from the CCA, but we agreed with it wholeheartedly."

John Hudson, the head of CBC television sports, had been lobbying for just such a change. At a 1978 luncheon speech given to the Canadian Ladies' Curling Association, he said that the Brier and the Canadian women's championship would have to invoke some kind of play-off if they were to remain on television. Broadcasts of curling were becoming increasingly popular, but the world men's and junior's championships had both adopted play-offs, which made them more exciting.

Hudson either knew something was up—although the sponsorship contract had not yet been signed—or had an intuitive flash. In any case, he eventually became the man calling the television shots for curling when he joined TV Labatt a few years later.

Under the new play-off arrangement, the traditional round-robin remained and the first-place team advanced to the final. The second- and third-place teams played in a semifinal.

The differences between sponsorship by Macdonald and by Labatt's were significant. Many of the players who competed in both eras noted a great sense of tradition with the first sponsor, but more of a big event with the second.

"It's like apples and oranges," said Rick Lang, the famed Northern Ontario curler who shares with Ed Lukowich the distinction of winning both the Macdonald Brier Tankard and the Labatt's Tankard. "Both were good at the time and both had great parts to them. To say which one was better is pretty tough. A lot of things with Macdonald had become traditions because they just kept happening. With Labatt's, it was a big show, an extravaganza."

Two-time Labatt Brier winner Rick Folk was less subtle in his analysis. To him the differences were obvious. "It was run differently," Folk stated. "They [Labatt's] really wanted to make it a first-class show. From a curler's point of view, they went out of their way. The functions were a little bit sharper, a little classier, and a lot more attention was paid to the curlers and their wives. The ice conditions were better, too. It was really like night and day."

When Macdonald ended its reign in Ottawa in 1979, there was an emotional farewell. Every living Brier-winning skip—22 in all, representing 34 championships—came to the nation's capital in the largest gathering of curling talent ever seen under one roof. Emmet Smith, the only living player from the first Brier, was also in attendance. As the week went on, the fans were treated to some exciting play by the winning Manitoba team of Barry Fry, but more and more, the championship became a teary-eyed farewell.

Just before presenting the trophy for the last time, David Stewart, the man in the coonskin coat, had some parting words:

"This marks the closing chapter of the 50th year of Brier curling, which originated in 1927. It is a pleasant and emotional moment as we bring to a close our participation in this great event which has brought Canadians together from all walks of life.

"The Brier has emphasized the fact that Canadians can get along with each other in sportsmanship and fellowship. Competing rinks have played together hard, but there can be only one winner. I make special mention of New Brunswick and Prince Edward Island rinks who have competed all these years, but have never won a Brier championship. Yet, they never complained or threatened to drop out. That's what curling is all about. I thank you all for your participation and help. I am very grateful."

9

Playoff Madness: The Early Eighties

While the Brier was getting a new look in 1980, there was one familiar feature: Saskatchewan's Rick Folk, who was playing in his third consecutive national championship. By virtue of his two previous performances, he went in as the favorite.

In 1978, after finally winning the Saskatchewan championship, Folk and his team posted an 8-3 record that left them a game behind the winning Alberta team of Ed Lukowich. A year later, the Saskatoon team finished with the identical mark and again was runner-up, this time to Manitoba's Barry Fry.

In 1980, Folk was determined to go the last step and claim the Brier crown. It was a dream with a long history.

Born on the Prairies, the soft-spoken Folk had naturally started curling at a young age. His family, all curlers, lived a block from the Nutana Curling Club in Regina, and by the time Folk was 10, he was racing home from school daily to pick up his curling boots, slip down the back alleyway and wait patiently for a sheet of ice to open up.

"It didn't matter if it was only for 10 minutes," remembered Folk, a round-faced man with a figure that earned him the nickname Pudge. "I'd be out there throwing rocks. Sometimes I'd wait hours just for the chance to throw rocks for a couple of minutes."

At playdown time, Folk was glued to the radio, listening in to the play-by-play while such Saskatchewan legends as Merv Mann and

Ernie Richardson battled it out for the right to represent the province. "I can remember hearing those brooms sweeping in the background," he said. "I got a real charge out of those games."

When he reached high school, Folk met up with the man who would become his closest friend and longtime teammate, Tom Wilson. The two played together on the high school team, Wilson (the elder by two years) skipping and Folk handling third duties. That team broke up when Folk left for university, but the pair had an enduring bond, and 10 years later, they reunited to play the competitive circuit in western Canada. This time, Folk skipped while Wilson played second.

From the start, the Folk team, which in its pre-Brier days was rounded out by Bob Thompson at third and Rodger Schmidt at lead, did not conform to traditional Saskatchewan curling standards. For one thing, in an era when most teams were switching to push brooms, the Folk squad stuck with corn. To anyone who saw them play, the reason was obvious.

Tom Wilson might have been the best sweeper in the game's history. Barrel-chested and burly, Wilson was as strong as a weightlifter and as relentless as a bull, and his power showed when he slung the corn. People standing anywhere near him while he swept would feel tremors up their legs.

Wilson treated his brooms as if his life depended on them. He had them custom-made with an extra-thick handle and would carefully tailor the corn to suit particular situations. If he wanted more corn on the ice, he chose one broom. If he wanted less, he chose another model. He methodically numbered his brooms and selected them the way a golfer selects different irons. But these brooms didn't last as long as golf clubs. A game, maybe a game and a half, and Wilson would have exhausted them.

As Folk pointed out, taking the corn out of Wilson's hands was like disarming him. "It would have been like giving a gunfighter a knife," he stated. "In my opinion, Tom is the best curler in the world to ever play his position. When he was in his heyday, his shotmaking and sweeping were just unrivaled."

The team also varied from the standard western style of play because they favored a draw game with lots of rocks in play. Wilson had spent some time playing with Lukowich, a noted master of the draw game, and quickly learned that this style was the key to success. He didn't have to convince Folk of the benefits because the skip had a touch that leant itself to a softer style.

"We were one of the few teams in Saskatchewan that preferred the messy game or what we called the Ethiopian offense, where anything goes," Folk said. "We knew you could go right to the top with that style and it was less likely to happen with straight bopping."

The final key to the team's makeup was its strict adherence to the rules of the game. The players weren't just being good sports— they wanted to intimidate other teams. During the late 1970s, advances in curling equipment were changing the way the game was played. Faster sliders meant problems with releasing the rock before the hog line. Push brooms could be used to sweep only a part of the running surface of the rock, causing it to curl more or less. Releasing the rock after the hog line and changing the curl of the rock were essentially against the rules.

Most teams didn't appreciate any of this rule-breaking, but few did anything to stop it. The Folk team took a stand. "We were one of the few teams that had the gumption to go up to the other team and say, 'Hey, look, you foul once more and we're taking the rock off.'"

Their gumption led to many heated moments. While most of the disagreements were verbal, it was not uncommon for Wilson to stop a rock halfway down the ice if he felt the player had released it over the hog line. The opposition might protest, but few were willing to do much more than that, with the scowling Wilson standing by.

"The guys we were playing against were really upset because we were the only ones that would say it to them," Folk remembered. "But privately, in the bar after, we'd have a lot of players come up to us and tell us it was about time somebody did what we did, because they'd had it done to them before."

The reputation the team gained for holding up its end of the rulebook did not exactly make them a fan favorite, but it gave the players an edge. Walking out onto the ice against Folk meant wondering if and when one of the team members would call an infraction.

"If the other teams were intimidated by us calling them on cheating, then good," Folk said. "They knew that if they came out to play against us and if they did anything outside of the rules that they were going to get confronted."

But some players of the time suggest that Folk was as much of a gamesman as the rest. He was accused of intentionally moving while standing behind the house during the opposing team's shots in order to distract the shooter. He was accused of palming the ice.

Folk vehemently denies he did anything other than pay back the offenders.

"In any of those situations, where the other team is cheating, you have three choices. You can ignore it, you can do it right back to them, or you can confront them and try to put an end to it. Most often we chose the third, but sometimes, we'd have to go with number two."

By the time they reached the 1978 Brier, they were regarded as a no-nonsense group with considerable curling talent. Unfortunately, the ice at that event was horrible and it severely hampered some of the team's ability. Nevertheless, their performance surprised Folk.

"We were a fairly experienced team at that point, but not at the Brier level," he said. "It was a real eye-opener to see the ice conditions we had to play in. We were a real finesse team that liked to think we could play any type of game. But when we got to that Brier, we could only use about a third of the sheet because the frost was so bad. It took us half a week to really adjust and realize that we just couldn't play our style of game."

Folk managed to keep calm, despite his enormous frustration. Here he was at the pinnacle of Canadian curling, and he might as well have been playing outdoors on a pond. It was almost sickening. Yet the team played on, grabbing runner-up laurels.

The next year, Schmidt left the team and was replaced by Wilson's brother, Jim, whom Folk says was even more fiery than Tom. The skip, who considered himself laid-back, was grateful for the Wilson spark plugs. "I never had to go to a curling rink and worry that my team wasn't up for the game. The Wilson boys were ready to pop at any time."

Jim was definitely strong-willed and deceptively powerful. His sweeping, while not quite up to his brother's, was certainly strong, and together the Wilsons made a Herculean front end.

Again, the Folk rink took the Saskatchewan title and moved on to the 1979 Brier. The ice in Ottawa was substantially better than the ice the previous year in Vancouver, but all was still not well. The rocks, borrowed from a local club, were nothing short of awful. Mismatched and pitted, they reduced shotmaking to a guessing game. A skip might throw his first stone perfectly to the button and on the second, with an identical shot, end up hogging it.

"We'd played with rocks that were five feet different in weight," Folk said, "but never 20 to 30 feet like these ones. That was an awakening, for sure. It was the same for all the teams but the rocks sure made us all look pretty stupid at times."

Halfway through the week, conditions had become so bad that the organizers called a meeting and made an announcement: if two thirds of the teams voted in favor, new rocks would be brought in. Naturally, Barry Fry of Manitoba, who was leading, didn't want to change. He and a few of the other contenders who generally played a hitting style were not having as much trouble and voted against. One team never bothered to show up for the special vote and so the bad rocks stayed, much to the dismay of the Saskatchewan team.

But once again they struggled on, finishing in a tie for second with Larry Pineau of Northern Ontario. Now they knew they had the talent to win it all, yet were not sure if they would ever make it back. "Coming out of Saskatchewan," Folk said, "you just never knew if you would get another shot."

Certainly the odds were not with them. No one had won three straight Saskatchewan titles since the Richardsons. With its deep pool of talent, the province was a competitive minefield that had claimed many curling careers.

Compounding the difficulty was the departure of Thompson, who had moved to Lethbridge, Alberta, for business. His loss meant throwing a new player into the mix, and no one was ever sure if that would work out.

But Ron Mills, the new third, seemed to be the perfect fit. Unlike Thompson or the Wilson brothers, Mills was laid-back, almost quiet. It became almost comical to watch the contrast between the front end and the third.

"It was kind of interesting watching them down there," Folk laughed. "You had the two fiery Wilsons and Ron, who had a tendency to daydream at times. You'd see the Wilsons keep Ron in the game and Ron keeping the Wilsons settled down. It really worked quite well."

Beating the odds, they made it back to the 1980 Brier in Calgary, the inaugural Labatt's shindig. Despite the fact that they were the favorites because of their previous record and their overflowing confidence, most of the fan and media attention was focused on the hometown Calgary, Alberta, rink skipped by 22-year-old Paul Gowsell.

Gowsell had won two World Junior Championships and had been the media darling of competitive curling for the previous two years. If the Folk team was non-conformist, then Gowsell was radical. He had literally changed the game, not only with his talented play but also with his outrageous attitude.

Gowsell and his team zipped around the country, playing hard and partying harder, picking up cash wherever they went. And curling fans flocked to see this young man with the unkempt locks and the scraggly beard as much for his shotmaking as for his performances. His antics on the ice left some people cheering and others in a state of shock; there were protests and plaudits, arguments and appreciation, but the one consensus about this brash, cocky kid was that he could curl.

His impact on the game was often overshadowed by his style, but his 1976 World Junior Championship rink was the first non-European team of note to abandon the straw and adopt the push brooms, leading the way for what has become the norm in nearly every curling club in Canada.

He was also one of the first to go hog-wild with the aggressive come-around game. "If there was a straw on the ice, he'd draw around it," remarked Ed Werenich, one of his combatants on the cash circuit.

Gowsell first rose to prominence in the 1975 Canadian Junior Championship in Edmonton. Along with teammates Neil Houston, Glen Jackson and Kelly Stearne, Gowsell dominated play with a devastating hit game uncharacteristic of his later style. ("I called it no-brain curling," commented Gowsell.) He also began to make a name for himself as a partier by inviting the entire closing party back to his hotel room. Police were called in three times to quiet the ruckus; the third time, they gave up trying and tossed everyone out.

That same team represented Canada at the 1976 World Junior in Aviemore, Scotland, a small resort town. The sleepy burg was woken up by the Calgary boys and their tactics.

One of the reasons the Gowsell team had latched on to the push brooms was because of their ability to corner-sweep the stone— what the rules now refer to as snow-plowing. This strategy would affect the degree of curl to the rock. They could also slow the rock down, if necessary, by dumping debris in front of it. Although these same tactics had caused Folk and Wilson considerable aggravation, they were nominally legal at that time. But for the host Scots, these strategies were an outrage and against the spirit of curling. But to Gowsell, it didn't matter—he had won.

He won another World Junior crown in 1978 in Grindelwald, Switzerland, but almost didn't get to accept his trophy. At the closing banquet, the long-haired Gowsell, despite wearing the Canadian team blazer, was prevented from entering the ballroom by a security guard, who growled, "This party is for curlers, not hippies."

After that good-bye to the junior ranks, Gowsell turned his attention to the men's circuit and began to rip through it as he had done the under-20 events. In bonspiel after bonspiel, he could be seen sliding out with his broom resting on top of his neck, collapsing at the hog line, yelling sweeping instructions while lying flat on his stomach. He would curse rocks and taunt opponents.

Ed Lukowich remembers the Gowsell of that period as one who brought a new energy to the game.

"He was the most animated and exciting curler I'd ever seen," Lukowich said. "It was really a thrill to play against him. He had very little fear of anything so he was willing to play almost any shot. Missing wasn't in his mind. He really believed he could walk on water."

There was also the matter of mind games. Gowsell would yell and scream, slap his broom up and down, flail around on the ice— anything to distract the other skip.

At one western cashspiel, Gowsell was up against the slow-playing veteran Larry McGrath. Gowsell became so pissed off at the snail's pace of the game that he ordered a pizza and had it delivered to sheet three of the host club.

One of the stops along the way was the Canadian Postal Championships, which were being contested in Regina that year. Accompanied by Grant Waterman of Labatt's, Folk showed up carrying the trophy and sat through a closing banquet that enthralled him about as much as watching someone get a haircut. To while away the hours, Folk and Waterman had quite a few cocktails, and by the time the evening wrapped up, they were feeling no pain. They decided that, with official duties completed, they would continue the evening, and went out on the town drinking and dancing until the wee hours. After a late-night pizza, they decided to make their way back to the hotel along with the Tankard, but Folk's stomach couldn't make it. With the perfect aim that made him such a great threat with a draw shot on the ice, Waterman recalled, he upchucked right into the Tankard, christening it as only the new champion could.

"I had to have a lid put on it after that," Waterman laughed later. "I figured it would be better not to have it hollow, so there weren't any more accidents."

To this day, the trophy awarded to the Canadian men's curling champions—although modeled after a beer tankard—has a hard plastic lid inside the rim about a half inch below the lip. The lid makes taking a victory swig out of it or putting anything else into it impossible. (In reality, officials discovered that the Tankard was constructed of a toxic material that is poisonous when mixed with liquid. Even the replica Tankards given to the winning teams are drilled with holes to prevent anyone from drinking out of them.)

The runner-up that year, Al Hackner, was about to follow in the Folk footsteps and learn that three times really is lucky. Like Folk's team, the Northern Ontario squad needed three tries to capture its own Brier championship after losing finals in 1980 and 1981. The team took a far different road, however, than the 1980 winner did.

Hackner grew up in Nipigon, about a half-hour drive from Thunder Bay. Like many kids in the small town, he grew up playing every sport offered. As he grew older, however, it came down to a choice between hockey and curling, and the roaring game won.

"I used to love to practice," Hackner remembered. "I just wanted to be the best I could. I didn't have any goals other than that."

In Nipigon, when Brier playdowns rolled around, it was a big feat to make it past the club level. After that, the teams usually became sacrificial lambs to the big squads from Thunder Bay, with which they shared a district.

Hackner grew to love curling with a deep passion, and by the time he was in his final year of high school, he had moved to Thunder Bay to curl on a successful school team. He also played men's competitive curling and threw rocks at every chance.

School began to lose importance, though, and his marks slipped. He didn't care about advancing to university; making it to the Brier was now at the top of the list. By the time classes ended for Christmas holidays, Hackner had said good-bye to the books and his school team and was concentrating on the men's play.

He had found his Eldorado. Curling was everything to him, even more than a serious job opportunity, although he signed on with the railway to keep the wolves from the door.

By 1979, Hackner had become a force in curling circles around the Lakehead. He had earned a reputation as a solid skip as well as a tenacious partier. The two seemed to go hand-in-hand for the man who had become known as the Iceman. It was curl hard all day, party hard all night.

Hackner didn't look like a wild man. In fact, he seemed almost shy. But when it came to the nightlife, he took on a different persona. He loved to stay up late, drink and tell lies. He enjoyed going out and partying until everyone else had gone home. He had incredible recuperative powers and, to the casual observer, seemed to be able to function on 30 minutes of sleep.

During a bonspiel, an early night for the Hack was 2:00 a.m., but he never let partying interfere with his curling. At that time, he was able to keep the two tracks of his life going at full tilt, without any spillover effect.

In contrast to Hackner was Rick Lang, the man Ed Werenich calls the best curler ever to play the game. Lang was a tiny kid who grew up in a middle-class neighborhood in Thunder Bay. He worked hard at school and was always popular with the crowd in spite of his size. By the time he was heading to high school, he was hardly 100 pounds soaking wet.

Obviously, hockey was not an option for a kid built like a soggy toothpick, so he took to curling and excelled. In 1975, he joined Bill Tetley's team and won the Brier, and returned in 1976, skipping his own team.

In the ensuing years, Hackner and Lang bashed heads along the playdown route. One was always knocking the other out of the picture and it didn't take long before both realized a compromise was in order. But the negotiation was easier said than done. Before the 1978 season, the two talked over the idea of joining forces but couldn't make the numbers fit—both were committed to other players and the friendships involved were stronger than the need for a winning curling team.

After suffering through another year of head-to-head struggles, however, the two decided it was time to work together.

"We were both committed to other teams but we decided to join forces, and each guy could bring one other guy," recalled Lang. "We gave up friendships in order to get a stronger curling team. Up to that point, curling had not been businesslike for us. Although we were dead serious and wanted to win, it had all been true friendship."

But suddenly, the individual urge to win took over. Both realized the pieces were all there, but to make them fit would mean cutting their buddies. It was a matter of putting curling ahead of anything else. Although they seemed to share nothing but curling, the two men held a common goal.

"We went together well because of our passion for the game," Lang remembered. "That was the strongest thing we shared. There's a lot of good athletes in this game but they don't win as much as the guys who really want it. Al and I both shared that same focus."

In the end, Lang had to drop Al Fiskar while Hackner said good-bye to Johnny Salo. (Luckily, the friendships, although shaken at the time, have grown strong once again.)

Two solid players, Kennedy and Nichol, formed the consistent, if not particularly dramatic, front end for Hackner's new team.

The team waltzed through the season, grabbing the Grand Prix title, Thunder Bay's biggest cash bonspiel, and then winning the Northern Ontario title with ease. For Hackner, it was off to the Brier, something that he had been working towards since leaving high school years earlier. Despite the team's good performance, he was not all that optimistic about their chances.

"I thought we had a decent team," Hackner remembered, "but not great. I felt if we batted .500, we would have been quite happy."

But the boys put on a bit of a winning streak, taking their first five games before losing a close one to Folk. And off the ice, they were doing pretty well, too.

On the way to the Brier, Kennedy had read a great deal about the exploits of Paul Gowsell. Despite the press clippings, Kennedy was sure that he was up to the talent—both on and off the ice—of the Gowsell team.

"Bruce definitely had this thing about Gowsell," Hackner said. "He'd read all this stuff that he was a great shotmaker and curler, but more than that, he could out-party anyone. So Bruce said, 'Well, let's check this guy out. He can't be that good.'"

Immediately upon arriving in Calgary, Kennedy, with Hackner and Nichol in tow, located the legendary Gowsell's room and began to drink with him. At first, Gowsell thought it was perfect —another talented team that could keep up with his. This was going to be a good Brier, he must have thought.

But things soon changed. The Thunder Bay boys were on a mission to dethrone Gowsell as the king of the party and they succeeded. After a few late nights in the Alberta team's room, the Northern Ontario squad arrived to find the door locked. Despite their banging, Gowsell was not answering.

"Bruce would stand in the hall and yell at them to open up, but they wouldn't," Hackner recalled with a sly smile. "Then he'd yell real loud, 'Well, let's go down and have one more in our room because these guys are sleeping.' Then we'd go back downstairs and go to bed."

It was the ultimate mind game between two party-hearty teams. Gowsell had met his match, and when the two faced off in the semifinal, Hackner had that one small edge.

After losing the 1980 final to Folk, Hackner returned to the Brier in 1981, full of faith in his team. "When you realize you can play," he stated, "you go out there with a lot more confidence. We just played a lot better, and going into the Brier, we felt we had a shot at winning it. It was a totally different attitude than in '80."

One thing that was not different, however, was the off-ice partying. They kept on drinking and staying out late. They took in the gatherings and then some, usually not getting back to the hotel until just before dawn

"We always liked our beers," the skip remembered. "Even between draws, we'd have a beer or two. Other teams thought that wasn't too good, but we felt that it was what we had always done, so why change now?

"Two beers isn't going to throw you off your game. People were always surprised to see us with beer in front of us, but that was the way we'd been doing it all our lives."

And with no curling until 2:00 p.m., the boys were able to sleep it off and get to the rink in fighting form.

Lang was about the only calming influence on the team of wild ones. He wasn't into the parties, at least not as much as Hackner was. But he didn't seem to mind the others carrying on as long as the team was winning.

"It didn't matter much that we were night and day in terms of lifestyle," Lang said. "Al was a real partier and I wasn't much of one. But that didn't bother me at all in those days. We were both headed in the same direction—it didn't matter how we got there."

The team won its first six games and ended up with a 9–2 record, claiming first place. Everything was unfolding as it should for the Northern Ontario squad. They had suffered through the old Brier adage that you have to lose a championship before you can win it, and they were now ready to claim what was rightfully theirs.

But something went terribly wrong.

In the semifinals, Manitoba's Kerry Burtnyk defeated Bob Ellert of Saskatchewan. If there was one team in the Brier that frightened Hackner, it was Burtnyk's.

"We had a tremendous amount of respect for Kerry's team," Hackner said, admiration still evident in his voice. "We had played them three or four times before the Brier and they were scary."

Terrifying might have been a more appropriate adjective for the youthful Manitoba team. In the province that arguably had the most competitive depth, Burtnyk had put up winning streaks of 40 games, hammering teams sporting sweaters filled with Purple Hearts. The players were fearless on the ice and, while not quite up to the standards of Gowsell, loved to partake in the office adventures that seemed to characterize all of the big curling bonspiels of the period.

That winter, they crossed the country, winning cars and big cheques, while ambling on without a care in the world. And rightly so—they were all young and single, with curling as their shared preoccupation.

On the front end, Ron Kammerlock and Jim Spencer could best be described as extreme. Third man Mark Olson was the rudder on the Good Ship Burtnyk, largely because he didn't drink. And at 22, Burtnyk had transformed from a shy kid into a cocksure skip.

"I don't think they knew how good they were," Hackner remembered. "We had confidence, but we knew we were going to have to play our best to win. And we did—for nine ends."

In that tragic final, the Iceman maneuvered his team into a 4-2 lead going into the final end and appeared on his way to the Brier title. But what happened next was a gut-wrenching scene he described as "a tragic conclusion."

"I remember thinking, all we have to do is peel out and we win," said Lang. "But I tried not to think about that. I tried to block out any thoughts about standing on the podium but they were swirling around in my head."

The game came unglued in an ugly fashion in that fateful 10th. Nichol fanned a hit attempt on a Manitoba guard and Burtnyk quickly buried a stone behind it. Lang then tried to extricate the shot rock but ticked the guard, moving it over about half a foot. Hackner made his attempt at removing the stone but kissed it, pushing it over towards the side board.

"It wasn't in by two inches, it was in by half an inch," Lang said. "It kind of hit the frost and just stopped."

Hackner was about to be sick. "I just looked down at the ice and thought about those three misses, all by a total of less than an inch. I mean, how much more of that last one do I have to hit to get it out? It was painful. When we saw that rock still in the rings, everybody just went numb. Everything just went so very fast after that. We didn't have time to think about things other than we just couldn't believe it was happening."

A slow buzz that had been brewing in the crowd became an excited cheer as Burtnyk went down to the hack to play an open draw for three points and a win. It was an incredible turn of events for Burtnyk—from vanquished to victor in the space of about 10 minutes.

The final stone was perfect, and halfway down the ice, the Manitoba skip went into a jumping victory spasm that only stopped when a teammate grabbed him. For the Thunder Bay team, however, the defeat was sickening.

"We were crushed," remembered Lang. "Kerry's team was great because they showed a lot of emotion, but I didn't know what we were supposed to do. If I knew we were coming back to the Brier the next year, it might not have been so bad, but we were right back to the club playdowns after that. God, it was so far to come back."

But the shock soon wore off. The four stunned curlers packed their gear in silence in the dressing room before Hackner finally spoke: "Where would we be if we'd won?" The answer was obvious and the four silver medalists pranced off to the bar to join the victory celebration.

"We never dwelled on anything very long except a case of beer," summed up Lang.

In 1982, Hackner again rolled through the country during the competitive circuit and again won the Northern Ontario crown. For the third time in three years, he was off to the Brier, and this time, he was going in as the favorite. That feeling was a bit uncomfortable as the team arrived in Brandon, Manitoba.

While sitting in their hotel room the day before play began, the team watched Rod Hunter, from Don Duguid's two-time Brier championship team, being interviewed on Brandon television. Hunter praised the Northern Ontario team. "No one has had a lock on a Brier like this since the Richardsons," Hunter forecasted. "They shouldn't even bother playing it."

For Lang, it was too quick a climb to the top ranks.

"Two years earlier, we walked in against Gowsell and Folk and they don't even know who we are," he said. "Then we're there and they're saying they should give it to us without even playing. Boy, we'd come a long way in two years."

Hackner was out to prove Hunter correct, except that he was relishing playing the games. He made sure he had fun, but this time nothing was done at the expense of the curling.

"It was a real quiet Brier," Lang remembered. "It was also the first Brier with a Patch [the huge bar attached to the curling facility that has become a traditional party place during the competition] but we didn't let Al know there was a Patch until Friday. He walked in there on Friday and his eyes just about fell out of his head. He said, 'What's this!' It was like a kid in a candy store."

After rattling off eight straight wins, the Northern Ontario team lost its last three games but still finished in second place, a game back of British Columbia's Brent Giles. After knocking off Manitoba's Mel Logan in the semi, Hackner was into his third straight final. Unlike the previous two years, however, the team knew if it didn't win this time, the players would be scarred for the rest of their curling lives.

"We were awfully nervous going into the final," Hackner remembered. "We felt we were the better team and we were playing a team that wasn't as strong as Burtnyk, so there wasn't any reason not to win. There was a lot of pressure and no one could eat any lunch. We were thinking a lot about not losing, not about winning."

One of the championship broadcast traditions of the final is an "up-close-and-personal" interview with the team that is shown during breaks by the CBC. As the team was leaving the arena after winning the semi, a producer for the people's network came up and asked if the team could arrive an hour and a half before the next day's final.

Hackner and Lang protested, feeling that an hour and a half was too long to be sitting around. But after much pleading from the staffer, they agreed. For some reason, however, the next day the boys mistakenly showed up two and half hours before game-time.

"We got there at 10:30 a.m. and there was no one around," Lang remembered. "We didn't know what was going on but it was too late to go back and there wasn't enough time to go anywhere else, really."

So the team decided just to wait it out in the rink. But Hackner had forgotten the pass and the security guard on duty, who knew nothing about curling, wouldn't let him in the building. The other three showed a great deal of compassion for their unfortunate skip.

"There was no one around to figure out the story, so we just walked in and left him there," Lang laughed. "Half an hour later, [CBC broadcasters] Don Duguid and Don Whitman came walking in with Al. The guard didn't know who Don and Don were either but Duguid threatened to punch him in the nose if he didn't let them in."

Reunited with his team, Hackner produced a telegram that had arrived just moments before. It read: "Dear Al and team: It's the seventh game of the world series, bottom of the ninth, runner at third, two out, 4-3 Cardinals. Tug McGraw walks to the mound and says to Steve Carlton, 'Isn't this fun?'"

"At first, we thought it was odd," Lang said. "But then we realized the message. It was asking us where we'd rather be—at home watching the Brier final on television with a beer in hand, or out there playing? We knew where we wanted to be."

That message, which came from a friend in Thunder Bay, may have shown them that the pressure they were feeling was all self-imposed. Lang says it set the team's collective mind a bit at ease and allowed the four to have some fun out there.

That fun translated into a victory as the Northern Ontario team finally grabbed its championship with a 7-3 win over British Columbia, thanks in large part to steals of single points in ends six, seven and eight.

Naturally, there was quite a celebration following the game. In fact, the team established a tradition that year by partying right through the night until it was time to leave for the airport the next morning. When they made it back to Thunder Bay, the airport was jammed and a packed hall had been booked for a city-wide celebration.

A few weeks later, the excitement hadn't died down. In a newspaper poll, Hackner was voted as the second-most recognizable man in the Lakehead, after the mayor, and there were even a few calls of "Iceman for Mayor."

10

The Dream Team

While Hackner and his team were taking top honors in the annual bragging contest between Northern and Southern Ontario, a new team was forming in Toronto that would seek to put an end to the north's domination and give the south a bona fide world-class team for the first time since Alfie Phillips, Jr., in 1967.

In 1979, Ed Werenich and Paul Savage had ended a turbulent eight-year partnership that had seen them make it to three Briers and win a plethora of big spiels. Although as players the two fit together as well as Hackner and Lang did, they were both quite fiery. On-ice battles were common, and when the winning stopped, the alliance disintegrated. The break-up wasn't an amicable one, either, as the two bad-mouthed each other around the Avonlea Curling Club.

Savage said that Werenich didn't know how to play at the highest levels, while Werenich shot back that Savage wasn't dedicated enough. It was petty and nasty, although most people felt the two had more in common than they were willing to admit.

They both went their separate ways in 1980, with Werenich ending up playing third for Joe Gurowka, the 1966 Brier runner-up, who would later become one of the Wrench's most hated enemies. That team didn't last long as the styles of the two main members clashed: Gurowka liked to hit while Werenich preferred to draw.

A year later, Werenich finally did what he had wanted to do all along—skip. With his team of Bob Widdis, Jim McGrath and Neil Harrison, he made it to the Ontario final, where fans first got a dose of the Wrench's stubborn attitude.

Before the playdown began, the Ontario Curling Association explained that the play-off method they would use was the same as the new-look Labatt Brier. Confusion arose, however, over a mistake in the printing of the program, which advertised an entirely different procedure regarding tie-breaks.

Werenich was incensed that the OCA couldn't make up its mind and refused to start the first game until the kerfuffle was corrected. While all the other games got under way, he sat behind his sheet, scowling.

Finally, he launched a formal protest by telling one of the OCA officials why he was angry and then began his game. Later, he learned that his protest wasn't being accepted because it had not been made in writing. The Wrench was not amused.

"I was pissed after that," Werenich recalled with some understatement. "I just couldn't believe what was going on."

The OCA, after some waffling, decided to go with the format as advertised in the program, leading many to wonder just how resolute the rules actually were. Werenich certainly instigated some of the outcry.

He got his revenge at the conclusion of the Ontario final, which he won. In the locker room after the game, when Leon Sykes, an OCA official, handed Werenich the Purple Heart, the Wrench took it, turned around and mooned Sykes, saying, "How do you think this would look on my ass, Leon?"

Werenich went on to the Brier in Halifax, posting a 7-4 record and losing a tiebreaker for a play-off spot to Saskatchewan's Bob Ellert. While he was disappointed with that loss, it was clear to Werenich that skip was his position. He was where he should have been from the start, he believed, and now that he had made it to the last rock, he wasn't about to change.

But even Werenich knew that his team needed some more talent if it was going to make it all the way. In 1982, after losing to Bruce Munro of London in the Ontario final, the Wrench called up his old teammate Savage and offered the olive branch.

"I suggested that he come and play vice for me," Werenich said.

"I really didn't know if he'd go for it, but he seemed to like the idea."

In truth, Savage says now, he had always been looking to play vice, but he had never seen anyone for whom he'd feel comfortable throwing third rocks.

The other two members were easy to find. Neil Harrison had been the consummate lead for most of his career, almost to the point of redefining the position. John Kawaja was a hotshot just out of juniors whose confidence surpassed that of the most seasoned veteran. Three years earlier, he had come second in the Canadian Junior Championship.

The new lineup became known as the Dream Team—although to some it was a nightmare.

Together, the four had as much ego as any team in curling. They were pretty darn sure of themselves as individuals; as a team, they were insufferable. They were way beyond cocky—they were downright nasty.

News of the team spread quickly through Toronto curling circles and opinion was divided: either they would win everything or they would kill each other by Christmas. The four players figured it would be the former.

"I knew there was something special," Werenich said. "We knew this team had a chance. There was a fair amount of criticism when we put it together. People were saying, 'It's four skips, it'll never work.' Everybody knew there was a lot of talent, but I wasn't concerned about the personalities or attitudes. I knew the chemistry would be there."

And it quite obviously was. The plump little firefighter and his cast of characters ripped across the country topping the money list with $40,000 in cash, four cars and four Purple Hearts.

The 1983 Brier was held in Sudbury and a large group of Werenich supporters made the trip. They were ready to see Ontario win its first Brier since Alf Phillips, Jr., had won in 1967, and the Wrench felt likewise.

"I don't know if we were the favorites going in," he said, "but we felt it was our Brier to win."

After their first four games, the boys were at 3-1, suffering a loss at the hands of Ed Lukowich's Alberta entry. But morale was still high and there was nothing but optimism.

Like Hackner's team, the Wrench's rink added the nightlife to its Brier schedule. Harrison, Kawaja and Savage especially loved to go out cavorting and carousing, while the Wrench preferred to sleep.

"Eddie loved his sleep," Savage said. "We'd go out and take it easy until Eddie said it was time for bed. He'd leave and we'd go a bit wild."

Paul was also a bit of a party-pooper, especially when it came to the end of the evening. When the night was over, he wanted to go to bed.

"I didn't mind having a nightcap," he said, "but I liked to have it alone, in my bed, watching the news. I wasn't like the other guys who would come back from the party and then have 40 guys sitting around in the room."

The players and their wives enjoyed giving Savage the gears about this attitude and teased him about "being on the rag." During one evening at dinner, when Paul was being particularly whiny, Barb Savage and Jane Harrison stuffed a sanitary napkin down his pants to press home their point.

Paul took offense at the joke and stormed out, to the delight of everyone else at the table. He left the players' hotel and found another where a number of friends from Toronto were staying and joined their party. Savage was having such a good time there that he ended up spending the night in his friends' suite.

Back at the players' hotel, Barb Savage was becoming concerned. Their dinner had wrapped up and she had returned to the room, expecting to find Paul. After an hour passed without any sign of the Ontario third, she began looking for him and soon enlisted others on the floor—including a funeral director from Kingston and a minister. But that search, too, failed to turn up any sign of her husband.

The tears flowed and the worry grew.

"I didn't know where he was and I was thinking I'd just cost the team a chance at the Brier," remembered Barb.

When daylight came, there was still no sign of Paul, and Barb was a wreck. To add to the problem, she and Jane Harrison had agreed to be interviewed on a local television station early that morning. Barb wasn't looking forward to it and decided to have a couple of drinks to calm her nerves. By the time the limo came to pick the women up, Barb had downed four caesars and was a mess.

But the show went on anyway, much to the torment of the interviewer. Never before has a television talk-show host worked so hard to pull answers out of a guest. While Jane would babble out the responses to questions such as, "Is it tough sitting in the stands watching your husbands?" Barb was almost comatose. Her face was puffy from crying and drinking, and she was in no mood to play patsy to any bubble-headed interviewer.

"It must be exciting to come out to the Brier for a week," remarked the interviewer.

"Yes," said Barb.

"You've been to a number of Briers, haven't you, Barb?" tried the host again.

"Yes," she said.

Thus it went on for 10 excruciating minutes. (To this day, the tape is one of the most-watched at the Savage household, and it usually leaves everyone who has seen it in tears.)

Luckily for Barb, when she came back from the television studio, her husband had returned, none the worse for wear, but wearing a big smile.

Not much ever upset Paul Savage, except when he was about to step out onto the ice.

"Paul was the Glen Hall of curling," Werenich said. "When the bagpipes started, Paul would have his head buried in the garbage can. Whenever he did that, we never lost. When Paul hurled, he curled."

And that week, they curled. The three players in front of Werenich were so good, the skip rarely had to make a tough shot.

"It was so easy," the Wrench proclaimed, "it was like cheating. I threw guards all week."

The Ontario four tied for first place with Alberta, but were relegated to the semifinal because of their loss to Lukowich earlier in the week. That pitted them against the veteran Bernie Sparkes.

Suddenly, the team that had been bursting with confidence all year began to twitch. Playing against the three-time Brier winner Sparkes put some question marks in the collective mind.

But those doubts were overcome in what curling observers remember as perhaps the greatest game in the history of the Canadian championship.

"It was probably the most incredible curling game I've ever

been involved in," Werenich said, his voice still filled with excitement. "I was sort of fired up playing Bernie because I always thought their team was a bit smug with their straw brooms and all."

But it was the Wrench who emerged satisfied, especially after completing a sensational triple takeout in the sixth end. It was a shot that clinched the game and sent the crowd into bursts of cheering that nearly tore the roof off the Sudbury Arena.

Even the veteran Sparkes knew he had seen an extraordinary game, although he still regards it as a tough loss. But 20 minutes after it was over, he went to Werenich's dressing room and congratulated him. "That was the most incredible display of shot-making I've ever seen," he said, shaking Werenich's hand.

The Sudbury Brier was the first time the CBC used wireless microphones on the players. It opened up a whole new world for viewers, allowing them to hear exactly what was being discussed before the shot was played.

The players had to keep reminding themselves about the microphones, however. Watch the language, the CBC told them. For Lukowich, it wasn't a problem. But for Werenich it was just impossible. Discussing a shot with Savage, the Wrench said he would release his rock on the narrow side of the broom, "and let the boys sweep the piss out of it." In the mobile studio outside the arena, the CBC technicians fell out of their chairs, some stunned, others howling.

But it is doubtful that many viewers turned off their televisions at that point because the game was enthralling. Thanks to a miss by Alberta third Neil Houston, Werenich had taken two in the first end and was playing everything defensively after that, hitting the majority of Alberta stones.

"I had no intentions of peeling out the game from there," Werenich admitted. "But after about the fifth end, I could sense they were getting frustrated, so I said to Paul, 'Why don't we see if we can peel for a few ends?'"

And the Ontario team became stronger with every end. Finally, in the 10th, down three points, Lukowich had one shot remaining and only a prayer of getting three. They held a team meeting at the hog line and that's when viewers heard the second microphone gem.

Alberta third Mike Chernoff surveyed the hopeless situation and then turned to his skip: "Well, what do you think?"

"I think these guys just won the Brier," was Lukowich's succinct reply.

And so they had. The Dream Team had lived up to its potential and had won the Canadian championship, surviving two tightly contested matches to do it.

Their victory led to a wild celebration, beginning with Don Kawaja, John's father, cajoling the manager of a Sudbury liquor store to open up and sell them some champagne. And the party didn't end on the evening of the win. While being driven home, Paul drank 24 beers between Sudbury and Toronto.

"I bought 12, drank them and had to stop in Parry Sound for 12 more," he laughed.

As the winners hailed from one of Canada's media centers, the team became the darling of the press. The players were sought out for interviews time and time again, and set up for a full rubber-chicken circuit.

At the time, Werenich describes himself as quite shy in front of a crowd. That may be hard to believe now, given his reputation as the most outspoken curler on record, but with the media demands, he gradually emerged from his shell. It did take some time, however. At a victory party at Avonlea shortly after the Brier win, the emcee asked Eddie to say a few words.

"I was so nervous, I just decided to go up and tell the dirtiest joke I knew," he said. "I figured I'd never get asked to say anything again." The joke was about a man obsessed with curling who visits the doctor. "The doctor asks him, 'What do you think of when you see a woman's breasts?' 'Oh, that's easy,' says the man. 'Double takeout.' 'What do you think of when you see her belly button?' the doctor asked. 'Oh, a draw to the button,' the man said. 'And what do you think of when you look a little lower?' said the doctor. 'Oh, I've got three of them on my team.'"

In 1984, it looked as though the Dream Team was going to waltz back to another Brier title. At the start of the year, they continued winning at a torrid pace, including a $60,000 first prize—the richest in curling to that point—at the World Challenge in

Calgary. By the time the playdowns for the Brier began, the squad had pocketed more than $80,000.

But some suggested success was going to their heads. They were jokingly referred to as Team Humble, and as columnist Ken Thompson pointed out in the *Ontario Curling Report*, "Just like the old song, it's hard to be humble when you're perfect in every way. And this team is as close to perfection as any we've ever seen."

Success for the Dream Team came at a price. They won the Ontario title again, but arrived at Victoria drained and with team morale at a new low. They were carping at each other, and when they took to the ice, things didn't go that well. They started off a lowly 1–3 and seemed to be beaten before they had begun.

After moving their record to 2–3 with an ugly win against New Brunswick, the team decided it needed to get away from the rink for a while. The weather in Victoria was beautiful and balmy, and so Werenich, Harrison and Kawaja decided to play golf. Somehow, the CBC got wind of the plan and sent a camera crew to tape the high-profile curlers as they played their round.

On the first hole, with the cameras rolling, Werenich decided to ham it up. He addressed the ball, waggled the club and then said, to no one in particular, "Gee, I don't know whether to play a fade or a draw here."

Without missing a beat, Harrison bleated back, "Better play the fade, Eddie, you haven't made a draw all week."

Despite its poor play, the team was still up to its usual antics. The four came up with a scam on Ed Lukowich that nearly gave the great curler a stroke. Earlier in the year, the team had been playing in Vernon, British Columbia, and had run up against Lukowich, who had left his 1983 team and was playing third for Frank Morissette. At one point in the game, the Ontario boys accused Lukowich of high-siding a rock while sweeping, an illegal move. Some heated words were exchanged but the matter was put to rest before the end of the game.

The next week, playing in Kamloops, the two teams met up in the hotel lobby and decided to have dinner together. That may have seemed like a good idea at the time, but the dinner slowly turned into a drunken war of words over the sweeping incident.

"The more we had to drink," remembered Savage, "the more heated the argument got. It got to the point where Lukowich said to me, 'If you call me a cheater once more, I'm going to belt you.' Then we began to throw slurs at each other. He had written a book [*The Curling Book*] and I was cutting that up, and he was cutting mine [*Hack to House*] up."

At one point in the taunts back and forth, Lukowich said to Savage, "Well, I plagiarized some stuff from your book." For some reason that statement stuck in Savage's mind, and when they learned that Lukowich was going to join them at the Brier in Victoria, the Dream Team came up with a scam.

Savage asked a lawyer friend of his to write up a fake letter informing Lukowich that he was being sued for $80,000 for plagiarism. At breakfast one morning during the Brier, Savage arranged for a bellhop to deliver the letter to the Alberta skip, while the Ontario team watched on from a booth on the other side of the restaurant.

Lukowich received the letter and read it over. His face turned white as he handed it to his teammates. He just couldn't believe what was happening. The other players on his team, who were all in on the gag, were trying not to snicker as Lukowich reread the letter one more time. Finally, just before he fell apart, he spotted the instigators—doubled over in laughter across the restaurant.

The golf and the practical joke seemed to be a good tonic for the team, because it won six of the next seven games and squeaked into a tiebreaker. After winning that match and then another tiebreaker, the players found themselves in the semifinal against Lukowich. They beat him 6-3.

In the space of a few days, the Dream Team had shown its mettle by going from also-ran to finalist. With the momentum building, Werenich and the boys seemed ready to take another Brier. At least, that's what the fans and media wanted to believe.

But despite all the wins, the team was still struggling. Werenich's advantage was his aggressive play, and the ice in Victoria wasn't cooperating. It was so dead straight that it became almost impossible to bury a rock behind a guard. In the team's two-year run, it had gained a reputation for going on the attack right from the coin toss.

"In the first end against a lot of teams, the other guys would throw one in the rings and Eddie would call for a corner guard," recalled Savage. "The other team would just wilt at the prospect of having to battle us. No one had seen a team play with as much confidence as us."

And with the tremendous team of shotmakers lined up behind the skip, they rarely got into trouble.

But their aggressive play was useless on the straight Victoria ice. It benefited the style of Mike Riley, a Manitoba player who could be extremely good—or extremely bad.

Riley had joined up with Brian Toews, John Helston and Russ Wookey without any real goal other than playing well. They were all friends, and even if they didn't do well, they would still enjoy themselves. But, earlier in the year, they knocked off Werenich in a big bonspiel in Winnipeg and began to realize that maybe they were better than just a good club team.

In fact, they went on to beat Werenich three times that year, surprising even themselves. With each big win, they chalked up confidence; after all, any team that manages to make it to the Brier from Manitoba must be doing something right.

Riley had finished in first place with an 8-3 record and gained a spot in the final. When it became apparent he would be playing Werenich for all the marbles, he wasn't about to knuckle under.

Riley challenged Werenich in the final, his play supported by the ice conditions. As Savage admitted later, on the few occasions during the game when the Dream Team overcame the straight ice and played aggressively, Riley did not panic.

"The fact that he didn't go crazy when we went to our game may have had a psychological effect on us," Savage said. "But what really gave it to them was Eddie's miss in the third."

The entire season for the Dream Team disintegrated as Werenich's final stone in the third end sailed by the Manitoba rock.

"I just floated it," Werenich stated matter-of-factly. "I knew I'd missed it as soon as I let it go. We never threatened them after that, never got it going even though we had chances."

And so, although the contest lasted 10 ends, it was already all but over. The Dream Team continued on for a few more years, but without the winning, it soon came apart at the seams. Werenich and Savage returned to their subtle sniping. Kawaja became more interested in the nightlife than the curling and Harrison just tried to hold the pieces together.

Life at the top of the curling world is difficult to maintain.

"Every game, the opposition is gunning for you," Kawaja reflected in later years. "It doesn't matter if you are playing against four grandmothers, they want to beat you because you are the champions. You can only sustain the intensity at that level for so long. And when you throw in all the time off from work and family, you just can't expect to keep it going forever. If you're not winning, it's not any fun anymore either."

By 1986, the team was a shadow of its former self. The splits in the ranks became gaping, especially between John—the only single member—and the rest of the team.

"John basically partied himself off the team," Savage said. "At one spiel in London, we were all going back to the hotel and John got out of the car and took off with Hackner. We knew that was trouble. The next morning, we were on the ice waiting for him to show up [the team was staying in a hotel attached to the curling club] to start the game, and he walked out looking like death with Clorets in one hand and Rolaids in the other. He looked at us and said, 'Come on, guys, we've got to start playing better.' We all just howled at that."

In the end, the four decided to part ways and stay friends. They knew that any more time together could do irreparable damage. They simply played their last game and split.

The Dream Team had brought curling into a new age of offense-dominated strategy. Their style and their savvy were perfect for television. The fact that they were from Canada's biggest city also helped focus attention on the roaring game. But above all, the combination of their talent and their personalities assured them a spot in Brier history.

11

The Hack Came Back

Nineteen eighty-five saw the return of a familiar face to the Brier. Al Hackner, after a two-year absence, was back representing Northern Ontario at the Canadian championship in Moncton, New Brunswick. He brought along Rick Lang, but Kennedy and Nichol were gone.

In their place were two fresh-faced youngsters with a lot of verve and energy. These qualities were precisely what had made the young pair attractive to the veteran skip and third.

"In 1983, after winning, we just ran out of gas," said Hackner. "In 1984, we had a good season and almost made it to the Brier, but we still weren't as strong as before."

The difference was the motivation of the front end. Kennedy and Nichol had slogged through the wars for too long and were now, like so many champion front ends before them, losing the edge.

"It was tough to get them to practice," Hackner recalled. "It was also tough to get them fired up; it was obvious they had lost their desire. Rick and I were still working hard so we felt there wasn't much point in practicing if they weren't. After the '84 season, I said we had to make a change and Rick agreed."

Their first choice was Bill and Jim Adams, twin brothers who had been successful juniors. But the Adamses declined, largely because they wanted to head their own team. Down the depth chart, Hackner and Long found Ian Tetley and Pat Perroud, two solid players who were only too eager to join up with the heavy hitters.

Tetley, the son of Bill Tetley with whom Lang had won the Brier in 1975, was a fiery, opinionated player who loved to throw big weight. Perroud was quieter, more laid-back than his friend, but he had a will to win. Together, they made a good combination, and what they lacked in experience, they made up for in desire.

Very quickly, the team gelled and became an intimidating unit. "At the start of the season, I wouldn't have thought we were capable of winning, but I found it amazing how quickly they came around," remembered Lang.

The team cashed in at almost every stop on the circuit, and then advanced to the Northern Ontario playdowns where they won the Purple Hearts. Off to Moncton they went, the front end with stars in its eyes, the top end with some anticipation.

"Pat and Ian had fit in so well," Lang commented, "going into the Brier, strictly shooting-wise, I thought this was the best team I had ever played on. It might not have been the whole package, but the shooting was great."

No matter how good they were, however, absolutely everybody that year was being humbled by a buzz saw named Pat Ryan. He skipped an Alberta team that walked through the round robin with a perfect 11-0 record, thanks to a devastating, molar-rattling takeout game.

Ryan would play hard early in the game, establish a lead and then hit everything in sight. His strategy wasn't popular with the crowd, but it allowed him to win.

Meanwhile, Hackner was toiling along, winning games in ugly ways.

"We started slowly," said Lang, "and we never got fast. The whole week was a struggle."

But in the end, they wound up a distant second with a 7-4 record. In the semifinal, they continued to get by and were handed a win on a silver platter when Saskatchewan's Eugene Hritzuk messed up down the stretch.

That victory put them into the final game, which provided one of the most exciting finishes in Brier history.

Playing Ryan was an unenviable task. Before the Hackner

squad even stepped onto the ice, they knew they could not afford to get down to the Alberta team. The Northern Ontario four's strength was their aggressive play, which often opened them up to surrendering a deuce, but against Ryan this strategy would spell instant death.

As the game went on, however, Hackner struggled. He was down 4–2 after six and was playing so poorly that he felt it might be over at any point.

"After seven ends, I thought if Ryan had been a little more aggressive, he could have just buried us," Hackner conceded. "But with the game he was playing, he just kept running. By doing that, he kept us in the game."

Lang concurred with his skip. "It was easily Ryan's worst game of the week. He should have been up about 7–2 going into the last end but they were only up two."

Against most teams, that lead might not have been insurmountable, but versus Ryan, it may as well have been 50 points.

"We knew the stats," Lang said. "They had put up some amazing numbers. They had only given up one two-ender all week and hadn't allowed a steal. And we all knew that. They were just awesome and we had been struggling. Let's just say the odds weren't in our favor. Not only did we have to take two, but then steal one, too. And not only did they have to miss, but we had to make them all. It just hadn't happened all week."

Notwithstanding his stellar record and the fact that he was leading going into the last end, Ryan felt something funny was bound to occur.

"I expected something silly to happen because it had been happening in Brier finals during that time," he stated. "Hackner had it happen to him and it just seemed that you could kind of count on something strange happening."

His premonition was correct. As the 10th end unfolded, the hitting machine began misfiring. For most of the end, it seemed Hackner would get his deuce, despite the fact that Ryan was doing everything possible to keep him from the task.

But when he came to throw his last brick, Ryan was confident he was about to win.

"There was only one shot I could make that would just about guarantee it and that was the hit-and-roll about a foot and a half," he said. "If I made that, it didn't appear that there was any shot that he would have."

Hackner disagreed. As Ryan prepared for his rock, he and Lang talked over the possibilities. There was a long raise or the chance of a double. Both, however, were long shots. "Some of the shots we were talking over were next to impossible," Hackner admitted, "but they were there. We were going to have a shot no matter what he did."

As Ryan sat in the hack, he was staring at a corner guard on his left, a Hackner stone open in the corner of the four-foot, which he was trying to hit, another Hackner stone at the top of the 12-foot, and one of his own at the back of the eight-foot. If he could hit and roll behind the corner to sit two, he believed the game would be over.

Ryan made his hit-and-roll, and walked down the ice with his broom held straight up in the air and a smile beaming across his face. His teammates congratulated him, second player Don Walchuck was leaping all over the sheet, and a photographer ran out on the ice to get the victory shot.

"After I threw it, I thought I had made the roll I needed. From the angle where I was looking at it, I had rolled perfectly behind the guard so that you couldn't see the outside edge of the shot. But I slid down the side of the sheet. From the center, looking over, there was a fraction of the rock open. From my perspective, it looked as though I had made the shot. But actually, I hadn't—I had lined it up."

From behind the sheet, Hackner saw the opportunity immediately. If he could navigate past the corner guard and hit all that he could see—about a half inch—the double was automatic and he would score his two.

"As soon as he rolled, I knew what we were playing," the Iceman stated. "They were acting like the game was over. Obviously they couldn't see the line. But it took a long time to call the shot. We had to get everybody calmed down and get the photographers off the ice."

Hackner and Lang never saw Ryan walk down the ice with his broom in the air—they were too busy picking out the ice for their last-chance shot. But they, like all curlers, know that celebrating before the end of the game is a bad omen. It's like asking for disaster, and Ryan was about to have it dumped all over him.

Although the odds on the final shot were long, there was something in the Northern Ontario team's favor: they knew the ice. Hackner had played three shots down that exact part of the ice in that end, including his first rock, a split.

"It was an extremely tough shot," Hackner remembered. "I'd made shots like that before in club games, razzler-dazzler shots to win games, but never in the position we were in—an arena full of people, the Brier on the line. I just said to myself, 'If I'm ever going to throw one more razzler-dazzler, let it be now.'"

Strangely, the teammates said little. Hackner deliberately made his way down the ice and went through his normal pre-shot routine. As he cleaned his rock off, he looked at Pat and told him and Ian that they were playing the double, just as casually as if it was a Saturday afternoon tag draw.

"My only thought process was to tell myself not to point it," Hackner recalled. "I told myself not to force the shot, just let it happen."

Behind the sheet, Ryan nervously looked on, telling third Gord Trenchie, "He's going to make this."

Hackner slid out with his famous upright delivery and cleanly released the rock. Immediately, Lang yelled for Perroud and Tetley not to touch it. The ice was so straight, jumping on it quickly may have caused it to back up. As the rock reached the hog line, it was obvious to everybody in the now deathly silent arena that the stone was very close. Lang gave two quick thrusts with his broom, urging the rock to curl just a tiny bit more and then— pandemonium.

"When it made contact with the first one, I knew he had it," said Lang. "When it hit the second one . . . there's never been a better moment in a curling arena."

The roar of the crowd could be heard back in Thunder Bay. "It went right through my body," Lang remembered. "I've never felt anything like that before."

Never before had someone played such a dramatic shot at such a critical moment. Yet Hackner slid down the sheet past Ryan and whispered quietly, "Sorry."

Lang was also trying to conceal his understandable excitement. A smirk was coming close to breaking into a full-fledged smile as he looked at his skip and said, "Nice shot, skipper. Now how the hell are we going to steal one?"

The players on both teams were now overwhelmed by the excitement in the arena. "I remember thinking, 'How are we ever going to settle down and play this end?'" Lang said. "Al and I got together with Pat and Ian to try and get them back in the game. It was a big shot but we still had another end."

That was precisely what Ryan was thinking.

"I wasn't rattled at all," he said. "They may have prolonged it one more end, but it's over—we're still going to win. That was how I was looking at it. I think my team was the same except for Gord. I don't know what was going through his head."

As play for the final end began, the crowd was still buzzing. And not only the spectators were feeling the effects of the big shot.

"I was so nervous after that I could hardly get my foot in the hack to start the next end because it was shaking so much," said Perroud.

The first half of the end was played clean, but when Trenchie went to throw his rocks, they blew up in his hand. He missed both, leaving two guards in play, and Hackner pounced. By the time Ryan came to throw the final stone, he was looking at a cold draw to a piece of the four-foot to beat out a Hackner rock that was shot. Hackner watched quietly to see where Ryan put the broom down. He knew that if the Alberta skip threw it an inch outside the four-foot circle, the rock wouldn't curl. As well, the intended path was close to a dangerous part of the ice for judging weight. The stone could very easily hit the slide path and race through the rings.

Sure enough, Ryan placed his broom in the straight spot.

"When the broom went down, I felt our chances were extremely good," Hackner said. "I didn't even think he was going to hit the rings. When it came across the hog line, I thought it was in the hack."

But the stone slowed ever so gracefully as it hit the circles. Lang, who usually handles the sweeping, just stood and watched, transfixed by the final rock. Sensing that Lang wasn't going to make it as the stone crossed the tee line, Hackner jumped out and swept it.

"When I looked down at the rock, I could see we were shot," Hackner said. "It was sort of a delayed feeling of 'I think we got it.'"

But the Iceman wasn't jumping in the air just yet. He straightened up to find himself swarmed by Ian Tetley bounding through the rings. Tetley's shoe landed about a foot from Ryan's rock just seconds after it had stopped.

Hackner quickly lassoed his overjoyed second, pulling him away from the circles as quickly as you could say Labonte.

"Ian," he barked. "What are you doing? You almost kicked that rock. Settle down, let's measure first, then we'll jump."

Looking back on his reaction, Hackner realizes that he may have snuffed out Tetley's excitement, but for good reason. "Sure, I probably spoiled the moment for him, but it would have been even worse if he'd kicked the rock. I think I saved his life."

For Tetley, it was a painful moment. He later confided to Perroud that Hackner had ruined the victory for him.

In fact, it was a strange victory for many involved. Lang, for one, was almost remorseful.

"There was almost a feeling of guilt towards Ryan," he admitted. "I really struggled with it after the win because of the situation with the teams. I never would have felt that way if we had been 11–0 and he was 7–4. But I really struggled with how to feel. I just didn't know how to react. They were the best team out there all week, the best team for nine ends of the final and then one shot and an extra end and we robbed them. We knew how Ryan's team felt because it had happened to us [in 1981]. It really took something away from winning."

But Hackner was once again on top of the world, and there was another world-class celebration. It lasted all night and into the next day when the teams all left for the airport. Since many of the squads were on the same flight to Toronto, Eugene Hritzuk hoped to continue the party in the air and had taken special precautions. He and his team arrived at the airport toting a large garbage can that was all taped up. When security guards asked them what was inside, they said it was lobster on ice.

But the grounds staff told the curlers that the can was too big to go on the plane. Hritzuk, undaunted, ripped off the top and displayed about 100 beers on ice that he had hoped to distribute on the flight. Then, at 10:00 in the morning, he began handing them out to anyone who wanted one, instigating an impromptu beer bash in the terminal. The watchful airport security, knowing full well that their guests were the Brier curlers, gave them some leniency. In half an hour, they would all be gone anyway.

There is a saying among Brier curlers that you have to lose one before winning. It had happened to Folk and Hackner and happened again in 1986, when Ed Lukowich grabbed the laurels in Kitchener. Lukowich had won a Brier before, in 1978. That year, he threw skip rocks although Mike Chernoff called the game. He had lost in 1983 and been a semifinalist in 1984. But he was hungry for another title when he arrived in Kitchener the March of 1986.

Some people consider Ed Lukowich, during his prime between 1978 and 1986, to have been the best ever to throw the stone. He also had a strong mind when it came to strategy. "When he got into his game," said one former teammate, "he was in his own little world out there. There could be bombs dropping all around him and he wouldn't know it."

Curling has been Ed Lukowich's world for most of his life. He has never held what could be called a steady job, preferring instead to try something new every five or six years or so. If a few more of his business ventures had been successful, he might have been called an entrepreneur. Over the years, he has been a teacher, a car salesman, and the owner of a curling shop; he's operated a mail-order business and even managed a roller hockey team. But despite all the changes, Lukowich has always landed on his feet. Indeed, he has done quite well for himself.

The main reason for his varied work record is that Lukowich has never let business stand in the way of his curling. That philosophy has helped him on the ice, but it has probably not given him much security. Still, it's hard to argue with success. He has been a world champion, authored three curling books, won hundreds of thousands of dollars in spiels around the world and, most recently, become commissioner of the fledgling World Curling Tour, a professional circuit of cashspiels.

In 1986, Lukowich was coming off a sensational year on the cash circuit. He and his team of John Ferguson, Neil Houston and

Brent Syme had meshed as a unit. At 40, Lukowich was the elder statesman on the team and seemed somewhat eccentric to the younger three. Lukowich's peculiarities didn't faze Ferguson and Houston, however—they had both played for Paul Gowsell, the king of eccentricity, who had hung up his slider. And what did it matter as long as Eddie was making everything?

The team's success had something to do with taking a page from Rick Folk's book. They had gone almost exclusively to the garbage game in a province full of hitters. Lukowich loved to play quiet bumps and freezes, and with his talented team supporting him, the job became much easier.

They handily won the Alberta title and went on to southern Ontario for the Brier where, thanks in part to a lackluster lineup, they became the favorites.

Lukowich curled extremely well in Kitchener, making plenty of the kind of clutch shots that had earned him the name Cool Hand Luke. The Alberta rink rolled out to a strong lead, winning its first nine games, and were loose. Lukowich combined that success in the arena with some fun off the ice as well; on a nightly basis, he headed out to the famously enormous bar in Kitchener named Lulu's, where he enjoyed himself until the wee hours. His appearance there became so regular that newspapers started referring to him as Ed Luluwich.

While he was having fun, many of the other teams were not so happy. Most of their displeasure was caused by the strong arm of the officials, who were making their presence felt for the first time in Brier play. Two CCA umpires sat at the hog lines and, like line judges in tennis, called violators who failed to release the rock in time. The watchdogs pulled 47 rocks from play, and were soon dubbed Hansen's Henchmen, after Warren Hansen, the Brier's head official. At every game, there were loud boos from the crowd and calls of "Let them play."

The players were incensed at this rigorous officiating. After all, every pulled rock gave the non-offending team two consecutive shots.

But the officials didn't faze the Albertans. Never one to disappoint on the curling ice, Lukowich finished a strong 9-2, tied with Ontario's Russ Howard, who was appearing in just his second Brier.

Lukowich received the bye to the final thanks to a tremendous round-robin victory over Howard's team, but a rematch was set up after Howard knocked off B.C.'s Barry McPhee in the semi-final.

The final was another classic matchup decided by two shots, one in the seventh and one in the ninth. In the seventh, Howard's second, Tim Belcourt, fanned a hit that eventually led to an Alberta steal of one. Two ends later, Howard had a chance to get two and take a 4-3 lead heading home. But his attempt at a hit-and-stick turned into a hit-and-roll from the rings, giving him only one.

"We just overswept that stone," Howard admitted later. "It was a panic sweep—we yelled on nerves and it never got to the face."

The crucial miss allowed Lukowich an open draw with his last rock in the 10th to take the title. This time, the win was all Eddie's. He had skipped, he had called the game and he had led his team to victory.

"I've been saying for the past three months that this is the best team in the world," Lukowich told reporters after his win. "Now, hopefully, I won't have to say that anymore."

Russ Howard hoped to continue the lose-one-win-one pattern in 1987 in Edmonton. He did not storm through Ontario as he had a year earlier. Instead, he took a more casual approach, playing in only a few spiels before Christmas. And then in the playdowns, disaster struck the team that had reached the Canadian final only a year earlier. It was knocked off by club teams and thrown into Ontario's Challenge Round, a last-chance dogfight with as many as 32 teams battling for one spot in the provincial final.

Howard somehow triumphed over that predicament and then knocked off the Wrench in the Ontario final to climb back to the 1987 Brier. He had survived a year of torment after losing the Brier to Lukowich in 1986. "That was the worst I'd ever felt in curling," Howard admitted. "I kind of had the feeling that it might have been my last chance to win and we threw it away. Of course, the whole world was watching you do that, too, and for a couple of months after, I was reminded of it."

That disappointment fueled Howard's determination the following year. He was not about to let another chance slip away. After an opening-round loss to British Columbia's Bernie Sparkes, the Ontario team of Howard, his brother Glenn, Tim Belcourt and Kent Carstairs won five straight. Experience was paying off.

"A year earlier, if we had lost to Bernie, we might have fallen apart," Howard said. "But we knew it was just one game in a long week."

By week's end, Team Howard sat atop the standings at 9-2. Once again, they were one win away from all the marbles.

And the opponent was a familiar face—Bernie Sparkes. Sparkes had finished at 8-3 and disposed of Newfoundland's Mark Noseworthy in the semi. He was looking to become just the fourth curler (joining Ernie, Sam and Arnold Richardson) with four Brier victories, after notching three as a front-end player for Ron Northcott in the 1960s.

In the final, it did look as though Sparkes was going to join that exclusive club. He led his team to a 7-6 lead after nine and seemed in control. But in the 10th, something went wrong. Instead of keeping everything clear, Sparkes let a tangle of rocks develop and then, by his own admission, he blew his final two stones.

"I just went brain-dead on my last two calls," he said later with regret. "Looking at it now, I made the wrong calls—I don't know what I was thinking."

Howard, with his last rock to come, was looking at a hit to score an incredible five points. That type of shot may have seemed too good to be true for the golf pro from Penetanguishene, Ontario. All he really wanted was to ensure his deuce, but that was still not an easy task.

"It was the toughest shot I've ever had to throw," Howard said. "At first we were going to throw a nose hit but we were afraid we might jam it [back on a B.C. stone] and only get one. So we decided to just hit half of it and that made the shot twice as hard."

Also adding to the pressure was knowing what would happen if he missed.

"On the way down to the hack, I tried not to let it enter my mind, but I couldn't help thinking what people would be saying if we didn't make the shot," Howard said. "If I missed that, I'd probably be bowling now."

But Howard is still curling. He executed the last brick to perfection, grabbed five points and vanquished the runner-up demons.

For Sparkes, the defeat was crushing. "To me, that was the hardest loss I'd ever had," he said. "It was so difficult to accept because you'd hoped for this your whole life. As a kid you'd dreamed of throwing the last rock of the Brier to win, and then all of a sudden it's there for you, and it doesn't happen. I found it really hard to take."

Sparkes curled competitively the next year but his heart wasn't in it. Losing to Howard sapped him of the desire, ending his brilliant career. "I had my run at it," he said. "When you get there that many times and have that many chances at it, the Big Shooter upstairs is telling me something."

In the win, however, Howard couldn't help but realize the magnitude of the Brier final as well, and years later, he tried to change his focus.

"It's such a big game," he pointed out. "Everything rides on it. No one remembers who loses but we all know the winners. Finishing second is not that bad when you think of how many people start out. Ever since that game, I've tried to look at it that way. [This attitude] might have actually hurt me because I might not get as pumped up going into the final. In the back of my mind, I don't think there's any shame in finishing second."

12

The Ryan Express

Another participant in the 1987 Brier was Pat Ryan. Although devastated by his loss in 1985, Ryan returned to the Brier in his hometown of Edmonton. Randy Ferby was now handling the third's duties, while Roy Hebert took over at lead. The team was looking forward to playing at home and getting the crowd's support.

Ryan knew that many of the recent Brier winners had suffered defeats before victory. If that trend held true, Ryan's team was certainly in line for a championship after its harrowing loss two years earlier.

As the hopes of almost all Albertans were squarely on the Ryan Express, the players felt the screws tighten just a little. But the team was already quite nervous.

"The expectations in that arena were that we were going to win the Brier," Ryan remembered. "We felt that, too, because we had knocked off who I felt was the best team in the country—Ed Lukowich—to get there."

But somehow, things slipped away. After an opening-round 10–1 victory over Nova Scotia, Ryan lost to the lowly Territories, and later to Prince Edward Island and Newfoundland—teams to which Alberta rinks simply did not lose. It was like the Montreal Canadiens getting beaten by a peewee team. The unruly redneck fans didn't appreciate the Ryan squad's performance. They expected winners.

As the record of the home team slipped further from a play-off spot, the taunting began. The catcalls started with a few yahoos yelling from the nosebleed section, but quickly escalated to a chorus of boos at Ryan's every move.

"It didn't matter what we did," Ryan said. "If the other team made an open hit-and-stick, the place erupted. If we did it, nothing. There were some catcalls coming out of there and then people started yelling personal things out. A lot of pretty negative personal comments were being yelled at us and they were done intentionally at the wrong times."

Such as when they were at the top of a backswing, or trying to concentrate on a pressure shot. It was a humbling experience, nothing like what Ferby and Hebert, two Brier rookies, had imagined the week would be.

"It wasn't that enjoyable because you felt that, when you walked out onto the ice, people were going to start throwing tomatoes at you," commented Ryan. "We wanted to play in the Brier, it wasn't that we were there to entertain people. We didn't think playing in the Brier meant we had to be a dart board for all these comments. We really weren't playing that bad, either."

Ryan ended up with a 6-5 record. But more importantly, he strengthened his resolve. If he ever got back to the Brier, he would tune out the crowd, he told himself. He would focus only on the job at hand.

Pat Ryan was born in Winnipeg, Manitoba, into a sporting family. His father encouraged him to play all kinds of sports and curling was one of them. Luckily, the club he joined, the Assiniboine Memorial, had an understanding icemaker who allowed juniors on the ice any time it wasn't being used. So Pat and his friends swarmed the club at every chance, throwing rocks and playing games early in the morning and late at night.

In 1970, Ryan snuck into the Winnipeg Arena to watch the final of the Brier. From high up on a catwalk overlooking the ice, he witnessed Don Duguid grab the cherished Macdonald Tankard.

"It didn't really mean anything to me at that point," Ryan said. "We were just a bunch of kids sneaking around and thought there would be some excitement at the arena."

Later, however, when he came to understand the Brier, he was in awe of every player who wore the Purple Heart. Playing in the Canadian Junior also gave him a taste of curling on a national level, and he took a liking to traveling across the country, playing in front of crowds and beating top teams. He began to gear his game towards the highest level.

After finishing university, Ryan was hired by Imperial Oil and transferred to Edmonton. There, he hooked up with Paul and Derek Devlin, and won the 1979 Alberta crown while playing second. His first Brier experience, however, was not a memorable one.

"What I remember about Ottawa was horrible conditions, rocks that wouldn't curl," said Ryan, whose slight build garnered him the nickname Flying Fury. "You had to throw them as hard as possible. It was a joke. I can't say that I experienced the sport of curling that year. It was Russian roulette—you didn't know if the rocks were going to slide or stop. They did not curl."

A year later, the Devlin team lost the provincial final to Paul Gowsell, and the following year, after a lackluster run, the team disbanded. At that point, Ryan decided he would try skipping. It was a big step, and he hesitated to take it.

"Being a second on a good team is one thing, but having good players play for you is something else," commented Ryan. "And the good players aren't necessarily going to play for you, because they may not think you're that good."

It took Ryan a few years to show that he had the right stuff to skip among the top ranks in Alberta. But those who watched him saw the steely resolve, the commitment of mind that would become his trademark. Pat Ryan never wavered from a goal, whether it was a longterm one such as reaching the Brier, or a shorter one such as making a shot. He was methodical and calculating. Every step seemed planned out and every move predetermined.

But no matter how good he became, he realized that shotmaking alone would not propel him to the national final. He needed something more.

"I couldn't find anything that would give us an edge," he said. "We were good curlers but so was everyone else."

Ryan finally found that edge in one of his co-workers at Imperial Oil, Duane MacPhail. Surprisingly, MacPhail wasn't a curler, but he had played hockey for Team Canada and had studied a bit of sports psychology. Ryan picked his brain, liked the ideas and soon signed him on as the team's coach at the 1985 Brier.

"He showed us a lot of what professional teams do to prepare for games and there's a lot of things that curling teams don't do but probably should," Ryan said. "It was mental preparation, aligning the team's thinking so you know where everyone is coming from."

All four players committed themselves to MacPhail's coaching and it seemed to work, right up until the final game of that fateful Brier.

In addition to MacPhail's words, Ryan learned several important lessons from that loss to Hackner in Moncton.

The first was that losing stayed with the team a lot longer than Ryan would have liked. The disappointment didn't really sink in at first. After all, in their first Brier together, the players had only lost one game. But, over the summer, they couldn't forget the defeat.

"Maybe you know you lost, but you begin to get reminded of it because people always come up to you and ask you about this and that," Ryan said. "That became a constant reminder. That was the part I didn't like. That's why I work my hardest in the final now because I don't want to spend the summer and the next year answering the same questions from the 100 people you meet every day."

Ryan also came to realize that, no matter how good a drawing team he had, if the boys couldn't peel, they would never win.

"We lost to Hackner because we couldn't peel in the eighth, ninth and 10th end," Ryan stated. "I decided after that, for my next team I was going to get guys who put a priority on hitting so we can defend a lead and we'll work on draws after that. I didn't want a front end that was going to make things tough for me."

The 1988 team was just what Ryan was looking for. Don Walchuk and Don McKenzie were reunited on the front end. They spent every minute of their daily practice sessions firing peels at each other. Randy Ferby at third did the same, although he mixed in a few draws.

The Ryan plan worked and the new Ryan Express became the best hitting team in the game.

"With that, we added another club to our golf bag that other teams didn't have," Ryan said. "It meant we could be aggressive, too."

With the mental and physical sides aligned, the Ryan Express roared through the competitive scene in 1988. They were devastating with their defensive hitting attack and won more one-point games than anyone could remember. The plan was to play hard in the first few ends, establish a lead and then pound the opposition into submission.

They arrived in Chicoutimi, Quebec, with some of the best teams in curling. Savage, Hackner, Burtnyk and Hritzuk had all made it, and observers predicted a close contest.

With such depth, no one expected any team to go undefeated. No one, that is, except Pat Ryan. The team hammered all 11 opponents to post a perfect round-robin record and move into the final. Once again, team preparation and Ryan's determination had put them in front.

The rest of the teams battled it out for the semifinal spots in front of a nearly empty arena.

Chicoutimi was certainly the most disappointing Brier of the Labatt era. There was little local interest and minimal crowd support. The indifference was reflected in the play that week; the games had a snoozy feel, despite all the big names.

When the round-robin portion of the competition ended, Ontario and Saskatchewan gained the berths for the semi. That was another classic matchup that would go largely unseen by the locals. Ontario's Savage had Werenich at vice, along with Neil Harrison at lead: three quarters of the old Dream Team was reconfigured. Graeme McCarrel was the only new member, replacing John Kawaja, who came along as the team's fifth player.

Hritzuk had come back with an entirely new foursome from the one that had collapsed in the 1985 semifinal against Hackner. This team seemed more confident, more mentally assured.

The first half of the contest went all Hritzuk's way, and after five ends he was holding a two-point lead. Savage was also holding something—his bowels. He was suffering from a long week in the Brier Patch and had been doing everything possible to hold matters in, so to speak, until the fifth-end break.

Just as the final rock came to rest, he made a beeline for the washroom but was intercepted by the CBC's Colleen Jones, who demanded a short interview. With sweat pouring down his face from stomach pains, Savage tried to look calm as he related what had happened so far in the game. But as soon as the red tally light of the television camera went off, he bolted, arriving at the men's room just in time. What the man known as the Round Mound of Come Around had forgotten was that he was still hooked up to the wireless microphone worn by each of the skips.

His relief in the washroom was heard by every CBC technician in the arena.

That would be the only satisfaction Savage would get that afternoon as Hritzuk dominated the Ontario four, winning 6-1 and going on to face Ryan.

The Alberta skip, meanwhile, was not in the best of health either. In fact, he was quite sick with strep throat and a wicked cold. But he refused any medication, fearing it would dull his senses for the big final. He had hoped that the day off between the end of the round-robin and the final would allow him time to recuperate, but when he woke up the morning of the championship game, he was still quite ill. In fact, he blacked out in the shower, almost hitting his head on the way down.

"If I bent over and stood up fast, I would have fallen over," Ryan admitted. "I was not in good shape. I could throw takeouts, but draws [which required him to bend over for a longer period of time] were not a good idea."

Considering Ryan's illness, it is not surprising that Hritzuk took command of the final game. He managed to score deuces while only giving up singles and, after nine ends, held a comfortable 7-5 lead. Ryan was not dictating the style of the game the way he normally did. Somehow, Hritzuk had been able to avoid the big hitting machine. Getting ahead early helped, and he never seemed to let the Albertans back in the game.

Flashes of 1985 went through Ryan's head. Could he possibly go undefeated in two Brier round-robins only to lose the final?

But while it had held control for the first nine ends, Hritzuk's team of Del Shaughnessy, Murray Soparlo and Don Dabrowski folded quickly in the 10th. Ryan was squeezing to get his two and didn't have much difficulty. With his last rock, Hritzuk was looking at three and attempting to lay a freeze on an Alberta stone near the back of the rings. At worst, he figured, there would be an extra end with Saskatchewan holding the hammer.

But then something happened to Eugene Hritzuk. Either the pressure got to him or he blew a head pipe, because, as he delivered his stone, it was obviously light. So light, in fact, that it was going to come up short of the hog line. Could the man who had made every shot that game suddenly pull out this dog?

The front end scrubbed the stone ferociously, but as it got over the halfway point of the sheet, everyone in the arena knew it was a hogged rock. The Alberta team jumped in celebration while Hritzuk came down the ice and turned the rock over. It was not clear whether he was checking for debris on the bottom or trying to crawl underneath it and hide.

For Ryan, it was a moment of relief.

"It sunk in right there," he said. "That was a big one, a monkey off the back. A lot of people had said we couldn't win the big one. We'd lost a lot of big games. In fact, I've probably lost more big games than anybody."

But it had finally come true: Pat Ryan had won his Brier. Despite his tough mental disposition, some doubt had crept in. But now it was erased.

"I suppose you never know for sure [if you're ever going to win]," he said. "You can't doubt yourself—you have to realize you're a human being. You stand in front of the mirror naked and then realize how crazy it is you're even in the Brier. You go for the ride. If you're winning, you're winning. If you're not, you're not."

The Ryan Express was definitely winning the following year. After losing the world championships in 1988, it picked up the next season where it left off, grabbing bonspiel titles in every part of the world.

But the hitting style was coming under increasing criticism. At the 1989 Brier in Saskatoon, people began to yell "Bor—ing" from the stands whenever the Ryan Express switched into demolition mode. Every discussion on curling seemed to center on how to make the game more exciting. Fingers pointed at Ryan.

He wasn't remorseful in the slightest. There was even talk of changing the rules to get rocks in play. Ryan took that as a compliment.

"Anyone can criticize me all they want," Ryan responded. "It doesn't matter to me because I have the blue ribbon and that's the way I had to play to win. I think I've figured out the game in this era."

But, by 1989, like so many successful squads before it, the team had begun to run its course. Pat, a financial manager, had accepted a job at a hospital in Kelowna, British Columbia—he has been one of the few top-ranked players who has managed to combine a successful white-collar career with curling—and moved there shortly after the playdowns began.

As Brier champions, the players had many opportunities to play around the country and the world during the year. The hectic schedule took them away almost every weekend. Ryan also had to fly back to Alberta for the playdowns, which they won for the third straight year.

But the pace was catching up with them. When they arrived at the Brier in 1989, they were spent.

"We were burnt out," Ryan admitted. "We had gone to the Brier three years in a row. We had no holidays left and we were all really tired. Every time you got off work, you were going to the airport to get on a plane and you'd be back late Sunday night and then back to work Monday morning. After three years in a row, you feel like you're playing your 100th straight Brier game. You don't even feel as though you've been off the ice."

Motivation became a problem as they journeyed to Saskatoon for the national final. As Ryan admits, at the start they were just going through the motions. To get over their apathy, they decided the best thing to do was to go out and look motivated, and hope that the pretense triggered something.

The plan worked. The Alberta boys finished atop the leader-board after the round-robin with an 8-3 record, and were into the final once again.

While Alberta was notching win after win, one of the most unusual episodes in Brier history was playing itself out. When it came to calling out sweeping instructions, no one bellowed as loud and as long as Ontario's Russ Howard. The skip screamed out a slew of sweeping commands on nearly every shot—as much to inform the sweepers as to release tension. The low, guttural sound he emitted earned him the nickname the Wounded Moose, a moniker coined by the *Toronto Star*'s Tom Slater.

But, as the week went on in the dry confines of the Saskatoon Arena, Howard's voice began to give out. By Tuesday, it was nothing more than a squeak and certainly no contest for the 10,000 whooping and hollering fans jammed into the facility. The skip's dilemma may have seemed humorous at the time, but to Howard it was no laughing matter.

"Losing your voice is almost like losing your eyes," Howard declared. "I couldn't communicate with the team at all."

While driving back to the hotel between games, Howard remembered that Paul Macdonald, a curling buddy back in Midland, had once experimented with walkie-talkie headsets. The two players had actually tested out a model on the main street of town.

As soon as Howard could tell the others his idea, they were off to Radio Shack to buy themselves some communication. The headsets were discreet, and when the team wore them out onto the ice for that night's game against Saskatchewan, no one even noticed. No one, that is, until the skip's commands started coming in over the walkie-talkies used by the officiating crew.

"Halfway through the game, Tim [Belcourt] came down to me and said Warren [Hansen] was mad at us because we were jamming the officials' frequencies," Howard remembered. "Then after the game, we shook hands and the officials met us on the ice. They weren't going to let us talk to the media."

Hansen had already been having a bad week. Umpires on the hog lines were strict in enforcing the hog line rule, and a number of rocks were pulled off the sheet, much to the displeasure of the crowd and the players. Ragnar Kamp, the skip of the Nova Scotia team, went so far as to threaten Hansen after one game, shaking a fist in his face and almost taking a swing.

Now, with the officials' frequencies jammed, Hansen was not in the best of moods.

The Howard four were ushered into a meeting room and Hansen asked them not to use the headsets. But Russ was not about to roll over quite so easily. He asked (in croaking whispers) where it said that walkie-talkies were against the rules, and Hansen couldn't come up with anything. He told Howard that the device was a problem because it was jamming their frequencies.

"I couldn't believe that," Howard said. "Here we were trying to win a national championship and these guys are just using these walkie-talkies to tell their buddy they want two creams in their coffee."

Tempers flared and voices—those remaining—were raised as the two sides battled back and forth. But without any rule against the headsets, Howard left the meeting determined to use them again the next day.

After the next morning's game, played with aid of the walkie-talkies, Howard was called into another meeting with the CCA. This time, however, it was the big boys, including the president, Joe Gurowka. To combat Howard's headsets, the CCA had taken the dramatic approach of creating a rule midway through the competition. Howard's communication device was now banned.

The CCA's contention was that there might be a third headset, and Howard could be communicating with someone in the stands. "What," Howard pointed out, "is someone in the stands going to tell me that would help my game?"

But the CCA stood firm, saying that walkie-talkies might be used down the road at junior events and the association wanted to nip things in the bud. Without the equipment, however, Howard's team was handicapped. It lost about a half-dozen stones because Russ couldn't emit so much as a peep, and the whole incident distracted the Ontario skip, who had been playing well up to that point.

"I got worse and worse after that," Howard said. "I shouldn't have, but I let it bother me quite a bit. That was definitely the beginning of the end as far as our relationship with the CCA went. I never really had too much time for those guys after that."

The 1989 final may have been the most boring game on record. The final score between Rick Folk's B.C. team and Ryan's Alberta four was 3-2 with six of the ends blanked. One missed shot by Folk in the sixth led to a score of two by Ryan and it was all over. The most unusual aspect of the game was that, with Ryan's move to Kelowna, the two skips were actually from the same curling club.

Although the Alberta team went on to win the world championship and played some European spiels the next year, the 1989 Brier essentially spelled the end for the Ryan Express.

Ryan's record to that point was incredible: four Briers as a skip, three finals, two perfect round-robins and two championships. He had established himself as a dominant player in the 1980s, but one who was perhaps misjudged by many.

The Pat Ryan seen on television looked like an icicle. He rarely showed any emotion, and his dark, darting eyes seemed to ward off any attempt by outsiders to intrude on his inner self.

"That was just the way we played," admitted the two-time champ. "We basically ignored the opposition out there all the time. As far as we were concerned, there was no one else out there. We just looked at the game as a series of situations you're placed in and you have to make a shot."

Ryan had also separated his curling world from his business life, as far as possible. He declined interviews at his office and before each Brier set out a schedule of when he would be available to speak to the press.

He was also vocal when it came to fighting for the rights of curlers. He refused to wear a wireless microphone, saying that the curlers were always giving and not receiving anything back from organizations such as the CBC. He also tried to get the logo of his sponsor, Asham, onto the screen when he was interviewed by holding his glove, which had the name emblazoned on it, up around his shoulder. (Brier competitors may not wear any logos of personal sponsors at the national final.)

But those pragmatic traits belie the real Pat Ryan. Off the ice, he is a warmhearted man who still loves curling like a kid. He spearheaded the development of curling trading cards, certain that many people enjoyed the heroes of the game as much as he did. And at every Brier, Ryan makes an appearance on stage in the Brier Patch to do his Elvis Presley impression.

"I don't ever try to figure out what people think about me," Ryan admitted. "When you're in the spotlight, no matter what you do, there is a tendency for the masses and media to roll up your character into two or three adjectives and that then becomes you. All the players out there have pretty wide dimensions to their character."

13

Into the Nineties

There is a belief that Ontario teams always do well at Briers held in Ontario. Six of the seven championships that the province has won were captured at home. In 1990, hopes were high because the host city was Sault Ste. Marie.

Hopes were even higher when the final field was announced. Ed Werenich had made it back for Ontario but the rest of the field was virtually unknown. Five of the teams had no Brier experience whatsoever and only Werenich's squad had won it all.

This was yet another new-look team for the Wrench, and had been born three years earlier. After leaving the Dream Team, John Kawaja had moved out on his own, skipping a team on the southern Ontario competitive circuit. His first year was a disaster. He parachuted down the Queen Elizabeth Highway into Burlington to avoid the difficult Toronto playdowns. But he was humbled in the zone finals, losing to teams he knew he should have beaten.

The next year, he hooked up with two familiar names—Pat Perroud and Ian Tetley. The Hackner front end had transferred down to Toronto for work and immediately joined up with their former Dream teammate.

Deciding on the fourth player was a bit of a problem for Kawaja, who had promised to play with a teammate from the previous year, but Tetley and Perroud had brought along Russ Mellerup, who they said would make a great skip.

Kawaja regretfully cut his friend, anxious to see what Mellerup, an unknown product, could offer. It turned out to be nothing much, and by Christmas, Kawaja was back skipping and Mellerup was barely hanging on as lead.

At the end of that year, with Mellerup back in Thunder Bay, the remaining three knew they needed a skip and the Wrench was an easy conscript. With three young, experienced players willing to put up with the old man, he could hardly say no. In 1988–89, they burst onto the scene—with a resounding flop.

While all four players were world champions, times had changed, at least at the start. Werenich was coming off the worst stretch of curling in his career, Kawaja had been mediocre, and Tetley and Perroud were still adjusting to life in the big city. Things moved slowly but steadily. The more they played, the better they got, but when it came down to the battle for the Purple Hearts, Dream Team II was nipped by Russ Howard.

The next year, the team came out with the turbines already hot. Werenich was as good as he had ever been, making lots of big shots while cackling and joshing with anyone who would listen. As had been the case in 1983, he was benefiting from the fine play of those in front of him, especially Kawaja.

Kawaja had become serious about his curling again. He could sense something good was happening and the feeling fired him up. "When you know things are going well," he admitted, "you're willing to work a little harder, go that extra mile. That's what happened that year."

Although it had a high profile like the 1983 team, this new amalgamation had a different play-book. Instead of being aggressive end after end, the Wrench decided to emphasize more hitting.

"Instead of beating our heads against the wall, we just went for a lead and then played it clean," he said.

It wasn't exactly the Ryan Express, but there was no doubt the old drawmaster didn't want to get into too many 10-9 games anymore. He was fully prepared to let his three young charges, who called themselves the Bash Brothers, peel things out once they got the lead.

At the provincial final, Kawaja's problematic knee suddenly cleared up and he shone, leading them to the Ontario title. They were off to the Brier.

True to the Wrench's form they brought some controversy with

them. Between the Ontario championships and the competition in
Sault Ste. Marie, Werenich was planning something, but he would
tell no one, not even his teammates, what it was. He did drop a hint
in a *Globe and Mail* interview, however, saying that, even if he won
the Brier, he might not go to the world championship.

With the weak field, Werenich went in as the overwhelming
favorite, and couldn't make a move without signing an autograph.
But this constraint on his social life may actually have helped him
out by fencing him in a bit.

In any case, the four found some fun. They were loose and
enjoying themselves, both on and off the ice.

There were plenty of jokes to be told, and the boys took special
delight at the witticism of a couple of drunks, who were stumbling
out of the Brier Patch at the same time as the team.

After passing Kawaja's extremely attractive girlfriend, Laura
Barker, one said, "They should call her the Wrench."

"Why?" asked the other.

"Because every time I look at her my nuts tighten up."

On the ice, Werenich's team was oozing confidence. They rattled
off six straight wins to start the Brier and were hardly tested. They
were getting almost cocky when British Columbia's Craig Lepine
finally handed them a loss. But it would be their only one.

The team was so sure of its place in the final, they began to enjoy
themselves more and more. In between draws on Wednesday, they
went out and had a liquid lunch of whiskey sours. When they
started to play the next game, Kawaja slid down the ice just before
the first rock and spoke to Werenich.

"Don't give Pat any tough shots for a few ends," he advised
the skip.

"Why?" Werenich asked.

"He's smashed, he can hardly stand up," Kawaja said.

But they won that game and rolled on to a 10-1 mark. That
record gave them their spot in the final.

The championship game was decided in the second end. Youthful Jim Sullivan of New Brunswick had been a World Junior
champion, but that experience didn't prepare him for his match
against the wise old Wrench.

After scoring one in the first end, Sullivan attempted to mix it up
with the Ontario four. Rather than clear guards, he drew behind

them. That left a tangle of rocks about the house. Sullivan actually seemed to have things in control until his third, and cousin, Charlie Sullivan, hogged his final stone. That gave Werenich a sensational double takeout and led to a big score of three.

From there, the Bash Brothers took over and Werenich sealed the victory with a last-rock open hit-and-stick.

But the fireworks weren't over yet. The next few minutes were what Werenich would later describe as "the highlight of the Brier." In the media scrum after the game, Werenich was asked whether he would indeed go to the world championship.

"I've decided that I will go," he told reporters, "if the CCA removes Warren Hansen as the coach."

By tradition, the CCA appoints a coach for the winning team at the Brier, but this year's arrangement was never going to work. Werenich and Hansen had battled for a number of years over a number of issues. Eddie had blamed the CCA employee for the Olympic Trial fiasco in which Werenich was ordered to lose weight. And he also associated Hansen with other problems caused by the CCA, including the increased number of officials at games. Werenich so despised the association that in 1988 he advised them that he didn't want to be inducted into their Hall of Fame. They did so anyway, infuriating the Wrench even more.

"It's been well documented the runs he's taken at me," Werenich told the reporters about Hansen. "If we're going to go to the world championship and represent our country to the fullest, then I want to do it without him."

After leaving the scrum, Werenich retired to the locker-room to cackle with joy over the press conference.

"I've got to admit," he said later, "that was the best thing I've ever done. It was running down my leg I was so excited about that."

Meanwhile, it was the skip's turn to be a Bash Brother: the CCA executives were caught looking the other way.

Hansen was unaware of Werenich's statement until a reporter cornered him and asked him about the story. As more reporters gathered around him, it was clear he was stunned at the Wrench's demand.

"I never expected him to do what he did," reflected Hansen later. "I didn't think they'd want me, but I thought it would be resolved behind closed doors."

Sensing another mess, Hansen went to CCA president Ed Steeves and apprised him of the situation. He also told him that, no matter what happened, he did not want to coach the Werenich team.

Steeves, a retired politician, knew exactly what he had to do. Along with CCA general manager Dave Parkes, he went into the locker-room and spoke to the Wrench, who was sitting in all his glory.

"I understand you have a problem with Warren Hansen being the coach," Steeves said.

"That's right," Eddie replied. "We don't want a coach, and if we have him, we're not going. The CCA has never supported me so I'm not going to help you boys."

"Okay," Steeves proclaimed, "that's fine, he's gone."

It was a sweet victory for Werenich, one he cherishes as much as his two Brier titles.

"They had to drop him," he said. "I knew I had the hammer. In 1983 [at the world championship] in Regina, before we went out to play against Sweden in the semifinal, Hansen had come down with some stats trying to show us the other team's weaknesses. I was polite at that time, but really, how did he think we'd got there? On a wing and a prayer?"

And so Werenich won twice at that 1990 Brier (and again at the 1990 world championship), proving that, no matter whether he was on the ice or off, he made Briers lively. He had established himself as one of the best—and outspoken—players in the history of the championship.

The 1991 Brier was again played in Ontario, in Hamilton. But this time, a home-province team was not successful. After knocking off Werenich in the provincial playdowns, Russ Howard represented Ontario and finished a mediocre 6-5. In a return to the days of old, western teams led the way.

At the top of the pack was a group of defiant young Alberta curlers led by Kevin Martin. He had skipped the 1985 Canadian Junior championship and had won the provincial title at the age of 24. That victory sent a message to many that these kids could play.

Also in the pack was Randy Woytowich of Saskatchewan, a veteran of the cashspiel circuit who was playing in his first Brier, and British Columbia's Gerry Kent, also a Brier rookie.

The pre-Brier favorite, Rick Lang of Thunder Bay, had managed to make it to a tiebreaker but was beaten by Kent.

With three western teams in post-round-robin play, the curling style was predictable. À la Pat Ryan, it was get a lead and then start hitting. The fans in Hamilton did not appreciate this tactic and let the players know it with constant booing. But the crowd's disapproval wasn't enough to distract the competing teams.

In the semifinal, Martin nipped Kent 4-3, setting up the final, which everyone in the stands predicted would be a low-scoring affair.

It was unusual to have two rookie teams in the ultimate match. The thinking had always been that rookies didn't win Briers, they observed them. If they were lucky, they came back another year to taste victory. But with Woytowich and Martin in the final, a first-year champion was assured for the first time since Kerry Burtnyk had won in 1981.

Martin had stirred up some controversy during the week with his broom. While most players were using push brooms, the Alberta skip continued to favor a heavy corn broom that shed chaff in every direction. In games when the Edmonton rink was trailing, Martin would race halfway down the sheet to "assist" with the sweeping of one of his team's stones.

Up from the broom would burst a cloud of hay, the broom disintegrating with every lick Martin gave it. The idea was to mess up the ice and try to get a miss thanks to the corn lying on the ice. It wasn't against the rules, but many players felt it wasn't good sportsmanship. There were even charges that the Alberta skip would soak his brooms in 7-Up before the games so that the chaff would really stick to the ice. Martin vehemently denied any such tactic and just kept on winning.

The final game proved to be more interesting than most predicted. The two teams went at it offensively and after five ends the score favored Saskatchewan 3-2. Then, in the fateful sixth, Woytowich lost his way. He found himself in trouble halfway through the end, and rather than bail out, he attempted to shoot it out and wound up dropping four. An aggressive attempt at a comeback the next end proved equally disastrous as he allowed Martin to steal another two. The game was over shortly after.

For Martin, it was a dream come true—a Canadian Junior title and, less than six years later, a Brier. In the tunnel underneath the stands, as it lined up to begin the closing ceremonies, the team celebrated by pouring 7-Up over the skip's head. Did they choose the sugary beverage because the media had accused them of soaking their brooms in it, or because they actually had? Martin never said.

In 1992, the lose–win tradition was about to change. Instead of losing a Brier before winning it, Martin was about to initiate a pattern of a win followed by a close loss. But he came into the Brier with mixed emotions.

The cash circuit had gone well for the team from the Ottwell Curling Club in Edmonton. It had performed admirably, earning about $35,000. But a month before the Brier, the team had represented Canada in the Olympics, held in France. According to most of the players, that event may have been the most disappointing competition in which they had ever participated.

The ice conditions were past horrible. Two of the four sheets became unplayable just before the competition started, and the inexperienced French icemaker asked Martin for help. The young skip was obliging but the other teams protested, thinking Martin might tailor the ice to his liking. The schedules then had to be revamped to accommodate only two barely playable sheets of ice.

The rocks were no better. For some reason, the World Curling Federation chose to use brand-new stones at the Olympics, a practice that would never fly at a Brier. And the use of the four-rock, free-guard zone, a new rule intended to stimulate offense, was being inaugurated at the international level. This new regulation entirely changed the strategy and thinking of all teams. It was like learning the game all over again.

There were even more problems with organization, and the entire affair left Canadians upset and disappointed. After going unbeaten in the round-robin, Martin ended up being eliminated by Urs Dick of Switzerland in the semifinal match. That defeat relegated the team to a bronze-medal contest against the United States.

Perhaps it was the futility of the competition, but when it came

time to play that third-place game, Canadian third Kevin Park
showed up late. The team was already short because second Don
Bartlett was called away on a medical emergency. With substitute
Jules Owchar filling in, they ended up beginning the game with
only three players.

In the end, they lost to the United States and went home empty-
handed and looking a little less like a team.

That was the first sign of a split in the ranks between Martin and
Park. By the time they reached Regina and the Brier, the cracks
were gaping.

The seams had begun to split the summer before. After winning
the Brier, Martin had been invited to play as a celebrity in a golf
tournament. In a lucky draw, he ended up winning a new automo-
bile. Park felt that because the team had won the national title,
Martin should share the prize with his teammates.

"As a skip, I would have split it four ways," Park told reporters.
"He gets in there because of what we did as a team and then he
wins a car. I know what I would have done."

As play began in the Brier, the team had one thing going for it
—they were curling well. But mid-way through the week, the
tensions of a long year in the public eye came to a head. Martin
lashed out at the media for what he felt was their unfair treatment
of his team. He accused the press of making up stories up and
picking on his team. He was also livid that the controversy surrounding his broom had not died down, and that people still
accused him of cheating.

"There's a lot of pressure on us to try to win, and to have to read
the papers in the morning while you're having a coffee that you're
an idiot and a cheat and you do all these things, well, that doesn't
really get you up for the game," Martin said.

"If you guys want to be fiction writers, then write novels," he
sniped at reporters.

On the other side of the coin was Manitoba's Vic Peters, one of
the easiest-going players ever to hit the Brier. Over the previous
decade, Peters had won almost every big competition except for
the Manitoba title, and although the fans didn't know him when he
arrived, competitive curlers were picking him to win it all.

Peters had a comfortable attitude about him that allowed his
team to stay on an even keel. His shotmaking was never in

question, and in Regina he just kept rolling along, piling up the wins and looking like a Brier veteran.

When the round–robin had ended, Peters had compiled a mark of nine wins against two losses, good for top spot. Next in line were Martin and Ontario's Russ Howard, both at 8-3. Howard had enjoyed an incredible year, banking more than $100,000 and cutting a wide path through curling circles.

He had a different front end from the one that had helped him win the 1987 Brier. Gone were the grind-'em-out duo of Kent Carstairs and Tim Belcourt. In were Wayne Middaugh and Peter Corner, two finesse players who had dominated junior curling around Ontario and had enough zest for the game to reinspire the Howard brothers.

The semifinal game was a contrast in teams. Howard and company were so together, they might as well have been joined at the hips. Martin's players, while still curling effectively, were a mess of personalities. It didn't take long for Howard's tight team to overtake Martin's frayed four as Ontario won 7-4.

It had been a long year for Martin and the burnout showed. Park spoke out to the press about his relationship with his skip, effectively severing all ties. "Overall, I agree with the way he calls the game," Park told the *Globe and Mail*. "There's the odd shot I'll disagree on, and as a skip, he's got to make the final decision. But I still think that he should at least be willing to listen to what I have to say and look at it constructively. But he takes it as an insult when I suggest something."

Asked whether he would return to the team, Park answered, "We'll discuss it, and if he's willing to meet me halfway then I'm probably willing to go back. But if he wants to keep on with the dictatorship that he likes to run, well, then I'll have to look elsewhere." In the end, the two split.

With the Martin melodrama over, the focus shifted to the final game between Howard and Peters. The two teams were experienced at big games, although Howard hoped his previous Briers would give him an edge.

But Peters, Don Rudd, Chris Nuefeld and Dan Carey prevailed, thanks to just one miss in the ninth end of an otherwise well-played but boring game. Glenn Howard came up well short on a freeze attempt and Peters stole a point. Although he hit and rolled out in the 10th to force an extra end, Peters made sure of things in the 11th, grabbing another Manitoba championship.

"We beat the best team in the world twice to win this thing," he said afterwards, referring to his final-game and round-robin victories over Howard. "As far as I'm concerned, Russ was the best team in the world this year. That's the way you want to win it. That's the way I always hoped it would be."

The Martin jinx would claim Peters the following year in Ottawa, as the defending champion came close but could not win a second title.

If ever a team was destined to win the Brier, it was in 1993. Russ Howard had completed one of the most incredible curling seasons in history, raking in $100,000 and winning practically every game his team played. They were feared by everyone.

During the TSN Skins Game, a made-for-television high-stakes shoot-out, wireless microphones picked up the opposition, Manitoba's John Bubbs, discussing a shot against Howard. Bubbs told his third, Mark Olson, that if they played a guard, it would leave Howard a very difficult shot to get one.

"Yes, John," Olson said. "But let's not forget, this is Russ Howard we're talking about."

Howard went on to win the Skins Game, and the first Seagram's V.O. Cup, the championship of the new World Curling Tour. He then rolled his well-oiled machine into the nation's capital to try to get revenge for his final-game loss the year before.

Being a perfectionist does not always mean you are perfect. But it does mean you spend a great deal of time trying to be.

That is certainly the case with Howard. Anyone who knows the 38-year-old skip realizes that, although he is a talented curler, he is rarely satisfied for very long. He is constantly trying to improve himself, to move up one more notch. That determination has kept him at the top of his game and made him arguably the best player of his era. Some curlers have even gone so far as to suggest that his team of brother Glenn, Wayne Middaugh and Peter Corner is the best ever to play the game.

Howard's obsession with excellence dates back a long time. It's something he may have inherited from his father, Bill, an avid curler who was known for his friendly but intensely competitive nature.

Bill Howard managed the grocery store in Midland, Ontario, where the family has lived all its life. (The team curls out of nearby Penetanguishene.) After 32 years in the grocery business, he retired and began to look after the local curling club, which gave his two sons plenty of access to the ice. And it was a rare day when Russ wasn't on the ice, trying to improve his delivery.

"He's always been a perfectionist," said Glenn Howard about his brother. "In everything he's ever done, in sports, in school, he's just never been satisfied. He always tries to do better.

"On probably 95 per cent of the shots he's played over the last 15 years, he always comes up and asks me how I thought he threw it. He wants to know all the time. Even in a club game, he's trying to throw it perfect."

Howard could also fill a video with footage of his best shots and still have some highlights left over. When lining up shots, he can see more angles than Minnesota Fats. He has a textbook delivery that could be used as a training guide, and he can call the game three or four shots ahead of where it is.

But not everyone admires Howard. Ed Werenich hasn't always been one of Howard's biggest fans, although the two curlers have come closer in recent years.

"He grates on you with that yell," stated Werenich, who feuded with Howard for more than a decade. "I've had a lot of people who come up to me and say, 'Please beat him, I'm sick of him and tired of that yell.' He also doesn't accept his misses very well. He just looks around and says, 'What happened? It couldn't have been me.'"

Nevertheless, even Werenich has respect for his arch-rival.

Howard has also been accused of having a great deal of luck. On at least four occasions in the Ontario championships, crucial opposition stones picked up hairs and had some effect in turning close games into Howard wins.

"We've had some good breaks," Howard acknowledged. "But no one ever talks about our bad breaks. We get picks, too. I think that all evens out. And you have to be good to be lucky. If you look at our record over the years, I don't think you could do all that on luck."

From others, the admiration flows a little more freely.

"They are a very talented team and Russ can always come up with the big shot," said Ed Lukowich.

"I respect him," stated Pat Ryan "He's smart, he's paid his dues. He's lost some big games and obviously learned from it."

Howard does miss the occasional brick, of course, but he also believes the more important the shot or the game, the better his team plays.

"I think under pressure we play incredibly well," he said. "And that's probably what I'm most proud of, how consistently well we've played in big spiels over the years."

Howard's residence at the top of the curling charts is certainly unique. Few teams are able to last through the intense competition without straining relationships or losing a mental edge. But Howard has done it. He attributes part of that success to his second championship team. After winning it all in 1987, Howard went into a curling depression.

"I wasn't enjoying curling," he remembered. "I didn't feel mentally strong. Everything was very, very tiring."

Relationships with his old team of Carstairs and Belcourt became strained in 1989, two years after their world title. Carstairs and Howard had been best friends. Belcourt was also very close. But when the team stopped winning, the friendship soured. Howard felt his strategy was being questioned. He began to lose confidence.

After the semifinal appearance in 1989, Howard had had enough and announced his retirement to the other three. But the competitive fires failed to cease burning. Deep inside, Howard still yearned to win. Like a racehorse let out of the barn, he wanted to run again.

Howard found the perfect recipe for success in a matchup with the brash young front end of Middaugh and Corner.

"Right from the start, there was a tremendous respect for each other," Howard said. "When I'm on the ice, I try 110 per cent and I want my team to play the same way. I get that with these guys every time out."

Middaugh's ebullience was a key factor. He took to curling as if he was on a caffeine high, constantly buzzing about, chatting people up and always finding the bright side to every situation. Corner was quieter, but no less dedicated.

Glenn Howard had developed into one of the best thirds in the world since his days as a top junior in the province. Like his brother, he was a perfectionist but perhaps a little looser.

In Ottawa in 1993, there was no shortage of curling talent. Rick Folk had returned, this time with Pat Ryan at third in what had been dubbed the Super Team. Rick Lang was also back looking for his fourth Brier win, and Peters, of course, was hoping to defend.

A betting man might have picked any of these teams, along with Howard, to be the winner. But no one could have predicted the turmoil that resulted when all four teams ended up in a tie for first place.

Heading into the final round of play, the chance of a four-way tie for first place became a definite possibility. Warren Hansen, the CCA's director of competitions, called a meeting of his officials and laid out the plan of attack in the event that such a possibility became reality. At that gathering, CCA head official Bob Decker informed Hansen that he believed the Manitoba team felt it would get first place if it won its final game. Manitoba had defeated Ontario, British Columbia and Northern Ontario in the round-robin. But that wasn't to be the case, Hansen insisted.

Because a play-off system involving such a bye would mean that one team would be pushed back two games, the round-robin records could not be used. Instead, there would be a series of tiebreakers, with opponents decided by a throw-off. However, as Hansen told the group, everything was still moot. The right combinations of wins and losses had to materialize in the final round.

Manitoba's spokesman in the entire matter had been its fifth player, John Loxton. He had read the rulebook and had spoken to several CCA officials and fully believed his team should get first place. There was also some confusion because rules for deciding a four-way tie were different in two publications: the rulebook and the competitor's guide. Interpretation seemed to be the key.

Just before the final round, TSN commentator Vic Rauter called Hansen over to an ice-side monitor. The graphics people were putting up the tiebreaker scenario to be relayed later to the television audience, and Rauter wanted to ensure they had it right. As Hansen was reviewing it, Peters walked by and glanced at the set.

He immediately stated that what was on the screen was wrong, because he would be given a bye to the final if he won his last game.

Hansen disregarded the comment, saying that nothing would happen until Peters won.

But Peters did win and the four-way tie did occur. The simplest solution would have been to have had two semifinal games and one final, but the CCA had set up a format for television that guaranteed just one semi. Four games would be played to eliminate one team.

When Peters and his team learned of the decision, they went ballistic. In front of the spectators and the media, the players, officials and CCA directors began shouting and pointing fingers at one another.

"This is ridiculous!" screamed Peters. "There's no credit at all for beating those three teams."

Dan Carey was more succinct. He stormed across the backboards, yelling, "This is shit!"

Hansen, a veteran of many curling incidents, was amazed. "What happened went beyond my wildest dreams," he said later. "It was just incredible."

Manitoba Curling Association officials immediately launched a protest, and while that was being heard, Hansen was trying to regroup and return the Brier to normal. He instructed Decker to try to get the four teams together and start the shoot-out. "Above all, Bob," he told the burly umpire, "don't get into a discussion with the Manitoba team."

But the Manitoba team was already going nose-to-nose with CCA director Bob Heartwell, the tournament liaison for the national body's board of directors.

The battle became a comedy fit for the Keystone Kops— everyone running about and no one knowing exactly what to do.

What became apparent, however, was that the Manitoba team had blown its head pipes. The once stable and consistent team was rattling off the sideboards in all the confusion, not realizing that, in only a few minutes, they would have to play another game.

"Peters got all wound up but there was no reason for them to do so," stated Pat Ryan, who believed that it was better to go with the flow. "The fifth man [Loxton] changed their expectations by telling them they would be in the final. That was clearly never the case. Because of that, I think he eliminated them from the Brier. They just never stopped complaining about it."

Indeed, when the tiebreakers were eventually held, Peters went down to defeat twice and had to relinquish his crown. It was an unpleasant end for the personable Manitoba skip, who left the ice shaking his head, saying, "I don't understand the whole thing. It's absolutely crazy."

Howard, continuing his roll, moved into the final, leaving Lang and Folk to knock heads in the semi.

Folk advanced to meet the Ontario dynamo that the press was now calling the best team in the world.

Going into that game, Folk was not 100 per cent. His knees had been giving him trouble and the extra games on Friday had not helped.

"Warming up for the game, I knew my knees weren't feeling too good," he said. "I hardly threw any rocks in the warm-up. It didn't affect me when I threw, but if I stayed in my slide position afterwards, it hurt."

Even with perfect knees, it is unlikely Folk would have beaten Howard that day. As he admitted later, "We made a couple of errors against a team that didn't make any."

Howard's team was commanding, building its lead early in the game and then cruising to the victory. After the fifth end, the Ontario foursome didn't throw anything but hits as they glided to another Brier crown, capping a sensational season.

The same two teams met in the 1994 final, but for the first time in anyone's memory, the Howard team was not the seamless unit it had been. They were still playing well and playing together, but there was something a bit different about them at the Brier in Red Deer, Alberta.

The first sign of change came in a Wednesday morning show-down with British Columbia. During the game, Glenn Howard balked a couple of times as he was preparing to deliver the stone. He stared scornfully into the crowd at every hesitation, looking directly at Gord Judzentis, a particularly vocal B.C. supporter. The Ontario vice, normally a model of concentration, was becoming frazzled at what he believed was an attempt to distract him. Although Russ didn't seem to be bothered, he came an inch too far

with his final draw in the 10th end and, in an extra end, allowed
Folk to take the all-important match.

At the end of the game, Glenn walked over to the boards to
confront his enemy, and a verbal sparring match took place.
Despite the efforts of B.C. second Bert Gretzinger to calm him
down, the younger Howard argued on, finally leaving after making his point.

The taunting continued in the afternoon when Ontario lost
another game, this time to winless Saskatchewan. The team
appeared confused and off-stride for much of the contest and
allowed Saskatchewan skip Doug Harcourt to steal a point in the
10th for the win.

Glenn was incensed by this time, and as he walked off to a
chorus of boos, gave the fans an "up-yours" salute.

Over in the media scrum, Russ was trying to mitigate the damage. "I knew if we didn't try to sugar-coat things, it would only get
worse," he said. "I tried to say it was just the tension at losing and
that Glenn didn't really mean it."

But Glenn had his own thoughts and shared them with the
media. The next morning, when Russ opened the *Edmonton Journal*,
he knew it would be a long day. In big, bold letters was Glenn's
quote: "This is the most ignorant crowd I've ever curled in
front of."

Glenn was not only mad at the fans but was also disappointed at
his brother for not supporting him. He considered Russ's dis-
claimer an act of treason.

Over the remainder of the week, things got uglier. One CCA
official told Tom Slater of the *Toronto Star*, "We were expecting a
redneck crowd at this Brier." But even the association couldn't
have imagined how nasty the situation would become.

"There were a lot of really hurtful things being yelled," said
Russ. "It was embarrassing for our wives more than us."

After the round-robin, there was more controversy to deal
with. Folk had ended that stage of the competition in first, Manitoba's Dave Smith was second, and Howard was third.

Unfortunately, the rule for selecting stones for the semifinal and
final had not been thought out in practical terms. It stated that the
first-place team chose first, selecting any color and any set of rocks

it wished to use for the final game. Then followed the second-place team, which had first choice of stones for the semifinal. Finally, the third-place team took for the semi whatever color the second-place team had not chosen. But by selecting first, Folk's team felt that it was losing an advantage to the second-place team.

"The way the rule was written, it sounded like all three teams were going onto the ice at the same time," said Ryan. "The intention was that the team that has won the round-robin has an advantage which they have earned. And we had earned the advantage of choosing the color we wanted for the final game. But because the rule was poorly written, we said we'll choose, but we'll choose after the semifinal."

Instead of making their selection, Folk and his team told the CCA that they didn't have time and left the arena.

"We were really amazed that they were trying to make us pick our rocks for the final before we knew who we were playing," Folk said. "It took all the advantage away from us."

So Smith and Howard chose their stones for the semifinal, Smith taking red and Howard yellow. The next day, just before the Smith-Howard contest, the CCA pulled the Folk team into a meeting. According to the rules, the team was supposed to pick before the semifinal began, but Folk and Ryan were still trying to press their point and hold out until after the game.

"Ryan was quite vocal in there," said Warren Hansen, one of the CCA's officials at that gathering. "He really has missed his calling. He should be a lawyer."

But this was one case he was not going to win. Moments before the semifinal game was set to start, the CCA issued an ultimatum: pick your rocks or we will pick them for you.

Folk chose yellow and left to watch the game.

After the contest, which the Ontario team won using the yellow stones, matters began to spin even faster. The Howard team was now upset, thinking that Folk had chosen yellow deliberately to prevent it from using the same rocks in both the semifinal and final.

Now it was Glenn and Russ's turn to berate Warren Hansen. Although the CCA wouldn't admit they were wrong, they did allow Howard to take any rocks—regardless of color—for the final. (The handles would be switched to give them eight red rocks.)

When Folk got wind of that concession, he flew into another rage, demanding to know why Ontario was getting an advantage. The explanation just didn't sit well.

"That incident with the rocks, allowing them to choose any stone, that really made me mad," Folk said. "I got together with some of our association people [protests or complaints about the CCA are made through the provincial association representatives], and I told them I was really disappointed and upset at how Ontario was able to warp the rules and how it was handled. But that was the end of it. 'Tonight,' I told them, 'I start focusing on the game.' All that stuff just made me more resolved that, come that final, we were going to win."

Thus a somewhat trivial incident had grown into a major part of the final. It also made the two teams hungrier to beat each other.

Unlike a year earlier, Folk was at 100 per cent. He seemed more focused than in Red Deer, more committed.

"I think Rick was definitely in command of himself," observed Ryan. "He was hungry and he went out with the mind-set that he wouldn't give the opposition any credit for having any talent. No one was going to be good enough to beat us."

The game was decided in the first half. In the fourth end, Howard's final stone wrecked on a guard and allowed Folk to score three. Gambling in the fifth, Howard lost another two and that mistake seemed to seal it up for the British Columbia team.

In the sixth end, Folk believes that the Ontario team was trying out a little gamesmanship in hopes of getting back in the match. Just as he was delivering his first rock, Middaugh and Corner began moving down the sheet, even though front ends are required to stay stationary while the opposition is delivering. And Folk had to stop his delivery with his final stone when Russ's broom whipped out to the side, causing a slight distraction. The B.C. skip stood up in the hack and told Howard to keep his broom still.

"I knew what was going on right away," Folk stated. "This was the sixth end after we'd just stolen a couple—they were trying to get to us."

Howard scoffs at that theory, saying both incidents were honest mistakes. "If that were true, why wouldn't we have kept doing it? They were accidents."

Tensions increased between the two teams. With so much riding on the game, feelings were not about to be spared. Neither side admitted to any dislike of the other, but both teams had lost Brier finals in the past and were keen not to let it happen again.

"When you're on the ice, you have to try and beat your opponent," said Howard. "You hate him because he's trying to beat you but you don't hate him as a human being. Folk's team are all great guys off the ice, real gentlemen. But when we're out there, it's no holds barred."

Ryan offered a similar sentiment. "When I was in Alberta, I had to play Lukowich all the time and I hated the fact that he would always snuff me out. I hated having to play him, but I didn't hate him. Respect is the proper word for what goes on between us and Russ. When you've got two really good teams going for the Brier and you know the loser gets that summer of humiliation, there's a lot on the line. Your intensity has to go up for a team you know can beat you."

And so the two great teams pushed each other to the limit. Folk eventually triumphed by an 8-5 margin and took his second Brier title. He also became the first skip to win representing different provinces. Ryan became only the second player after Howard "Pappy" Wood to win as a skip and then later as a third.

Moments after the 1994 closing ceremonies, the ice was taken out of the Centrium in Red Deer, all the trophies were put back in their cases, the signs were taken down, visitors began to pack for the journey home, and Rick Folk and his team began their celebration. For yet another year, the Brier had ended. Old stories had been told and new ones had been created. Champions had been crowned and losers had been consoled. But across the country, in small and big centers, players were already planning for the next Canadian Men's Curling Championship—the next Brier.

Epilogue

Going Big Time

As plans were being laid for the 1995 Brier in Halifax, changes were happening quickly on many fronts. Wayne Middaugh had left Russ Howard's team to form his own squad. Al Hackner and Rick Lang, after five years apart, were reuniting for another run. Ed Lukowich was contemplating the end of his competitive career, and Rick Folk was wondering if his wonky knees would hold up for another season.

The CCA was also looking to the future. Nineteen ninety-five would be the first year of the new Season of Champions, a marketing campaign designed to enhance curling's profile. Instead of a logjam of national and international finals in March and early April, events would be spread out from January through Easter.

Increased television coverage and more revenue from sponsors meant a financial windfall for the CCA and the World Curling Federation. The two organizations had jointly hired the St. Clair Group, a Toronto marketing firm, to sell their properties, and the results had been encouraging. Ford took over the world championship, Unitel the Mixed, and the Canadian Imperial Bank of Commerce the Seniors. Labatt's and Scott remained with the men's and women's championships respectively.

The CCA was also addressing the players' concerns. More and more, curlers were demanding a share of this lucrative pot of gold. With the demands placed on the players, they deserved some compensation.

Howard's team had shown officials that playing in the Brier had cost each player in the neighborhood of $2,000 in expenses and lost wages. Considering the profits generated by the host committees, which ranged from an average of about $350,000 to a high of $1 million, it was hard to deny the curlers compensation.

The CCA started the bidding by offering to sell a crest on the jersey of every player and reward each team with $8,500. But the players would have no say as to which corporate logo they would have to wear—the crest would be sold by the St. Clair Group on the players' behalf.

For high-profile players such as Russ Howard, this system was not acceptable. Theoretically, he could wear the crest of Bell Mobility (his sponsor) all year and then, if he made it to the Brier, be forced to wear the logo of a competitor such as Cantel.

The debate testified to the growing popularity of curlers as well-known sports figures.

Russ Howard, sensing he was marketable, hired an agent at the start of the 1993–94 season and received some endorsement money. But he knew the big payoff would come if, like skiers or golfers, he could wear corporate logos at the top event, the Brier. His agent, Randy Paul of the Landmark Group, said it would be possible for Howard to receive $50,000 for doing so.

Howard had asked to wear the Bell Mobility logo in the 1994 Brier but was refused permission by the Ontario Curling Association, which he was representing. However, his demands had pushed the issue of player compensation to the forefront, and the CCA could no longer ignore it.

Endorsements are one more step towards what seems to be an increasing professionalism. No longer is it possible for a local club team to sign up and make it to the Brier. Now it takes a winter of commitment, practice and bonspieling. Fewer and fewer teams enter the Brier playdowns each year. Most know the national championship is the reserve of the Russ Howards and Rick Folks of Canada.

Back in Halifax, the host committee was trying to organize everything from souvenir sales to who would pour the beer in the Brier Patch. More than 1,000 volunteers would be needed to help make the event a reality and (they were hoping) to turn a profit for the group. Money raised is usually put back into the local curling association for junior development or capital curling costs, but the slice of the pie is shrinking. Rights fees (increased in 1995), arena rental, entertainment and other costs eat up a lot of the revenue, making it tough to turn a buck. The organizing committee is no longer three trustees—it is a corporation with a million-dollar budget.

As the Brier enters this new phase, the CCA hopes to move it to larger arenas, such as Maple Leaf Gardens in Toronto and Calgary's Saddledome. The executives believe the days of holding the tournament in 5,000-seat arenas are numbered. They honestly feel that curling can grow in popularity and compete with NHL hockey and NBA basketball, and believe that its inclusion as a medal sport in the 1998 Olympic Games could be the catalyst.

Whether all of these dreams come true is anybody's guess. In some ways, the game's loss of innocence has already been sad. The gentlemen who shook hands at that first meeting in Toronto back in 1927 would likely go into shock if they saw the Brier today. Corporate advertising, television coverage drawing upwards of three million viewers, player agents, hundreds of media people covering the event—it is big time.

But at least one simple ritual remains—the players still shake hands before and after games. That tradition will likely never change, for it seems that every curler feels a respect and affection for the grassroots of the game. Thank goodness for that.

Appendix

Past Brier Champions

Teams are listed in order of skip, third, second, lead.

1927   Nova Scotia   Halifax Curling Club
Murray Macneill, Al MacInnes, Cliff Torey, Jim Donahue
Record: 6-1   Site: Toronto

1928   Manitoba   Strathcona Curling Club
Gordon Hudson, Sam Penwarden, Ron Singbusch, Bill Grant
Record: 9-2   Site: Toronto

1929   Manitoba   Strathcona Curling Club
Gordon Hudson, Don Rollo, Ron Singbusch, Bill Grant
Record: 9-0   Site: Toronto

1930   Manitoba   Granite Curling Club
Howard Wood Sr., Jim Congalton, Victor Wood, Lionel Wood
Record: 8-2   Site: Toronto

1931   Manitoba   Strathcona Curling Club
Bob Gourley, Ernie Pollard, Arnold Lockerbie, Ray Stewart
Record: 8-1   Site: Toronto

1932   Manitoba   Granite Curling Club
Jim Congalton, Howard Wood Sr., Bill Noble, Harry Mawhinney
Record: 6-2   Site: Toronto

1933   Alberta   Royal Curling Club
Cliff Manahan, Harold Deeton, Harold Wolfe, Bert Ross
Record: 6-1   Site: Toronto

1934   Manitoba   Strathcona Curling Club
Leo Johnson, Lorne Stewart, Lincoln Johnson, Marno Fredrickson
Record: 7-0   Site: Toronto

1935   Ontario   Thistle Curling Club
Gordon Campbell, Don Campbell, Gord Coates, Duncan Campbell
Record: 6-1   Site: Toronto

1936   Manitoba   Strathcona Curling Club
Ken Watson, Grant Watson, Marvin MacIntyre, Charles Kerr
Record: 8-1   Site: Toronto

1937   Alberta   Royal Curling Club
Cliff Manahan, Wes Robinson, Ross Manahan, Lloyd McIntyre
Record: 9-1   Site: Toronto

1938   Manitoba   Glenboro Curling Club
Ab Gowanlock, Bung Cartmell, Bill McKnight, Tom McKnight
Record: 9-0   Site: Toronto

1939   Ontario   Kitchener Granite Club
Bert Hall, Perry Hall, Ernie Parkes, Cam Seagram
Record: 9-1   Site: Toronto

1940   Manitoba   Winnipeg Granite Club
Howard Wood Sr., Ernie Pollard, Howard Wood Jr., Roy Enman
Record: 9-0   Site: Winnipeg

1941   Alberta   Calgary Curling Club
Howard Palmer, Jack Lebeau, Art Gooder, St. Clair Webb
Record: 8-1   Site: Toronto

1942   Manitoba   Strathcona Curling Club
Ken Watson, Grant Watson, Charlie Scrymgeour, Jim Grant
Record: 8-1   Site: Quebec City

1943–45   **No Championships**

1946   Alberta   Sedgewick Curling Club
Billy Rose, Bart Swelin, Austin Smith, George Crooks
Record: 9-2   Site: Saskatoon

1947   Manitoba   Deer Lodge Curling Club
Jimmy Welsh, Alex Welsh, Jack Reid, Harry Monk
Record: 9-0   Site: Saint John

1948   British Columbia   Trail Curling Club
Frenchy D'Amour, Bob McGhie, Fred Wendell, Jim Mark
Record: 8-1   Site: Calgary

1949   Manitoba   Strathcona Curling Club
Ken Watson, Grant Watson, Lyle Dyker, Charles Read
Record: 9-0   Site: Hamilton

1950   Northern Ontario   Kirkland Lake Curling Club
Tom Ramsay, Lenny Williamson, Bill Weston, Bill Kenny
Record: 7-2   Site: Vancouver

1951   Nova Scotia   Glooscap Curling Club
Don Oyler, George Hanson, Fred Dyke, Wally Knock
Record: 10-0   Site: Halifax

1952   Manitoba   Fort Rouge Curling Club
Billy Walsh, Al Langlois, Andy McWilliams, John Watson
Record: 10-0   Site: Winnipeg

1953   Manitoba   Dauphin Curling Club
Ab Gowanlock, Jim Williams, Art Pollon, Russ Jackman
Record: 9-2   Site: Sudbury

1954   Alberta   Edmonton Granite Curling Club
Matt Baldwin, Glenn Gray, Pete Ferry, Jim Collins
Record: 9-1   Site: Edmonton

1955   Saskatchewan   Avonlea Curling Club
Garnet Campbell, Don Campbell, Glen Campbell, Lloyd Campbell
Record: 10-0   Site: Regina

1956   Manitoba   Fort Rouge Curling Club
Billy Walsh, Al Langlois, Cy White, Andy McWilliams
Record: 9-2   Site: Moncton

1957   Alberta   Edmonton Granite Curling Club
Matt Baldwin, Gordon Haynes, Art Kleinmeyer, Bill Price
Record: 10-0   Site: Kingston

1958   Alberta   Edmonton Granite Curling Club
Matt Baldwin, Jack Geddes, Gordon Haynes, Bill Price
Record 9–2   Site: Victoria

1959   Saskatchewan   Civil Service Curling Club
Ernie Richardson, Arnold Richardson, Garnet Richardson, Wes Richardson
Record: 10–1   Site: Quebec City

1960   Saskatchewan   Civil Service Curling Club
Ernie Richardson, Arnold Richardson, Garnet Richardson, Wes Richardson
Record: 9–1   Site: Fort William

1961   Alberta   Alberta Avenue Curling Club
Hec Gervais, Ron Anton, Ray Werner, Wally Ursuliak
Record: 9–1   Site: Calgary

1962   Saskatchewan   Regina Curling Club
Ernie Richardson, Arnold Richardson, Garnet Richardson, Wes Richardson
Record: 9–2   Site: Kitchener

1963   Saskatchewan   Regina Curling Club
Ernie Richardson, Arnold Richardson, Garnet Richardson, Mel Perry
Record: 9–1   Site: Brandon

1964   British Columbia   Vancouver Curling Club
Lyall Dagg, Leo Hebert, Fred Britton, Barry Naimark
Record: 9–1   Site: Charlottetown

1965   Manitoba   Winnipeg Granite Club
Terry Braunstein, Don Duguid, Ron Braunstein, Ray Turnbull
Record: 9–1   Site: Saskatoon

1966   Alberta   Calgary Curling Club
Ron Northcott, George Fink, Bernie Sparkes, Fred Storey
Record: 9–2   Site: Halifax

1967   Ontario   Parkway Curling Club
Alf Phillips Jr., John Ross, Ron Manning, Keith Reilly
Record: 9–1   Site: Ottawa

1968   Alberta   Calgary Curling Club
Ron Northcott, Jim Shields, Bernie Sparkes, Fred Storey
Record: 9–1   Site: Kelowna

1969   Alberta   Calgary Curling Club
Ron Northcott, Dave Gerlach, Bernie Sparkes, Fred Storey
Record: 10–0   Site: Oshawa

1970   Manitoba   Winnipeg Granite Club
Don Duguid, Rod Hunter, Jim Pettapiece, Bryan Wood
Record: 9–1   Site: Winnipeg

1971   Manitoba   Winnipeg Granite Club
Don Duguid, Rod Hunter, Jim Pettapiece, Bryan Wood
Record: 9–2   Site: Quebec City

1972   Manitoba   Fort Rouge Curling Club
Orest Meleschuk, Dave Romano, John Hanesiak, Pat Hailley
Record: 9–1   Site: St. John's

1973   Saskatchewan   Regina Curling Club
Harvey Mazinke, Bill Martin, George Achtymichuk, Dan Klippenstein
Record: 9–1   Site: Edmonton

1974   Alberta   St. Albert Curling Club
Hec Gervais, Ron Anton, Warren Hansen, Darrel Sutton
Record: 8–2   Site: London

1975   Northern Ontario   Fort William Curling Club
Bill Tetley, Rick Lang, Peter Hodgson, Peter Hnatiw
Record: 9–2   Site: Fredericton

1976   Newfoundland   St. John's Curling Club
Jack MacDuff, Toby McDonald, Doug Hudson, Ken Templeton
Record: 9–2   Site: Regina

1977   Quebec   St. Laurent Curling Club
Jim Ursel, Art Lobel, Don Aitken, Brian Ross
Record: 9–2   Site: Montreal

1978   Alberta   Medicine Hat Curling Club
Ed Lukowich, Mike Chernoff, Dale Johnston, Ron Schindle
Record: 9–2   Site: Vancouver

1979   Manitoba   Deer Lodge Curling Club
Barry Fry, Bill Carey, Gordon Sparkes, Bryan Wood
Record: 10–1   Site: Ottawa

1980   Saskatchewan   Nutana Curling Club
Rick Folk, Ron Mills, Tom Wilson, Jim Wilson
Record: 10-2   Site: Calgary

1981   Manitoba   Assiniboine Memorial Club
Kerry Burtnyk, Mark Olson, Jim Spencer, Ron Kammerlock
Record: 10-3   Site: Halifax

1982   Northern Ontario   Fort William Curling Club
Al Hackner, Rick Lang, Bob Nicol, Bruce Kennedy
Record: 10-3   Site: Brandon

1983   Ontario   Avonlea Curling Club
Ed Werenich, Paul Savage, John Kawaja, Neil Harrison
Record: 12-1   Site: Sudbury

1984   Manitoba   Pembina Curling Club
Mike Riley, Brian Toews, John Helston, Russ Wookey
Record: 9-3   Site: Victoria

1985   Northern Ontario   Fort William Curling Club
Al Hackner, Rick Lang, Ian Tetley, Pat Perroud
Record: 9-4   Site: Moncton

1986   Alberta   Calgary Winter Club
Ed Lukowich, John Ferguson, Neil Houston, Brent Syme
Record: 10-2   Site: Kitchener

1987   Ontario   Penetang Curling Club
Russ Howard, Glenn Howard, Tim Belcourt, Kent Carstairs
Record: 10-2   Site: Edmonton

1988   Alberta   Ottewell Curling Club
Pat Ryan, Randy Ferbey, Don Walchuk, Don McKenzie
Record: 12-0   Site: Chicoutimi

1989   Alberta   Ottewell Curling Club
Pat Ryan, Randy Ferbey, Don Walchuk, Don McKenzie
Record: 9-3   Site: Saskatoon

1990   Ontario   Avonlea Curling Club
Ed Werenich, John Kawaja, Ian Tetley, Pat Perroud
Record: 11-1   Site: Sault Ste. Marie

1991   Alberta   Avonair Curling Club
Kevin Martin, Kevin Park, Dan Petryk, Don Bartlett
Record: 10–3   Site: Hamilton

1992   Manitoba   Winnipeg Granite Club
Vic Peters, Dan Carey, Chris Neufeld, Don Rudd
Record: 10–2   Site: Regina

1993   Ontario   Penetang Curling Club
Russ Howard, Glenn Howard, Wayne Middaugh, Peter Corner
Record: 11–3   Site: Ottawa

1994   British Columbia   Kelowna Curling Club
Rick Folk, Pat Ryan, Bert Gretzinger, Gerry Richard
Record: 11–1   Site: Red Deer

Index